Spirituality

as Ideology in

Black Women's

Film and

Literature

Spirituality as Ideology
in Black Women's Film and Literature

JUDYLYN S. RYAN

University of Virginia Press

CHARLOTTESVILLE & LONDON

University of Virginia Press

© 2005 by the Rector and Visitors

of the University of Virginia

All rights reserved

Printed in the United States of America

on acid-free paper

First published 2005

9 8 7 6 5 4 3 2 1

Library of Congress Cataloging-in-Publication Data

Ryan, Judylyn S., date

Spirituality as ideology in Black women's film and literature / Judylyn
S. Ryan.

p. cm.

Includes bibliographical references (p.) and index.

ISBN 0-8139-2369-7 (cloth : alk. paper) — ISBN 0-8139-2370-0 (pbk. :
alk. paper)

1. African American women in motion pictures. 2. African American
women motion picture producers and directors. 3. American literature—African American authors—History and criticism. 4. American
literature—Women authors—History and criticism. 5. African American women—Intellectual life. 6. Women and literature—United States.
7. African American women in literature. 8. Spiritual life in literature.
I. Title.

PN1995.9.N4R93 2005

791.43'6522—dc22   2005001760

This book is lovingly dedicated to the memory of my grandmother Mrs. Hilda Walcott, who first demonstrated that the purpose of life is to make more life possible; to the memory of my father, Mr. Joseph Ryan Sr.; to my mother, Mrs. Sybil Ryan; to my other mothers, Mrs. Stella Phillips and Mrs. Marilyn Joseph; and to all those sent to remind me that having a revolutionary consciousness means nothing without the spirit of power, of love, and of a sound mind.

CONTENTS

ACKNOWLEDGMENTS

I would like to express my appreciation to the various individuals and institutions that supported me in the process of researching, writing, and revising this book.

Thanks to the Women's Studies in Religion Program in the Divinity School at Harvard University for providing the opportunity to move beyond my own disciplinary boundaries as a literary/film scholar and to think about the multiple meanings of spirituality from the perspective of the religious studies scholar. As a research associate and visiting lecturer in the program during the 1994–95 academic year, I benefited from the community of feminist/womanist scholars, especially the weekly sessions with my colleagues in the program, and with the WSRP's former/founding director, Constance Buchanan.

In the course of writing the book, I was partially supported by a Minority Faculty Development Grant from Rutgers University, New Brunswick. While revising, rethinking, and rewriting the manuscript, my participation in an NEH institute on Black film studies at the University of Central Florida in the summer of 1999 expanded my understanding and interrogation of Black women's cinema.

I would also like to acknowledge the support of colleagues in several professional organizations who attended conference sessions at which I presented portions of the book, and whose interest provided much needed fuel. (Thanks to Anthonia Kalu, Joseph McLaren, Hermine Pinson, and Ingrid Reneau for always showing up.) Financial support from Rutgers University, New Brunswick, and from Ohio Wesleyan University made it possible for me to attend those conferences.

I owe a special debt to Anthonia Kalu for taking time away from her own writing to help me untangle the knots I occasionally worked myself into as I tried to understand various aspects of African ethics and African women's roles. In addition to many illuminating conversations, her published work on African literature, African women, and Igbo thought was an invaluable source of knowledge. For her generosity, thorough readings, timely suggestions, unsolicited kindness, and intellectual support, I offer sincere thanks.

This book began as an attempt to teach a course on Black women writers and filmmakers. Along the way, it has profited from the necessity of presenting portions of the analysis to both undergraduates and graduate students. In particular, the graduate students in my spring 1995 seminar at Harvard Divinity School and the students in my graduate seminar in the Program in Literatures in English at Rutgers University, New Brunswick, challenged me to clarify and simplify my arguments. The book has been enhanced by their engagement.

For their friendship, love, intellectual camaraderie, and constant community, I thank Heather Ampofo-Anti, Kwabena Ampofo-Anti, Anthonia Kalu, Kelechi Kalu, Estella Conwill Májozo, Hermine Pinson, and Ingrid Reneau. Thanks also to my best friend and sister, Althea Phillip, for frequent words of encouragement, for believing in me and in the importance of this project. To my siblings—Irma, Cynthia, Jennifer, John, "Shane" (Joseph Jr.), Carol, Andrea, and Verlene—and to the extended circle of the Ryan, Richards, Smith, Scipio, Campos, and Grier families, I offer thanks for keeping me grounded and connected. (A special thanks to my sister Jennifer for the books and conversations that sparked my early intellectual development.) To my niece Crystal, thank you for adding contour and color and excitement to my dreams and for allowing me to share and support yours. Thanks to my father for being a source of comfort and security that I took for granted, and whose passing has left me without half of my covering. To my mother, Mrs. Sybil Ryan, I offer loving thanks for always being there—in person, and in prayer; for caring and worrying (equally) about all nine of us; for being a daily example of godliness.

I am especially grateful to Cathie Brettschneider, my editor at the University of Virginia Press, for seeing the book's potential in its embryonic state, for patient and persistent interest throughout the stages of its development, and for being a wise advocate. Thanks, also, to the anonymous readers at the Press for providing the critical responses that helped me to identify those places where my analysis needed greater depth and clarity.

Sections of chapters 1 and 2 were previously published as an article titled "Spirituality and/as Ideology in Black Women's Literature: The Preaching of

Maria W. Stewart and Baby Suggs, holy" in Beverly Mayne Kienzle and Pamela J. Walker (eds.), *Women Preachers and Prophets through Two Millennia of Christianity,* copyright 1998 The Regents of the University of California, and are reprinted here with the permission of the University of California Press. (A special thanks to Emilie Townes for taking the time to read and comment on an early draft of that article.) Another article, based on a section of chapter 4 and titled "Outing the Black Feminist Filmmaker in Julie Dash's *Illusions,*" was published in *Signs,* copyright 2004 by The University of Chicago. All rights reserved. That material is reprinted here with the permission of the University of Chicago Press. Extracts from the book *i is a long memoried woman* by Grace Nichols, copyright 1983/2004 Karnak House, are reprinted with the permission of the publisher.

Finally, and firstly, I thank God from whom all blessings flow.

Spirituality
as Ideology in
Black Women's
Film and
Literature

Introduction

The History

When I began work on this manuscript, my goal was to draw attention to the frequency with which contemporary Black women writers and filmmakers explored spirituality in their works. In fact, the film that crystallized my awareness of this pattern was Julie Dash's *Daughters of the Dust* (1992). Prior to Dash's film, several literary works had provided equally extensive depictions of spirituality, among them Simone Schwarz-Bart's *The Bridge of Beyond* (1970), Toni Cade Bambara's *The Salt Eaters* (1981), Mariama Bâ's *So Long a Letter* (1983), and Toni Morrison's *Beloved* (1987). However, after viewing *Daughters of the Dust*, I realized that spirituality was not simply being depicted as an aspect of the characters' lives. Rather, spirituality had a more integral function in the work, a function connected to the artist's vision and to the objectives she set out to accomplish through the film or literary text.

In the early stages of writing, therefore, I focused on the ways in which spirituality anchored or encapsulated a set of ideas related to the Black woman artist's view of human relationships and human possibilities. Spirituality, I argued, is the foundation on which the Black woman artist constructs her vision of empowerment. It sustains the mechanisms of transformation that Black women's narratives generate for the characters, actors, readers, and viewers, as well as for other writers and filmmakers, critics, and scholars. These spiritual elements appear in varying form: from Toni Morrison's returned-from-the-dead protagonist in *Beloved,* to the Unborn Child narrator in Julie Dash's *Daughters of the Dust;* from the fusion of psychosocial and spiritual healing in Estella Conwill Májozo's *Come Out the Wilderness* to the charting of spiritual emancipation in Euzhan Palcy's *Sugar Cane Alley;* from the ancestral consciousness of Grace Nichols's *i is a long memoried woman* to the architectural configuration of self-possession in Maureen Blackwood's *Home Away from Home;* from the creative agency and autonomy of the priestess in Ntozake Shange's *Sassafrass, Cypress, and Indigo* to the priestess's challenge to an elitist and masculinist liberation theology in Zora Neale Hurston's *Moses: Man of the Mountain;* from Ama Ata Aidoo's vatic *Anowa* to Zeinabu irene Davis's prescient *Mother of the River.*

When I realized that spirituality was not simply an aspect of the characters' lives but had explicit functions in advancing the artist's vision, I faced several challenges. First, I had to construct a definition of spirituality that would encompass these two distinct aspects while clarifying its connection to African American and other diaspora cultures. This challenge was compounded by the fact that the works did not focus on specific denominational theologies. Looking to the literary and cinematic works themselves, I extrapolated a definition of spirituality as a combination of consciousness, ethos, lifestyle, and discourse that privileges spirit—that is, life-force—as a primary aspect of self and that defines and determines health and well-being. Health and well-being are broadly conceived to include nonmaterial—that is, psychological/emotional and ethical—aspects, as well as material aspects of life.

I also had to find a way of identifying and classifying narrative elements that could be linked to the operation of spirituality in the work. To do so, I followed the guidelines provided in Toni Morrison's essay "Rootedness: The Ancestor as Foundation," in which she acknowledges that she consciously works to have her fiction reflect a Black cultural and spiritual worldview. Morrison describes these cultural and spiritual components as "elusive but identifiable" aspects of Black literature (342). Encouraged by that assessment, I tried to identify influences that shaped the form of the work and that expressed particular ethical and philosophical values, by examining those works that most explicitly and extensively relied on an African spirituality. In other words, I attempted to gauge how specific philosophical and ethical values shaped the form of the work and could be connected to underlying spiritual principles.

Starting with an investigation of traditional African religions, I identified an *ethos of interconnectedness* that could be readily discerned as a recurring feature of Black women's literature and cinema. Since the primary goal within an African cosmology is to attain and preserve a righteous equilibrium of interdependent relationships, when and where Black women artists represented this cosmology in their literary and film works, they *necessarily* affirmed an ethos of interconnectedness. Indeed, through their narrative engagement with an ethos and ideology of interconnectedness, these Black women artists revealed distinct ways of being human, with attendant responsibilities.

I surmised that specific denominational theologies were not represented in the works because the artists had already extrapolated—consciously or unconsciously—the philosophical and ethical principles from those theologies, an easy task given the ways in which various cultural practices and traditions are already infused with these principles. Throughout African diaspora experience, for example, the widespread practice of claiming and enacting kinship responsibilities toward children who are not part of one's biological lineage is consistent with the traditional African proverb "It takes a village to raise a child." This proverb underscores both the collective nurturing a child needs and the collective responsibility for nurturing. Like the nurturing practices it authorizes, the proverb derives from and expresses an ethos of interconnectedness. It illustrates how oral traditions and cultural practices are infused with specific philosophical and ethical values. I used the literature and films to determine which principles were drawn from, and could be located within, a traditional African religious cosmology. Based on this mapping, I concluded that the operation of an African spirituality could be detected even when there was no explicit focus on spirituality in the lives of the characters, as exemplified by Toni Morrison's *The Bluest Eye* (1970), Sherley Anne Williams's *Dessa Rose* (1996), and Maya Angelou's film *Down in the Delta* (1998).

The issue that intrigued me—and that eventually led to the current title—was the striking contrast between the careers of these Black women artists and the characters, plots, and settings they developed in their works. Several of these artists had come of age during the civil rights, Independence, and Black Power campaigns of the 1950s and 1960s. In their career paths and professional achievements, they had fulfilled the civil rights vision—a vision shared by progressive movements elsewhere in the diaspora—that focused on "institutional gains" and professional advancement. Yet their novels and films did *not* depict Black women characters pursuing and attaining college degrees, awards, prizes, and elite positions as the tokens of success, nor did they represent the college classroom, the courtroom, or the corporate boardroom as the site of empowerment. To the contrary, journeying to the past—and, frequently, to the Slavery[1] past—was presented as the primary avenue of empowerment.

This contrast between the lives of Black women artists and those of their characters raised several questions. Why had these artists supplanted the civil rights vision with a vision of transformation that requires a return to sites of oppression from which the characters typically retrieve different symbols of success? Why had they chosen to use spirituality as a vehicle for transformation in their works? And why had they created a model of self-empowerment that involves the discovery (or recovery) of independent (spiritual) agency before and beyond any institutional endowment? While I could not fully formulate answers to these questions, I was sure of two things. First, that the placement of the Black woman protagonist outside of mainstream institutional settings was deliberate. And second, that the depiction of her use of a self-affirming spiritual agency to sustain a broad human community and, simultaneously, to transcend structures that deny the right of a creative and fully democratic participation on the basis of gender, race, and class was equally deliberate.

Two texts—one literary, the other scholarly—provided the clues I needed to solve the puzzle. The first was Ama Ata Aidoo's play *Anowa* (1970). Set in Ghana in the late nineteenth century, the play focuses on a young woman who, at an early age, is identified as a "born priestess." One of the primary traits of the priestess is that she carries within her the life-force—in the form of vision, memory, knowledge, and grace—which must be distributed to sustain the community. Despite her obvious calling, Anowa doesn't pursue a formal apprenticeship to be initiated as a priestess. Instead, she marries Kofi Ako, who—with her assistance—rises to prominence and comes to represent a new breed of economic and political leadership. As Aidoo's play demonstrates, the priestess's commitment to and responsibility for group preservation can be fulfilled outside of religious institutions. In fact, Anowa's calling to the priestess role directs her to the sociopolitical and economic arena in which her creative agency and vision are most urgently needed. Aidoo's portrait of Anowa illustrates that, in the post-Slavery, post-colonial, and post–civil rights eras, the Black woman bearing life-force fulfills her responsibility by embracing diverse roles in civil society.

The second text, Anthonia Kalu's essay "The Priest/Artist Tradition in [Chinua] Achebe's *Arrow of God*," corroborated my reading of Aidoo's play. In that essay, Kalu demonstrates that while participation "in group preservation . . . is normally the responsibility of only priestly elders" (52), Achebe displays this authority in his writing. To the extent that Achebe embraces and is qualified to fulfill this responsibility, Kalu explains, he enacts a priestly demeanor and role. Based on the criteria set forth in Kalu's analysis, I surmised that, in the contemporary era, the role of film or literary artist is one of the many offices through which the Black woman priestess fulfills her responsibility for group preservation.

Spirituality as Ideology, therefore, makes a two-pronged argument: that spirituality functions as a life-affirming ideology in Black women's art, and that, in the choices informing narrative construction and characterization, Black women filmmakers and writers embrace the role and responsibility of the priestess, bearing and distributing life-force to sustain the community of viewers and readers.

Given the large numbers of literary and cinematic works—each with fascinating plots and endearing characters—that conformed to and exemplified my preliminary hypotheses, deciding which works to include in the study was a heartrending task. Every work I included seemed self-indulgent; every "cut," an unforgivable omission. Finally, I decided to ground the study in an analysis of a diverse selection that would include short films and feature-length works, poetry, novels, drama, and memoir. With two notable and necessary exceptions—*Beloved* and *Daughters of the Dust*—I decided not to focus on works that had previously received extensive scholarly treatment. In addition, I determined that it was important to include works from different regions of the diaspora, to the extent that my scholarly background allowed. Thus, the scope of this study is diasporic—in terms of its investigation of these women artists' vision and their works in relation to the African cultural domain, cultural consciousness, cultural forms, and cultural histories. As such, it reflects my own critical location as an African diaspora woman scholar, writing about, and working primarily with cinematic and literary works in English.

The Argument

Spirituality as Ideology evaluates the ways in which Black women film and literary artists utilize a diverse range of African diaspora spiritual traditions. It analyzes the ways in which spirituality shapes the Black woman's definitions of self, freedom, and artistic and political vision through an in-depth examination of the cultural, ideological, and theoretical significance of this vision in the Black experience. In so doing, it enlarges the scope of African diaspora cultural studies by redefining the philosophical and ideological direction that specific cultural and artistic tropes were designed to advance. For example, my investigation of the ways in which spirituality shapes narrative choices and assists philosophical goals in Black women's literature and film clarifies and expands upon the pioneering work of Henry Louis Gates Jr. in identifying the concept of "signifyin'" as a rhetorical and structural principle. In his book *The Signifying Monkey*, Gates employs the term "signifyin'" to refer to the relationship among various texts within the African American literary tradition. While "signifyin'" provides an important critical lens for understanding the rhetorical structure of specific works and the intertextual relations among Black—especially male—writers, it does not provide a framework for interpreting or critiquing the philosophical significance of these dynamics or discursive practices. The focus on spirituality—particularly the ethos of interconnectedness, what I term the *democracy of narrative participation,* and other related aspects—extends Gates's project by combining an analysis of formal / narrative elements with an interpretation of philosophical, ethical, and ideological goals that African diaspora artists advance in their works.

In addition to its exploration of spirituality as a source of knowledge and way of knowing, *Spirituality as Ideology* examines the ways in which Black women's literary and film texts critique and mediate the cultural, social, and historical conditions surrounding their production. While most discussions of Black women's engagement with, and contribution to, the discursive space of the culture (the social text) assume an oppositional or reactive stance, I argue that the disposition reflected in Black women's art tends to be proactive rather than reactive, and that oppositionality is not a prominent feature. One reason for this choice is that, by itself, oppositionality lacks autonomy and remains locked in the crippling gravitational pull of hegemonic discourses. Indeed, autonomy is achieved and preserved only when oppositionality is located within a larger vision that is self-designed and proactive. To the extent that Black women's texts articulate and are informed by a preexisting cultural vision, they must be seen as more than oppositional. In addition to their autonomous stance, several strategies assist the negotiations within Black women's literature and cinema. These include the juxtaposition of different time periods, the depiction of intergenerational transfers, journeying and migrations, and ritualized transformations that are central to the deployment of spirituality and the agency it generates.

By their own admission, Black women literary and cinematic artists define self and artistic vision to include both singular and collective dimensions. Therefore, this study constitutes a collective *auteur* criticism, one that presents a progressive unfolding of a *collective* Black woman's artistic vision.[2] Techniques of cinematic narration utilized in Black women's films are particularly important to this study since they illuminate the domain of the spiritual by reconstructing narrative subjectivity in ways that allow the viewer to experience and affirm different/distinct ways of knowing. Equally important, these cinematic techniques illuminate the work's ideological design. The transformative objectives to which these works are directed are both encoded in, and require the deployment of, cinematic techniques that empower both the film's subjects and its viewers. In *Daughters of the Dust*, for example, the camera narration allows viewers to register the metaphysical presence of the Unborn Child narrator. Through the camera narration of her presence and her successful intervention, the viewer is positioned to access new ways of knowing. Similarly, the camera unveils the temporal layering of the past and present on Ibo Landing in the closing sequence when Nana Peazant recalls/rehears a conversation between her younger self and her young husband. The camera reveals that the domain of the spiritual coexists with the material, the past with the present, and that both influence events in the present.

Spirituality as Ideology accomplishes several goals. Specifically, it illustrates the centrality of spirituality to Black women's vision of transformation. Second, it demonstrates that Black women's texts inscribe their own interpretive blueprint and, in so doing, provide a new paradigm for reading artistic, cultural, and social texts, which I call the *paradigm of growth*. Third, it provides an interpretive model for examining a broad range of texts by Black women artists by unveiling the ways in which ideological and spiritual objectives coincide in these works. Fourth, it offers a theoretical framework for looking at the growing body of Black women's film by exploring the reciprocal gaze among filmmakers and writers and the distinct intertextuality forged by these exchanges. Finally, it charts the dual engagement with spirituality and ideology as an aspect of intertextual relations among Black women artists of the diaspora.

The book's interdisciplinary approach intersects with several discourses in film studies, literary history and criticism, theology, and critical pedagogy. Despite the increasing number of feature films by Black women artists that have followed *Daughters of the Dust* in gaining theatrical distribution, scholarly attention to Black women's cinema is still an underdeveloped area. This study follows the pioneering examples of Gloria Gibson and Jacqueline Bobo in seeking to alleviate the shortage of scholarly analyses of Black women's cinema. It also adds to the growing body of literary criticism of Black women's writing. However, while most recent studies offer comprehensive analyses of nineteenth- and early twentieth-century Black women's texts, this book focuses on contemporary writers and filmmakers. Nevertheless, in order to provide historical clarity, I include an analysis of the preaching careers of two nineteenth-century Black women: Maria Stewart, and Toni Morrison's fictional priestess Baby Suggs, holy. Analytically, these two figures are used to establish a historical precedent for the conjunction of spirituality and ideology in Black women's contemporary art. This approach emphasizes the historical nexus among spiritual, cultural, and sociopolitical identities. At the same time, the discussions of texts by Stewart and Harlem Renaissance writer Zora Neale Hurston foreground those literary ancestors whose works set a precedent for the deployment of spirituality by contemporary artists.

The discussion of theology in chapter 1 provides a new way of viewing the connections among New World African diaspora religious traditions. It challenges the widespread and reductive assumption that Afro-Christianity shares no philosophical commonalities with Santería, Candomblé, Voodun, and other diaspora religious traditions that are not christological. My approach follows the Black women's texts discussed here in focusing on forms of spirituality shaped by diverse theologies and *not* on the theologies themselves. For example, while I note Dash's incorporation of elements of Yoruba/Santería in *Daughters of the Dust,* this analysis does not provide a phenomenological reading of religious elements. Rather, my analysis focuses on the ways in which an understanding of their spiritual identities shapes familial relationships and responsibilities, on the narrative construction of various modes of resolution, and on the ideological directions they outline for viewers.

I examine the theological foundations of spirituality and outline the different cosmological understandings that inform African theology. I also explore the ideological functions Western theology has served in legitimating hegemonic agendas. This analysis explores the ways in which Black people's identities were reconfigured by European imperialism and American Slavery. It also examines their resistance to these assaults, as well as their continuing commitment to the goals and principles of the paradigm of growth, through choices informing vernacular exegesis. Building on ethicist Peter Paris's work in *The Spirituality of African Peoples,* I identify an ethos of interconnectedness that informs diaspora religious and cultural traditions. I argue that this ethos is a primary aspect of Black women's artistic vision in film and literature.

In addition to sharing a common ethos, the narrative focus on the realm of the ancestors, the realm of the living, and the realm of the unborn that typifies Black women's literature is recreated in Black women's cinema as a layered double-vision.[3] I illustrate that Black women filmmakers use cinema to unmask other realms of experience—the realm of the hidden past, and the realm of hidden/suppressed dimensions of the present. This visually layered double-vision enables the Black woman filmmaker to support the epistemological project of the Black woman writer by cinematically enunciating what she knows, what she sees.

Apart from examining looking relations among filmmakers and literary artists, I analyze the strategies by which Black women filmmakers inscribe a unique artistic subjectivity within the arena of filmmaking and conclude that the techniques they use promote new forms of visual literacy. This is significant because for Black women and many other independent filmmakers, the primary challenge posed by Hollywood's hegemony is that of generating new modes of visual literacy that can enable viewers to become more competent and self-consciousness interpreters. These filmmakers acknowledge that creating film texts that supply "correct" and/or corrective readings inevitably promotes new relationships of dependency, unless viewers are simultaneously assisted in attaining interpretive autonomy and in crafting new looking relations. Lasting transformation begins not simply with new critiques but with an exposure of the process by which narratives are constructed and deployed. Accordingly, I examine the many ways in which Black women filmmakers embrace the responsibility of narrative construction, and their reliance on spirituality in promoting what is at once an ideological and a pedagogical agenda through the artistic exploration of African diaspora experience.

This book provides a way of discussing and interpreting spirituality that is culturally and artistically indigenous. Following Karla Holloway's and Kimberly Rae Connor's explorations of spirituality as a primary aspect of Black women's literature, I suggest how an informed attention to both christological and nonchristological modes of spirituality can enhance critical and pedagogical approaches to both literature and film. Spirituality, I argue, is not simply depicted as an event; rather, it is deployed as a mechanism of transformation that resuscitates and invigorates specific cognitive capacities. For Black women filmmakers and writers, it is a means of expressing a distinctly Black female epistemology in their works. While most theories of knowledge presume that epistemologies are "universal," this analysis argues that modes of knowing are as distinct as cultures themselves. The vast body of "scientific knowledge" developed in the nineteenth century purporting to prove Black people's subhumanity and/or genetic inferiority indicates that theories of knowledge and epistemological inquiry are neither "universal" nor immune to sociocultural influences.

Given the hegemonic functions of Eurocentric epistemologies that proliferate in the Western academy, it is easy to see why contestations over knowledge as well as ways of knowing have been at the heart of Black people's quest for both human and civil rights in the modern era. The (frequently discredited) modes of knowing that African peoples developed and relied on before, during, and after Slavery to construct strategies for growth further indicate that epistemologies are culturally informed. In referring to Black women's ways of knowing, this analysis recognizes the distinctiveness of Black women's sociocultural experiences, roles, and histories, and the epistemologies concomitant with those realities.

The Structure

Acknowledging the distinctiveness of Black women's ways of knowing is absolutely essential to any effort to interpret Black women's art and the vision(s) of transformation encoded therein. Since spirituality is a key aspect of Black women's ways of knowing, *Spirituality as Ideology* emphasizes the role of the artist as theorist, theologian, and priestess, exercising spiritual agency *through* the work of art. The chapter titles reflect that emphasis.

Each chapter explores a specific aspect of the priestess's spiritual agency. In chapter 1, "Interpreting Spirituality," I delineate the parameters of my argument by identifying spirituality as a primary characteristic of Black art. This chapter outlines a spiritual continuum characterized by an ethos of interconnectedness common to both New World African religions (including Santería, Voodun, Hoodoo, Candomblé, *and* Afro-Christianity) and traditional African religions. Here I demonstrate how the African cosmology engenders this ethos of interconnectedness and shapes an enabling vision of Black women's spiritual and sociopolitical leadership beyond the boundaries of religious institutions. I discuss the connections among spirituality, ideology, and epistemology in Black culture and in Black women's lives and retrace historical definitions of spiritual/cultural community and the identities they assign. I argue that Black women artists share a commitment to dismantling what I call the *paradigm of resistance,* that is, the binary interpretive framework within which Western interpretations of African diaspora artistic and expressive cultures have been traditionally located. I use an interpretive methodology to show how these women artists reaffirm the paradigm of growth, a multidimensional interpretive lens that recognizes interdependent relationships.

Using the careers of two nineteenth-century Black women preachers from history and literature—Maria Stewart, the first woman political speaker in the United States, and Baby Suggs, holy, the spiritual center of Toni Morrison's *Beloved*—chapter 2, "Embracing Responsibility," examines the contours of Black women's spiritual authority. As "imagined contemporaries," these two Black women figures enable a perspective that clarifies the relationship between spirituality and art. I engage Stewart's career as a historical precedent for the view of spirituality in contemporary literature and film by Black women artists. Here, I argue that for Black women, authority rests upon *embracing responsibility,* not just *asserting rights.* This responsibility extends to cultural, spiritual, and political constituencies. The congruity between Stewart's vision and Morrison's representation of Baby Suggs supports a view of spirituality both as a source of authority and as a vehicle for exercising righteous/transformative agency.

In chapter 3, "Bearing Life-Force," I examine the enactment of political leadership through the priestess/prophetess role. As transformative agents, priestesses and prophetesses engage a traditional role involving vision, memory, knowledge, grace, and other aspects of the life-force whose equitable distribution makes more life possible. Responsible narrative construction enables distribution of these aspects in ways that stabilize the Black community while transforming it. As priestesses, Black women exercise righteous/creative agency by mediating between cultural/spiritual community, its oppressors, and divinities and/or ancestors. They consciously present themselves, their vision, knowledge, memory, and work as offerings designed to strengthen the life-force of the community.

While preaching is perhaps the most obvious channel through which life-force is distributed, this chapter demonstrates that several other less prominent channels are accessed and/or created by Black women. Indeed, the typical depiction of the Black woman priestess does not present her in a religious office. Instead, Black women writers and filmmakers typically present the priestess in a range of secular roles as wife, midwife, mother, grandmother, artist, activist, warrior. Frequently perceived in a liminal position, the priestess symbolizes Black women's unsanctioned, illicit, self-styled, and veritable agency. I use Hurston's *Moses: Man of the Mountain,* Ghanaian writer Ama Ata Aidoo's play *Anowa,* and African American writer Ntozake Shange's *Sassafrass, Cypress, and Indigo* to explore and emphasize the priestess's changing role in various sociopolitical contexts—postemancipation, colonial, and post–civil rights—and examine her function in enabling various collectives to fashion avenues for promoting growth while mediating freedom and new forms of enslavement and/or restriction.

Chapter 4, "Reversing Dispossession," discusses Black women's cinema and its role in recasting history. It offers an in-depth analysis of Julie Dash's recasting of U.S. national history, Black film history, and Hollywood history in *Illusions,* and her deployment of techniques that disclose and transform what James Snead calls "structured absence." Like Maria Stewart and Baby

Suggs, holy, Dash displays the spiritual authority of the Black woman priestess in embracing the responsibility to provide enabling visions of the past and the future. In the construction of a narrative that outlines the direction for future agency, Dash claims and enacts the priestess's role as an agent of transformation. *Illusions,* I argue, performs theories about Black women's position in the filmmaking industry by exploring their various roles as musical props, disembodied voices, and would-be producers. Using Janet Lyon's analysis of the genre of manifesto as one that "alternat[es] among the discourses of history, logic, and prophecy," I examine the gestures by which this film positions itself to function as a *manifesto* for contemporary Black women filmmakers, encouraging new modes of visual literacy by reinscribing future agency in a cinematic past. That is to say, Dash's imaginative positioning of a Black woman film producer in "Hollywood 1942" expands the artistic and ideological parameters for herself and other Black women in the contemporary filmmaking industry.

The role of female elders and ancestors in the intergenerational transfer of self-possession, with its dual significance as a cultural tradition and as a counterhegemonic strategy is the focus of chapter 5, "Renewing Self-Possession." Here, I argue that Black women filmmakers construct new patterns of looking that interrogate, subvert, and revise the classic cinematic gaze. In so doing, they expose and counter the debilitating consequences this gaze generates for (Black) communities as viewers and as film subjects. Their project is consciously aimed at renewing Black people's self-possession. Among other objectives, they seek to provide expanded roles and greater agency for Black women and Black men in film; to facilitate, thereby, Black people's self-empowerment through film; and, through encouraging new modes of critical viewing, to offer a new paradigm for constructing visual literacy and interpretive agency.

For these women artists, therefore, cinema is a site of contestation as well as a site of transformation and triumph. For example, for Zeinabu Davis, expanding agency/empowerment through film means supporting the training of women "of color" students and providing opportunities for them to gain valuable teaching and production experience.[4] In this way, she assumes the role of priestess as transformative agent as she embraces the responsibility of distributing knowledge, memory, and other aspects of life-force by becoming a vehicle for transforming the art and processes of narrative construction. In works such as Martinican filmmaker Euzhan Palcy's *Sugar Cane Alley,* and Afro-British filmmaker Maureen Blackwood's *Home Away from Home,* this involves the construction of what I call a *democracy of narrative participation,* that is, a well-developed pattern of representation in which characters who would otherwise be considered "marginal" are allowed to occupy the narrative foreground, endowing them with their full human complexity. The chapter also examines the role of what Toni Cade Bambara calls "spatial narration" in the formulation of new film genres.

Chapter 6, "Charting Futures," assembles the various interpretive angles into a comparative view of Black women writers and filmmakers as priestesses, harnessing their commitment to group preservation to the task of producing a desirable vision of the future. Through a close examination of the future directions unveiled in Guyanese writer Grace Nichols's narrative poem *i is a long memoried woman,* in Maya Angelou's feature film, *Down in the Delta,* and in African American writer Estella Conwill Májozo's memoir, *Come Out the Wilderness,* I show how the artist's creative and mediational role is aimed at positioning readers and viewers to claim more enabling interpretive choices on their own behalf.

Interpreting Spirituality

I don't regard Black literature as simply books written *by* Black people, or simply as literature *about* Black people, or simply as literature that uses a certain mode of language in which you just sort of drop g's. . . . I don't like to find my books condemned as bad or praised as good, when that condemnation or that praise is based on criteria from other paradigms. I would much prefer that they were dismissed or embraced based on the success of their accomplishment within the culture out of which I write.

—TONI MORRISON, "Rootedness: The Ancestor as Foundation"

In this first chapter, I introduce several key concepts that help to illustrate how and why spirituality provides a useful context for examining Black women's cinema and literature. To do so, I outline a new interpretive approach that I call the *paradigm of growth*. The paradigm of growth accords with and highlights Black people's psychosocial self-definitions that predate oppression/Slavery. Its primary axis is the definition of Black people as human agents, motivated by what I take to be a transcultural human commitment—a commitment to growth. Since this paradigm acknowledges the many proactive concerns of Black women artists, it facilitates a more thorough analysis of Black women's art. Elsewhere in the chapter, I show how this paradigm of growth derives from and reflects specific principles of traditional African religious cosmology.

Diaspora Identities and the Paradigm of Growth

In "Rootedness: The Ancestor as Foundation," Toni Morrison redefines Black literature, its characteristics, and its functions, pointing to a crucial distinction between "race" and Black culture. Morrison's observation of this distinction is part of a larger project by African diaspora artists and scholars to decentralize the pre-text of race and instead to relocate and enlarge the view of the preexisting text of culture. A primary motivation fueling this project is the fact that the ideology of race has historically denied that Black people were and are bearers, shapers, and producers of culture. The distinction between race and culture coincides with the distinction I make between what I call the paradigm of resistance and the paradigm of growth.

The paradigm of growth provides a theoretical rubric under which a diverse range of interpretations can be located. This model reflects a view of culture as a map that is constantly evolving, charting the direction in which a people has chosen to grow. Taking its orientation from this definition of culture, the paradigm of growth supplants the paradigm of resistance that has prevailed in most theoretical approaches to African diaspora cultural studies.

Within the Western academy, the paradigm of resistance[1] develops from an external historical narrative—ubiquitous in the social sciences—that designates race-centered crisis as the point of origin for African diaspora cultures and for all related arts. This narrative designates Slavery, racism, colonialism, and other hegemonic practices as determining events and the inevitable starting point for the critical analysis of African diaspora cultures—indeed, all "minority" cultures—and related arts. Not to be confused or equated with the tradition of resistance in African American letters,[2] the paradigm of resistance often conflates privilege and power, defining the latter solely as coercive agency. Given its starting assumptions, the paradigm of resistance is reactive; typically recognizes only oppositional (human) relationships (for example, "us" versus "them"); assumes a unidimensional goal; and imagines human communities comprised of the "powerful" and the "powerless." The assumptions that constitute the paradigm of resistance can distort scholarly analyses. As Deborah King notes, for example, the view of Black women "as powerful, independent subjects" has been obscured by "scholarly descriptions [that] have confounded our ability to discover and appreciate the ways in which black women are not victims" (72).

A typical articulation of the assumptions underlying the paradigm of resistance can be found in sociologist Orlando Patterson's *Slavery and Social Death* (1982). In his comparative analysis of the psychosocial dynamics of slavery, Patterson argues that one of the primary aspects of the condition of slavery is "the slave's natal alienation." Says Patterson: "Not only was the slave denied all claims on, and obligations to, his parents and living blood relations but, by extension, all such claims and obligations on his more remote ancestors and on his descendants. He was truly a genealogical isolate" (5). On the basis of this assumption, Patterson concludes that "slaves differed from other human beings in that they were not allowed freely to integrate the experience of their ancestors into their lives, to inform their understanding of social reality with the inherited meanings of their natural forebears, or to anchor the living present in any conscious community of memory" (5). Contrary to Patterson's claim, however, enslaved Black people maintained a private life—what W. E. B. Du Bois described, in *The Souls of Black Folk* (1903), as a life "within the Veil"—in and through which they preserved and experienced familial, psychological, and spiritual connectedness despite the "secular excommunication" to which White enslavers assigned them. Although Patterson asserts that "we know next to nothing about the individual personalities of slaves, or of the way they felt about one another," the vast body of writings by enslaved Africans confirms that far from experiencing "natal alienation," enslaved Africans utilized their (complex definitions of) kinship networks as a resource for negotiating the psychological and spiritual assaults of enslavement.[3] Their ability to refashion and improvise new kinship configurations was one of several resources used to dispel the limited view of human relationships posited by the paradigm of resistance and structured into the very dynamic of Slavery.[4]

By contrast, the paradigm of growth contains radically different elements. It defines culture as a dynamic composite of instructions on a chosen direction for growth, which exist in the form of rituals, philosophies, artistic practices, memories/histories, and ethics. Although the paradigm of growth also responds to oppressive events as obstacles to growth, it views resistance by itself as an inadequate goal. At once a call to self-perpetuation and a response to any threatening debilitation, the paradigm of growth is proactive. It envisions and seeks to establish interdependent human relationships and pursues a positive multidimensional agenda. This paradigm regards crises in African diaspora history—Slavery, colonialism, neocolonialism, etc.—as interdictions against an independent and preexisting cultural vision. Most important, it differentiates privilege from power by defining power as both coercive/oppressive and creative/righteous agency. Within the Black experience, the paradigm of growth is an internally defined point of departure. In their insistence on foregrounding this internally defined vision, Black women film and literary artists reaffirm the significance of the paradigm of growth as a more viable cultural and interpretive blueprint.

In addition to designating a different conceptual starting point, the paradigm of growth illuminates specific features of Black women's literary and cinematic art. For example, one of the features that this paradigm reveals is a *democracy of narrative participation* that enables a more expansive presentation of characters who would otherwise be considered "marginal," endows them with their full human complexity, and allows them to occupy the narrative foreground. The term "democracy of narrative participation" enhances the discursive and theoretical potential of the concept of "democracy," whose original impetus—as articulated in the U.S. Declaration of Independence—was precisely the question of human rights and, linked to this, the rights of representation and of participation. While these rights have been given extensive consideration in relation to structures of governance and electoral processes, Black women's art demonstrates that a genuine commitment to democracy requires much more. Among other things, it requires representation and participation in national history, national cinema, national literature, and curricula. Examples of this democracy of narrative participation include the expanded focus on the White indentured servant Amy Denver in Morrison's *Beloved;* on the Unborn Child narrator in Dash's *Daughters of the Dust;* on the deaf protagonist, Malindy/Malaika, in Zeinabu Davis's *Compensation;* and on the residents of Palcy's *Sugar Cane Alley.* These representations indicate a conscious decision by the artist to reject the standard binary casting of central and marginal characters consistent with their goal of depicting and establishing interdependent relationships.

Democracy of narrative participation enables the artist to expand the narrative to reveal that even individuals whose presence is temporally or socially limited have full personalities and unlimited human agency. Through such characters, artists create opportunities for readers and viewers to increase their own human agency, thus extending their transformative impact beyond the fictional realm to the social universe in which the work of art is designed to function. In so doing, they attest to the efficacy of the priestess's work (in art) for the community and society.

Morrison's commitment to redefining Black art in relation to philosophical and ethical aspects of culture is consistent with the paradigm of growth.

While noting and re-creating its "elusive but identifiable style in [her] books," Morrison links this "style" to a Black spiritual/cultural worldview. In "Rootedness," she asserts that this identifiable Black style is achieved in "the construction of the book and the tone . . . which . . . [blends] the acceptance of the supernatural and a profound rootedness in the real world at the same time with neither taking precedence over the other" (342). The conjunction of spirituality and epistemology outlined in Morrison's analysis is significant because the culturally grounded redefinition of Black literature she provides contrasts sharply with standard definitions of Black literature as "oppositional." "Oppositionality," clearly, has multiple meanings, which include the sense of counterhegemonic praxis, as discussed in bell hooks's "Oppositional Gaze." While Black women filmmakers and writers are obviously committed to counterhegemonic *praxis*, they nevertheless reject "oppositionality" as a subject positioning or definition of *subjectivity*. The oppositional model holds that Black literature's primary, if not sole, objective is to register a resistance to (its own) subordination. Indeed, Morrison's novels, like other Black women's texts, are widely regarded as works whose primary concern is the contestation between the powerful and the powerless.

Like their predecessors of the nineteenth century, many contemporary scholars are wedded to the view of Black women as powerless. This way of looking at Black women in literature and film gives rise to a prevalent assumption that Black women artists view and define themselves as powerless. In fact, Black women's texts clearly articulate their own empowered self-definitions. In an interview with Christina Davis, Morrison insists: "There's a gaze that women writers seem to have that is quite fascinating to me because they tend not to be interested in confrontations with white men—the confrontation between black women and white men is not very important, it doesn't center the text. There are more important ones for them and their look, their gaze of the text is unblinking and wide and very steady."[5]

As early as 1861, Harriet Jacobs's *Incidents in the Life of a Slave Girl* provided a typical assertion of Black women's independent and empowered self-definition. Recalling her enslaver's sexual aggression against her, Jacobs wrote, "The war of my life had begun; and though one of God's most powerless creatures, I resolved never to be conquered" (17). Jacobs's resolution "never to be conquered" expresses her awareness of the many instruments—legal and otherwise—used to render her "one of God's most powerless creatures." Her text clearly indicates that the contestation revolved around more than her enslaver's assertion of a right to sexual dominance. It involved his demand that she acquiesce to *his* definitions and assume the demeanor to match those definitions. Jacobs's resolution "never to be conquered" despite her subordinate status delineates her claim to an interpretive agency and her view of her own empowered Black female subjectivity.

As with many Black women artists, Jacobs's claim to interpretive agency has its source in the linkages, embedded in the family, that the Black experience makes between spirituality and culture. Jacobs's family, especially her grandmother, provided affirming definitions of her human worth, rights, needs, responsibilities, and capacities. This instilled in her the habit of self-definition and of claiming and exercising interpretive agency, especially in situations where her social status called for full submission. On the strength of this discursive agency, Jacobs rejects Dr. Flint's definition of her as powerless. Significantly, Jacobs's narrative refutes Orlando Patterson's claim regarding the "natal alienation" of enslaved Black people. In addition, it is important to note that the Black woman's response to social subordination and aggression is through a positive employment of the gaze. Instead of responding to Dr. Flint's negative gaze, Jacobs looks at herself using the authoritative text of the Black experience whose focus is enabled and stabilized by an ancestral paradigm that emphasizes growth. This is what Morrison refers to as a "gaze of the text [that] is unblinking and wide and very steady."

Like Jacobs's text, Ntozake Shange's contemporary novel *Sassafrass, Cypress, and Indigo* begins with a declaration of the empowered and defining self that informs Black women's texts: "Where there is a woman there is magic. If there is a moon falling from her mouth, she is a woman who knows her magic, who can share or not share her powers" (3). "Magic" and "powers" are equivalent in this description. Here and elsewhere, Black women artists embrace a definition of power summed up by South African educator Mamphela Ramphele as "a range of interventions of which an agent is capable." They view power as coterminous with human agency, that is, humanity itself. This view of power and human agency authorizes Black women's creativity—in literature, cinema, the visual arts, and the performing arts. In general, disempowerment reflects a cognitive dissonance as happens when individuals or groups are prevented from perceiving their own real and potential agency. Since mis-naming is a primary means of generating this cognitive dissonance, the Black woman's positive gaze at herself diffuses the impact of the aggression posed by external definitions like the one Dr. Flint imposed on Harriet Jacobs. By using the authoritative text of Black spirituality and culture, Black women writers and filmmakers both note and critique the hierarchical structures that configure and distort human relationships. Through the use of the democracy of narrative participation, which enables the creation of characters that are fully centered and human, their texts insist that power is an inalienable human birthright.

Logically, therefore, Black women's texts do not endorse the myth of a contestation between the powerful and the powerless. Historically, their texts' "unblinking . . . and very steady gaze" explores contestations over naming, definitions, and privilege. The cultural and social contestation depicted in Black women's texts involves both characters committed to the pursuit of privilege and those committed not simply or simplistically to refusing privilege but to critiquing and revealing its dangers. While power, as argued above, is an innate human attribute, privilege—whether in the form of a special benefit, advantage, or honor—is usually arrogated by and for select individuals or groups.

To the extent that legitimate dispensations of privilege occur in most societies, these usually rest upon earned right and demonstrated responsibility and are frequently moderated by structures of accountability so as not to endanger collective well-being. Here, however, privilege is defined (consistent with its historical construction in the West) as opportunity and/or immunity severed from right and responsibility and reassigned on the basis of race (Whiteness), gender (maleness), and class (wealth). This privilege is most potent when these characteristics exist in combination, but it is also significant even in singular allotments. Predictably, this construction of privilege is loaded with the potential for harm to the self and to others. At the same time, however, its acceptance requires neither formal nor informal gestures, no conscious or unconscious responses. Rather, it is the refusal of this view of privilege that provokes the crisis of a protracted struggle to reconnect opportunity and/or immunity with responsibility, conscience, and consciousness.

Although Black women's texts assert their empowered self-definitions, these definitions are routinely dismissed by contemporary critics preoccupied with positing an oppositional gaze as the inevitable point of departure for Black artistic production. This preoccupation reflects an unwarranted disregard for the existence of a proactive, autonomous demeanor on the part of Black women artists. But, contiguous with Black intellectual traditions rooted in transformative visions, Black women's literature and films reveal a disposition that seeks to explode the binary oppositions that endorse binary distributions of institutional power.

Morrison's statement "I don't regard Black literature as simply books written *by* Black people, or simply as literature *about* Black people, or simply as literature that uses a certain mode of language in which you just sort of drop *g*'s" notes and rejects mainstream designations of Black literary culture that weld Black literature to the taxonomy of race/biology and that mark it as the practice of "defective orthography."[6] In exposing and rejecting these presuppositions, Morrison maintains discursive space for a revised definition of Black artistic expression that links the attainment of an identifiably Black artistic style to the depiction and re-creation of an African[7] cosmology in the text. As she insists in "Rootedness," "It is indicative of the cosmology, the way in which Black people looked at the world" (342).[8] Barbara Christian concurs by pointing to the successful re-creation of this cosmology in several Black texts. As a result, in "Fixing Methodologies: *Beloved*," she calls for a critical methodology that "acknowledges the existence of an African cosmology, how that cosmology has been consistently denigrated in the West, and its appropriateness for texts that are clearly derived from it" (7). In subsequent sections, I extend both Morrison's and Christian's analyses through a close examination of the stylistic, structural, and thematic elements of Black women's film and literature.

Spirituality and Epistemology

Morrison's discussion of the formal and philosophical principles of Black expressive culture identifies aspects of African spirituality, "what I suppose could be called superstition and magic," as an epistemology, "another way of knowing things." While outlining the historical origin of the European novel in the eighteenth century, Morrison emphasizes the novel's ideological function and asserts, "My sense of the novel is that it has always functioned for the class or the group that wrote it" ("Rootedness," 340). For the Black novel, Morrison finds that spirituality serves epistemological functions and assists its ideological objectives, objectives that begin with healing. In the Black novel, this conjunction of spirituality and epistemology enables the depiction of protagonists who invariably withstand various ideological assaults and develop their own liberating ideologies.[9]

As defined above, spirituality refers to consciousness, ethos, lifestyle, and discourse that privileges spirit (that is, life-force) as a primary attribute of self, and that defines and determines health and well-being. This last is broadly conceived to include nonmaterial, that is, psychological/emotional and ethical, as well as material aspects of life. Spirituality, as depicted in Black women's literature and film, is recognizably African/Black but rarely conforms to any single traditional[10] African religion. Instead, its contours are shaped by the core ethical and philosophical values around which several traditions cohere within the African cultural domain.[11] Black women artists depict this Africa-centered[12] spirituality in varying configurations along a syncretistic range.

The primary components of traditional African religion include belief in God, belief in divinities and other spirits, belief in the sustaining presence of ancestors, and belief in the practice of magic. Theologian E. B. Idowu, in *African Traditional Religion: A Definition,* defines magic as the "attempt on the part of man to tap and control the supernatural resources of the universe for his own benefit" (190). In traditional African religion, magic is situated within a nonlinear concept of time. According to ethicist Peter Paris, this religious cosmology is characterized by a "diffused monotheism" in which divinities are derived from and are ministers of a single Deity and features a notable acceptance of the interconnectedness of male and female aspects of Deity. In his transnational analysis titled *The Spirituality of African Peoples,* Paris details four "related and overlapping dimensions of African cosmological and societal thought." He identifies these as:

(1) the realm of spirit (inclusive of the Supreme Deity, the subdivinities, the ancestral spirits) which is the source and preserver of all life

(2) the realm of tribal or ethnic community which, in equilibrium with the realm of spirit, constitutes the paramount goal of human life

(3) the realm of family, which in equilibrium with the realms of tribe and spirit, constitute the principal guiding force for personal development, and

(4) the individual person who strives to integrate the three realms in his or her soul. (25)

These elements map a cosmology in which being and kinship encompass the dead, the living, and the unborn; in which kinship and communication between the living and ancestors are neither ruptured nor interrupted by death; in which every aspect of human activity involves spirituality; and in which a primary goal is to preserve and/or restore an interdependent equilibrium among animate and inanimate beings. Within this cosmology, the expression of spirituality is not restricted to religious praxis. Theological investigations must, therefore, consider a variety of cultural forms and practices.

For contemporary Black women literary and film artists, this Africa-centered spirituality has an important epistemological function. It provides a means of accessing knowledge, including knowledge of what things can and must be known, and for what specific purposes and circumstances. The centrality of spirituality, therefore, enhances the work's epistemological value. As Karla Holloway notes in *Moorings and Metaphor*, "black women's literature reflects its community—the cultural ways of knowing as well as ways of framing that knowledge in language" (1), and these "ways of saying is a dimension of . . . spirituality" (2).

Because of its epistemological potential and its affirmation of culturally specific knowledge and ways of knowing, several scholars in the social sciences and the humanities have turned to Black women's art as a means of illustrating and confirming the ideological, theoretical, and epistemological issues that are central to their various analyses. This is especially true of Black women scholars. In her discussion of the methodologies used in her study titled *Black Womanist Ethics*, ethicist Katie Cannon observes, "I have found that this literary tradition is the nexus between the real-lived texture of Black life and the oral-aural cultural values implicitly passed on and received from one generation to the next" (5). Indeed, by employing Alice Walker's discussion of the term "womanist" to ground their own critical project (womanist theology), Black women theologians and ethicists attest to the centrality of Black women's art to Black women scholars. As a further example, sociologist Patricia Hill Collins's *Black Feminist Thought: Knowledge, Consciousness, and the Politics of Empowerment* relies extensively on Black women's literature and music in "plac[ing] Black women's experiences and ideas at the center of analysis" (xii). Similarly, Angela Davis's *Blues Legacies and Black Feminism* turns to Black women's musical expressions of the early twentieth century as a basis for assessing "past and present forms of social consciousness" and in "establishing the historical antecedents of contemporary Black feminism" (xi).

Numerous other examples demonstrate that Black women's art serves an important epistemological function in enabling contemporary scholars to authenticate knowledge and experience that are frequently misrepresented in, or excluded from, official histories. Morrison calls this artistic recovery of erased knowledge and experience "literary archaeology." Several scholars have commented on the epistemological objectives that motivate this artistic "archaeology." For example, in her analysis of Morrison's *Beloved,* Mae Henderson observes that Black women writers advance a twofold project: "the exploration of the black woman's sense of self, and the imaginative recovery of black women's history" (65). In "The Silence and the Song: Toward a Black Woman's History through a Language of Her Own," Barbara Omolade explains that, "History books and social scientific studies about Black women have yet to capture, touch, or transmit their historical experiences and visions with the truth and depth of the poetry, songs, and novels written by Black women about Black women" (104). Omolade further notes that "The ways of knowing which have developed in the West betray an obsession with rational thought; an inability to connect body, mind, and spirit" (106). The epistemological approaches of Black women literary and film artists characteristically acknowledge the interconnectedness of aspects of self/being. Consequently, as Omolade notes, they employ "a tremendous repertoire of historical methods," including dreams, visions, "rites and rituals . . . intuition, feelings, seeing, speaking, and singing" (106). This "repertoire of historical methods" derives from and attests to the specificity of a Black woman's epistemology, which designates, validates, and transmits culturally specific ways of knowing. It determines what knowledge is valuable, for what purposes, what responsibilities this knowledge confers, and what functions these have within the community, and beyond.

The interconnectedness of scholarly methodology and fictional analysis employed in Black women's scholarship exemplifies Morrison's vision of a balance between "a profound rootedness in the real world" and a reliance on externally "discredited knowledge," "with neither taking precedence over the other" ("Rootedness," 342). As a product of the imagination, fiction is often viewed as a type of "discredited knowledge," and indeed it presents itself as invention. In "The Site of Memory," Morrison notes: "Fiction, by definition, is distinct from fact. Presumably it's the product of imagination—invention—and it claims the freedom to dispense with 'what really happened,' or where it really happened, or when it really happened, and nothing in it needs to be publicly verifiable, although much in it can be verified" (112). While much fiction upholds the veil drawn between the imagination and the reality on which it feeds, Black women's fiction lifts this veil and offers itself as truth. Black women's fiction evinces a "profound rootedness in the real world" and typically begins with and acknowledges the lived, historical event that is transformed in the telling. This is well illustrated in Morrison's *Beloved*, which develops around the lived experience of Margaret Garner, a refugee from Slavery. Pursued by her former enslavers, Garner tried to kill her children—and succeeded in one instance—to save them from the horrific life she was forced to endure. Explaining the imperatives behind this fiction-cum-history genre, Morrison notes, in "The Site of Memory": "the crucial distinction for me is not the difference between fact and fiction, but the distinction between fact and truth. Because facts can exist without human intelligence, but truth cannot" (113). Grounded in the paradigm of growth, this approach simultaneously insists that the (institutional) privilege that denied Margaret Garner's right to power must not coerce Morrison, the artist, to surrender the Black woman's right to self-empowerment. The Black woman artist's resolution to tell the truth through art makes it possible to maintain the distinction between fact and truth, privilege and power.

Contemporary Black women literary and film artists have created works in which the characters display aspects of divinity, especially the capacity for righteous/creative agency and access to other ways of knowing. In these works, spirituality constitutes the foundation on which the artist constructs her vision of empowerment, and from which the characters derive knowledge of self and strength. For example, in Morrison's *Beloved* (1987), when

Baby Suggs, holy, priestess and preacher, exhorts the members of her community, she insists "that the only grace they could have was the grace they could imagine. That if they could not see it, they would not have it" (88). In Ntozake Shange's *Sassafrass, Cypress, and Indigo* (1982), Indigo, too, functions as priestess and healer. The narrator notes that, "A woman with a moon falling from her mouth, roses between her legs and tiaras of Spanish moss . . . is a consort of the spirits" (3). In Grace Nichols's *i is a long memoried woman* (1983), as the protagonist emerges from the traumatic birth of the "middle passage womb," the narrator/priestess observes: "being born a woman / she moved again / knew it was the Black Beginning / though everything said it was / the end" (7). In Paule Marshall's *Praisesong for the Widow* (1983), the Igbos' ability to choose life and reject the most intensely nightmarish aspects of the American experience is motivated by their ability to "see in more ways than one" (37).

The concept of "seeing in more ways than one" is evidenced in Black women's film in which the narrative voice is linked to the visual/historical, a style that validates the Black woman artist's effort to distinguish fact from truth. Typically, the character's engagement with an affirming ancestral gaze frames the film's exploration of spiritual agency, a technique that also appears in Black women's literature. In Zeinabu Davis's *Cycles* (1989), a film dedicated to "the goddess within us all," several women enter the dream consciousness of the sleeping Rasheedah to provide the assurance she needs, consoling her with the chant "You're doing okay; you're going to get better." In Julie Dash's *Daughters of the Dust* (1992), Nana Peazant urges her grandchildren to "call on your ancestors to guide you" as they prepare to travel north, to the mainland. And in Maya Angelou's *Down in the Delta* (1999), Loretta's renewed relationships with Uncle Earl, Aunt Annie, Jessie, and "Nathan" prompt a discovery of new ways of knowing herself. In each instance, the character's expanded access to sources and modes of knowing help to stabilize identity and strengthen (familial) relationships.

Spirituality and Ideology

Although the cinematic and literary works discussed in this study occasionally incorporate various configurations of religious praxis, the prominence given to elements of New World African religions has several distinct implications for theological discourse and for interpreting the transformative/emancipatory design within the works themselves.

As defined within Western tradition, theology is discourse on the existence and nature of the divine in a universe that is theocentric. Given the thesis that all human life is, to varying degrees, created in the likeness of the divine image, Western theology seeks to identify the rights and responsibilities of the human person through an assessment of God, the prototype of righteousness. As an extension of this theological praxis, physical variations within the human community—ostensibly the basis of race—have historically been construed as degrees to which specific groups "resemble" the invisible God.[13] The resulting hierarchy of "god-likeness" has (had) both ideological and sociological functions in determining the global distribution of rights and resources.

From an African cultural/spiritual and theological perspective, righteous agency need not be the exclusive province of Deity. In the context of traditional African religions that posit an anthropocentric universe, the divine nature or power of the divine is diffused and does not occupy a static and monolithic center from which various measurements can be extrapolated. In this cosmology, power is the salient characteristic of Deity, and it is directed toward attaining and maintaining a righteous equilibrium of interdependent relationships among animate and inanimate beings, an agenda that does not countenance hegemony.

South African educator Mamphela Ramphele, whose career exemplifies the ways in which spiritual agency informs Black women's civic roles, defines power in ways that reveal the diffusion of the divine nature throughout the universe. According to Ramphele, power connotes "the use of resources of whatever kind to secure outcomes, power then becomes an element of action, and refers to a range of interventions of which an agent is capable" (12). Their belief in the responsibility to exercise this capacity prompts Viola, the Christian convert, to disparagingly remark of her kinfolk in Dash's *Daughters of the Dust,* "They don't leave nothing to God."[14] By contrast, in the closing section of *i is a long memoried woman,* when the titular narrator stands "with all my lives / strung out like beads / before me," she asserts her own responsibility for claiming and exercising righteous agency with the declaration:

> It isn't privilege or pity
> that I seek
> It isn't reverence or safety
> quick happiness or purity
>   but
> the power to be what I am/a woman
> charting my own futures/ a woman
> holding my beads in my hand (79)

From this perspective, it is easy to see how every human activity is an expression of spiritual agency. Indeed, one need not focus on overtly religious phenomena in order to depict or detect expressions of spirituality. Since the primary goal within an African cosmology is to attain and preserve a righteous equilibrium of interdependent relationships, when and where Black women artists represent this cosmology in literature and film, they necessarily affirm an ethos of interconnectedness. Black women's narrative engagement with an ethos and ideology of interconnectedness reveals distinct ways of being human, with attendant responsibilities.

To understand the full significance of this ethos of interconnectedness and the specific ways in which it disrupts a hegemonic apparatus that Morrison dubs "civilization," one has to return to the site of Slavery. Since Slavery launched the production of epistemologies that defamed Black people's culture and experiences, it is a necessary point of departure for reconstructing a liberating epistemology. More important, one has to examine the traditional African cosmology in which these structures of interconnectedness were developed and which were partially eroded and reconfigured by Slavery.

Within traditional African cosmology, cultural nationality and spiritual identity are coterminous. Cultural nationality refers to one's participation in a specific ("ethnic") heritage/tradition. Spiritual identity refers to the same participation/positioning, viewed from a different angle. For example, being Igbo is a description of cultural and spiritual identity and membership. The role assigned to the community of ancestors is the crucial link that fuses cultural and spiritual identity. As Idowu explains:

> The ancestors are regarded still as heads and parts of the families or communities to which they belonged while they were living human beings: for what happened in consequence of the phenomenon called death was only

that the family life of this earth has been extended into the after-life or su-
per sensible world. The ancestors remain, therefore, spiritual superintend-
ents of family affairs and continue to bear their titles of relationship like
"father or "mother." (184)

Africans in the "New World" faced a loss of identity from Christendom,
an agency that gained both its authority and an ideological "immunity from
prosecution" from the institution whose surface features it appropriated—
Christianity. Although the terms "Christendom" and "Christianity" are frequently used synonymously, this analysis identifies radical differences between the two.[15] In writing his 1845 autobiographical narrative, Frederick
Douglass was compelled to add an appendix to clarify this difference.
"What I have said respecting and against religion," Douglass wrote, "I mean
strictly to apply to the *slaveholding religion* of this land, and with no possible reference to Christianity proper; for, between the Christianity of this
land, and the Christianity of Christ, I recognize the widest possible difference" (120). Writing before Douglass, in his 1829 *Appeal,* David Walker was
even more adamant in his insistence on the distinction between state-
sponsored Christendom and the Christianity of Jesus Christ, declaring that
"the Europeans and their descendants," "the White Christians of America,"
were "in open violation" of the teachings of Jesus Christ (55). "Can any thing
be a greater mockery of religion," he asked, "than the way in which it is con-
ducted by the Americans?" (63). Douglass's and Walker's analyses posit a
distinction between Christendom and Christianity that is essential for any
accurate evaluation of the history of contestation involving Black people's
identity. Acknowledging this distinction enables one to understand why,
during and after Slavery, Africans in the New World were able to utilize
Christianity as a vehicle for their own empowerment.

Although the term "Christendom" is now simply used to mean Christians worldwide, in twelfth-century usage it carried an increasingly em-
phatic geopolitical inflection, referring to those "countries professing
Christianity collectively." As evidenced by the role this "collective" has
played in world history since the fifteenth century, Christendom refers to
the conglomerate of those nation-states for whom racial identity (Whiteness), regional/territorial identity (Westernness), cultural identity (Euro-
peanness), and theological subscription were alchemized. Christendom

denotes both a regional *constituency*, and a state-sponsored *agency* responsible for unleashing a veritable holocaust on several non-White, non-European cultures—as well as Jewish communities in Europe.

As an agency, "Christendom" refers to that branch of the European imperialist apparatus disguised under religious rhetoric that espoused the goals of territorial expansion, colonization, and the accumulation of wealth—through the exploitation of human labor and natural resources. Like any hegemonic agency, Christendom, in order to more effectively "govern," needed to erase and elide the identities of the peoples it sought to dominate. Christendom operated and operates still on the presupposition of an entrenched cultural/racial hierarchy that coincides with, and is masked by, a theological hierarchy of believers and unbelievers.

One of the most obvious signs of this operation is in the customary expansion of the biblical categories of "Jews," "Gentiles," and "Church" to include—in most translations—a fourth category: "Heathens." In this expanded nomenclature, "Gentiles" denotes those non-Jews who are White, while "Heathens" denotes those non-Jews who are non-Whites. And while "Jews" and "Gentiles" can become part of "the Church," even "Heathen converts" remain outside this new definition and privileged relationship to God. As a further expropriation, the term "Christian" is used to refer to Europeans as a racial/cultural group, a departure from New Testament usage, where it designates a covenant relationship that is neither racially, culturally, nor regionally exclusive. Thus, as Winthrop Jordan notes in *White over Black*, "From the first, then, vis-à-vis the Negro the concept embedded in the term Christian seems to have conveyed much of the idea and feeling of *we* as against *they:* to be Christian was to be civilized rather than barbarous, English rather than African, white rather than black" (94). Although the practices within Christendom—including the theologizing of race, missionary-style colonization, assigning "Christian"/European names, and the institution of Slavery itself—did not have biblical sanction, they were essential to the advancement of European imperialism.

"Christianity," by contrast, refers to a body of *teachings* that has been given very diverse theological interpretations and applications in the two millennia since Jesus and his disciples first articulated them. The New Testament term used to refer to the global aggregate of those who accept Jesus and his teachings is "the church." Christianity *proposes* a new identity. For

those who accept the invitation to be "in Christ," prior identities are subli-
mated. This transformation stems from a new relationship with God and
God's creatures (beginning with the self) that, as a sustained commitment,
engenders a renewed character and revised identity. The term "conversion"
is commonly used to designate this voluntary commitment. While most
studies posit a singular definition of "conversion," this analysis recognizes
two distinct meanings. On the one hand, "conversion," as an element of colonization, refers to the process of assigning a new and putatively "superior"
cultural subjectivity, contiguous with the mandate of Christendom. On the
other hand, as Kimberly Rae Connor observes in her analysis titled *Conversions and Visions in the Writings of African-American Women*, "conversion"
designates a self-empowering "sacralization of identity," a process of "affirming qualities of selfhood and womanhood and claiming them as sacred" (4). In that sense, conversion represents a counterhegemonic act of
reclaiming discredited aspects of self. This understanding of conversion
undergirds my analysis of the two "imagined contemporaries"—Maria W.
Stewart and Baby Suggs, holy—in chapter 2. (Olaudah Equiano's two conversion experiences, recounted in his eighteenth-century autobiography,
illustrate the radical differences between these two modes.) As Paul summarizes it, "So if anyone is in Christ, there is a new creation: everything old
has passed away; see, everything has become new!"[16] Elsewhere, Paul explains this transformation as a volitional sublimation of various aspects of
personal identity.[17]

Because of somewhat parallel mechanisms of sublimation, the ideological demands of Christendom could be and were superimposed on the ontological demands of Christianity. As a result, African peoples—converts
and nonconverts alike—during and after Slavery, were required to divest
themselves of important aspects of their cultural and spiritual identity and
assimilate to a European cultural paradigm, beginning with the exchange of
African names for "Christian," that is, European, names.

An agenda to colonize, Christendom was skillfully disguised by a putative
mission to convert and presented the first threat to cultural/spiritual connectedness. For fifteenth-century Africans, conversion—as an act and process of relinquishing prior beliefs, customs, practices, in order to adopt new,
different, and "better" ones—was unthinkable, if not ontologically impossible. Among other things, this would have involved a radical and untenable

disconnection from kin (living and dead), a removal from self. The relocation and renaming of African peoples via the trans-Atlantic slave trade prioritized and facilitated the imposition of a "new" cultural/spiritual subjectivity. More than the force with which this "superior" cultural/spiritual cosmology was imposed, the ubiquitous practice of unnaming and renaming jeopardized the spiritual/cultural kinship among African peoples as it was designed to render them strangers to, and alienated from, themselves.

Despite the widespread enforcement of Christendom's ideological, cultural, and theological mandates, Africans in the diaspora maintained key aspects of their cultural/spiritual identity. Describing the development of diverse New World African religions, Albert Raboteau notes that "new as well as old gods have come to be worshiped by Afro-Americans, but the new, like the old, have been perceived in traditionally African ways" (16). While the persistence of this cultural design has been acknowledged in the case of Candomblé, Santería, Voodun, Hoodoo, and other nonchristological diaspora religions, this view has generally not been extended to Afro-Christianity. However, in looking at the development of Afro-Christianity among the Gullah, historian Margaret Washington Creel notes that they "converted Christianity to their African world view, using the new religion to justify combating objective forces, to collectively perpetuate community-culture, and as an ideology of freedom. Thus it was less a case of Christianity instilling a sense of resignation because of beliefs in future rewards than of an African philosophical tradition being asserted in the slave quarters" (74). As Paris explains:

> Due to the circumstances of their departure from Africa, Africans had no choice but to leave their cultural artifacts on the continent. Yet they did not arrive on these shores as a *tabula rasa*. Rather, different groups brought their respective cosmological understandings with them and gradually shaped a new world of spiritual and moral meaning by appropriating and interpreting various elements in their new environment in accord with their African cosmologies. . . . The preservation of their spirituality under the conditions of slavery was an astounding accomplishment, due principally to their creative genius in making the Euro-American cultural forms and practices serve as vehicles for the transmission of African cultural elements." (35)

Consequently, when Zora Neale Hurston writes, in "Characteristics of Negro Expression" (1937), that "The Negro is not a Christian really" (56), she is not accusing Black people of religious insincerity. Hurston's extensive knowledge of the cultural and spiritual life of Africans in several diaspora communities—the subject of her fiction and anthropological research—warrants a more complex interpretation. Given her awareness of the concurrence of cultural and spiritual identity, Hurston is simply acknowledging that Christendom could not and did not eliminate an African cultural/spiritual belonging. Read: "The 'Negro' is still an African." Hurston's interpretation is based on her observation of "those elements which were brought over from Africa" ("The Sanctified Church," 105) and subsequently unnamed. Morrison, too, asserts that this Africa-centered spirituality-cum-epistemology has been actively unnamed. As she notes, the only terms available for designating "other way of knowing things" were "superstition and magic."

Until recently, African religious traditions were widely regarded as an absence of religion. The dearth of names, labels, terminology in the West and in the Western academy for describing this and other key aspects of Black peoples' lives in the diaspora, as on the continent, is intimately connected to the fact that the African cultural domain has been designated as the absence of culture, so that one need not assign any further definitions. This designation perpetuates both a "conceptual gap" and a "functional lexical gap." Philosopher Bill Lawson explains that a "functional lexical gap"—"the lack of a convenient word to express what [one] wants to talk about" (76)—can exist even when there is no conceptual gap. The persistence of lexical gaps—the lack of "concise descriptive words," Lawson notes, "hampers the framing of appropriate social policy" (77). The existence of a conceptual gap—in this case, the lack of understanding of the complexity and integrity of the African cultural domain—impairs communication and thereby social relationships. For the Black woman artist, this situation evokes the need to deploy the paradigm of growth in the establishment of interdependent human relationships.

Hurston's critical, interpretive intervention in *naming* the necessary point-of-departure for contemporary Black women literary and film artists attests to her awareness of the utility of this approach. Hurston underscores the historical context of, and necessity for, a renaming and reaffirmation of spiritual/cultural identity when Janie observes, in *Their Eyes Were Watching God,* that "Nanny's head and face looked like the standing roots of some old tree that had been torn away by storm. Foundation of ancient power that no longer mattered" (15). Hurston's carefully cryptic syntax here prompts several questions: In whose judgment does this foundation "no longer matter"? From whose/what perspective might this foundation still be relevant? And what, after all, is this "ancient power"? Black women literary and film artists have been among the first to engage these questions.[18] They interrogate assumptions of fragmentation and debilitation and respond with the common vision of (inter)connectedness, with a primary emphasis on kinship matrices. They offer compelling answers to these questions by providing another view of Black peoples' histories, another repository of histories to be known, another way of knowing those histories.

While Hurston acknowledges the assault to which the African cultural/spiritual tradition has been subjected, she does not deny the reality of that "ancient power." Hurston's unequivocal rejection of a disempowered position in the sentence quoted above typifies the stance of Black women artists in revisiting Slavery. Paradoxically, returning to that temporal site facilitates an enabling encounter. On the one hand, it allows a recognition of, and reaccess to, the spiritual resources needed to withstand assault. On the other, it allows a rediscovery of new directions for growth. In sum, it facilitates a re-encounter with cultural philosophies and ethics that pre-date Slavery.

Slavery, with its systematic misnamings of African cultures and peoples—as *slave, colored, negro, coon, sambo, darky,* and so on—constitutes the interpretive context for revisiting an Africa-centered spirituality. This is indicated by its centrality in literature and film by contemporary Black women artists. For example, in Nichols's *i is a long memoried woman,* in Shange's *Sassafrass, Cypress, and Indigo,* in Palcy's *Sugar Cane Alley,* and in Dash's critically acclaimed film *Daughters of the Dust,* the history of Slavery and its continuing ramifications form the visible and invisible subtext. In Nichols's re-presentation of four centuries of African diaspora history that begins with Slavery, the titular narrator emerges from the "middle passage womb" to discover that, like broken waist beads, "my life has slipped out / of my possession" (21). The four centuries–long quest to re-collect and re-claim possession of her "beads" culminates with the closing piece, "Holding

My Beads," in which the narrator announces, "I am here / a woman. . . with all my lives / strung out like beads / before me" (90). The successful concatenation of her multiple lives coincides with her empowerment through this temporal and spiritual journey. Here, the ancestral voice spurns dismemberment, claiming a voluntary reconnection amid the dispersion.

In Shange's exploration of the role of the Black woman priestess, it is her encounter with the history of Slavery that propels Indigo toward a self-conscious understanding of her own calling and capacities. "The Caverns began to moan, not with sorrow but in recognition of Indigo's revelation. The slaves who were ourselves had known terror intimately, confused sunrise with pain, & accepted indifference with kindness. Now they sang out from the walls, pulling Indigo toward them." As she attempts to meet/read these voice, Indigo's "fingers grazed cold, hard metal rings. Rust covered her palms & fingers. She kept following the rings. Chains. Leg irons. The Caverns revealed the plight of her people, but kept on singing" (49). Through this encounter with Slavery, Indigo reconnects with her ancestors who assist her in defining her role and responsibility: "The slaves who were ourselves aided Indigo's mission, connecting soul & song, experience and unremembered rhythms" (45).

In Palcy's *Sugar Cane Alley*, the discovery of Slavery's still active infrastructure helps José to recognize the discrepancy between the schoolteacher's confident assertion that "Education is the key that unlocks the second door to our freedom" and the plantation model that locks the world's "black shack alleys" in the bottom tier of contemporary economic and social hierarchies. Palcy's narrative montage raises the question—articulated by the village elder, Mr. Medouze—of the extent to which the first door was really opened.

In Dash's moving presentation of the Peazant family, the recurring image of Black hands "scarred blue with the poisonous indigo dye that built up all those plantations from swampland" becomes a visual code for the history of Slavery that informs all situations and events in the present.[19] Consequently, although Slavery is not the explicit subject of the film, its shadow lurks in the story of the rape of Eula, Yellow Mary, and countless other "ruint" women, in the antilynching campaign with which Eli eventually becomes involved, in the undisputed kinship among all the inhabitants of these islands, and in the story of the Igbos that is recounted from different interpretive angles by Eula and Bilal Muhammed, respectively. Indeed, it is his transformative encounter with this history—as he journeys out to embrace ancestors represented in the wooden figure of an enslaved African floating in the waters of Igbo Landing—that enables Eli to understand the many dimensions of violation that Slavery entailed, and thereby the larger context of his wife's rape. The narrative and visual choices Dash makes enhances the implementation of the paradigm of growth by foregrounding specific goals—including the goal of (re)establishing interdependent relationships—and by encouraging the enactment of creative agency.

In each work, the ideological connection between the subversion of cultural/spiritual identity and Slavery is indisputable, as is the artist's commitment to revising, reclaiming, and renaming ancient identities, kinships, and responsibilities through the retelling of that past. Like the traditional Black priestess/prophetess, these Black women artists view survival and growth as primary aspects of an independent and comprehensive agenda. Working from that viewpoint, in which an Africa-centered spirituality—unrestricted to religious praxis—remains a central component, these Black women artists also fulfill important psychospiritual and sociopolitical leadership roles.

Black Women's Art and the Ethos
of Interconnectedness

Black women artists do not simply depict characters with spiritual authority; they facilitate and craft the parameters and dimensions of that authority. Each work manifests aspects of Black women's creative/righteous agency and testifies to the capacity of both the priestess functioning *within* the work of art and the artist-priestess acting *through* the work of art. In "The Race for Theory," Barbara Christian offers a crucial insight on Black women's art as a mode of theory. She identifies the operation of theory in narrative form—what she calls "theorizing": "I am inclined to say that our theorizing (and I intentionally use the verb rather than the noun) is often in narrative forms . . . since dynamic rather than fixed ideas seem more to our liking" (53). Christian's analysis dismantles the divide between theory and performance, suggesting that in works by Black women artists, theory is performed. Building on Christian's notion of performing theory or theorizing in narrative form, I extend the discussion here to the Black woman writer and filmmaker performing theology or theologizing through an in-depth exploration of her deployment of the paradigm of growth and the democracy of narrative participation.

Such a repositioning is sanctioned by the rearticulation of an ethos of interconnectedness *within* and *in the very form* of Black women's literary and cinematic art. Using an interpretive methodology, it becomes possible to show how the ethos of interconnectedness originates in the paradigm of growth, which then shapes specific aspects of the text. These aspects advance the ethical goals that undergird African cosmology, thereby illuminating the philosophical importance of African diaspora cultural and artistic tropes.

Since artistic expression is one of the many forms in which the cosmological vision is encoded and disseminated, it follows that these expressions are designed to support specific goals. Among the ethical goals that inform African cosmology are those of preserving community, establishing interdependent relationships, and promoting interpretive autonomy. Examining the four aspects of interconnectedness represented in Black women's texts exposes this philosophical foundation. This represents a significant development in scholarly methodology.

To the extent that the analysis of African diaspora artistic expressions has been shaped by the paradigm of resistance, this has generated sociological readings of these expressions. In fact, since the paradigm of resistance coincides with and reinforces a narrative of Black pathology, it generates a preoccupation with sociological readings. These have been especially prevalent in literary studies. Recontextualizing scholarly analysis in relation to the paradigm of growth allows for a discovery and consideration of the philosophical goals and resources that reflect the cultural worldview underlying the creation of literature, cinema, and other artistic expressions.

The aspects of interconnectedness that shape and that are represented in Black women's literature and cinema include the depiction of kinship matrices, the deployment of a multidimensional narrative consciousness, the incorporation of multigeneric components, and the construction of a multidimensional time realm. For the Black woman artist, the configurations of kinship matrices typically assume global dimensions to cover cultural kin in several (diaspora) communities. Kinship matrices consist of several roles that have explicit and extensive sustaining functions and include living relatives, cultural kin, and, most important, elders and ancestors. Many Black women's novels and films first depict the unborn as the central aspect of interconnectedness of kinship among the living and the dead. The multiple dimensions of human connectedness are used to underscore the symbiosis between the development of the community and the development of the individual.

Second, in its progression toward re*member*ing community, the narrative consciousness in Black women's literature and film spans several perspectives, constituting a multidimensional narrative consciousness. Multidimensional narrative consciousness represents an expansion of the dialogic relationship between the individual and community that typifies African cultural expressions. For example, whereas call-and-response dynamics usually consist of a single leader interacting with an audience and/or participant community—in worship, dance, storytelling, and so on —multidimensional narrative consciousness allows for a rotating and sometimes migrating focus on individual or collective narrative voices in ways that support a democracy of narrative participation. This rotating focus makes it difficult, if not impossible, to undermine the identities of individual constituents within the collective. In Black women's texts, therefore, the primary objective is to reconcile these voices so that the woman, man, child, narrator, protagonist, listener, reader, viewer, traveler repossesses their (cultural/spiritual and) historical self-consciousness. The different stages of reconfiguring this multidimensional subjectivity are reflected in the multigeneric composition of the works that deploy the ethos of interconnectedness to inform the themes of reconnection and re-collection. In a successful work, this ethos of interconnectedness manifests itself in the metaphysical and psychic direction of the narrative journey, which is invariably retrospective.

Applying the ethos of interconnectedness, Black women artists facilitate the varied expressions of multiple genres—poetry, letters, songs, sermons, recipes, prayers—within a single work. This results in the fusion of theory, theology, and artistic praxis such that a layering of cultural forms involving significant elements from orature, music, religious practice, dance, herbal medicine, photography, visual art, and literature is achieved. Among other things, it is this layering that enables these works to theorize about the ideological function of art and the role of the artist as priestess/activist. Theorizing in this way makes for the uniqueness of the fourth aspect: the construction of a multidimensional realm.

The simultaneity of a narrative past, present, and future produces an artistic viewpoint in which ancestors, the unborn, and those previously marginalized can be seen as fully and actively contributing to the sustenance and connectedness of contemporary living. Analyses in subsequent chapters illustrate how this temporal layering of experiences in Black women's literature and film produces a dense epistemological field from which characters, readers, viewers, scholars, and other artists can gather critical insights.

Embracing Responsibility

Maria Stewart and Toni Morrison

If such women as are here described have once existed, be no longer astonished then, my brethren and friends, that God at this eventful period should raise up your own females to strive, by their example both in public and private, to assist those who are endeavoring to stop the strong current of prejudice that flows so profusely against us at present.

—MARIA W. STEWART, *Speeches and Essays*

My objective in this chapter is to demonstrate how and why the focus on the landscape of Slavery in Black women's art is such an important one, and why it is such a frequent complement to the deployment of spirituality. Specifically, I argue that the Slavery setting provides a view of Black women's spiritual authority independent of their social status. I use the careers of Slavery-era Black women preachers in history and literature to clarify the sources and definitions of authority in Black women's lives.

Black Women's Spiritual Authority

The depiction of Black women exercising spiritual authority—often within oppressive contexts—is one of the most significant ways in which spirituality informs the vision of transformation in Black women's literature and film. Telumée in Simone Schwarz-Bart's *The Bridge of Beyond,* and the titular protagonists of Gloria Naylor's *Mama Day,* and Zeinabu Davis's *Mother of the River* all display an awareness of their own creative agency and spiritual authority amid circumstances shaped by various forms of institutional oppression. These portraits of spiritually empowered and self-possessed Black women have their prototype in the nineteenth-century career of activist Maria W. Stewart.

Maria W. Stewart (1803–79), the first American woman political speaker, was an important contributor to the public discourse of her time. Born in Connecticut and raised in the activist Black Boston community, Stewart published essays and spoke publicly on a variety of topics during a period of about two years. As an empowered Black woman in an enslaving, patriarchal society, Stewart's career provides important insights on the use of spirituality as a source of authority and as a counterhegemonic resource. Her career illustrates that, in the context of Black women's lives, authority is based not simply on the assertion of rights but also on the embrace of responsibility—responsibility to meet the spiritual, psychological, and material needs of the cultural community. In attempting to fulfill this responsibility, Stewart displayed a remarkable degree of autonomy and authority amid a social and political context that severely curtailed Black women's freedom.

Stewart's multifaceted spiritual authority can be compared to that of Baby Suggs, holy (1795?–1865), the spiritual center of Morrison's *Beloved.* Morrison's portrait of Baby Suggs, holy, presents spiritual authority as a mode of (ethical) leadership that ensures the survival of her community and that assists the novel's ideology. The parallel aspects and implications of Stewart's and Baby Suggs's preaching/public speaking careers highlight the connection between the novel's prominent depiction of, and reliance on, spirituality, and its artistic and ideological objectives. This analysis compares Stewart's preaching ministry with that of Baby Suggs, holy; examines the congruity between Stewart's sociopolitical vision and Toni Morrison's; and evaluates the conjunction between Morrison's critique of the ideology of "race" and Baby Suggs's analysis of its spiritual and epistemological consequences through her extended meditation on "color."

Stewart's historical ministry and Baby Suggs's fictional ministry exemplify the ways in which aspects of African religion/cosmology inform Black people's engagement with Christianity—Afro-Christianity—and engender a transformative spiritual and social vision. The primary indications of the influence of an African cosmology appear in their unsanctioned belief in their own capacity for creative/righteous agency and in the fact that their vision of the role and responsibility of preacher is informed by, and expressive of, an ethos of interconnectedness that enabled these "imagined contemporaries" to fuse spiritual and sociopolitical leadership roles. In referring to Maria Stewart and Baby Suggs, holy, as "imagined contemporaries," I want to direct attention to the fact that while only Black women who were situated like Stewart—in the North, and as "free" persons—could write and leave textual record of their preaching, Stewart, Jarena Lee, Zilpha Elaw, Julia Foote, and Amanda Berry Smith were not alone in their preaching. Even more numerous were the (formerly) enslaved southern Black women who, like Sinda[1] and like Baby Suggs, holy, spoke to the spiritual and psychological needs of the majority enslaved Black population, without benefit of denominational affiliation or literacy. While the textual record posits a single location for the early nineteenth-century Black woman preacher, the juxtaposition of these two figures provides a more comprehensive description of the diverse locations from which Black women embraced responsibility and claimed spiritual authority. Equally important, the congruity between Stewart's and Baby Suggs's visions demonstrates the patterning of Black women's art from Black women's lived experiences. Morrison's portrait of Baby Suggs, holy, coincides with Stewart's view of spirituality as a source of authority and as a vehicle for exercising righteous agency. To the extent that it does so, it provides an important insight into the empowered self-definitions that nineteenth-century Black women crafted on the site of oppression.

Historical records give no indication of gender restrictions on Black women's participation in the spiritual life and leadership of the enslaved Black community in the early plantation era. Were gender restrictions already established in the spiritual/religious life among Blacks on the plantation, there would have been no lived foundation on which Black women could have based their authority and embraced spiritual/cultural responsibilities. Without such a tradition, the leadership, authority, and effectiveness of women like Baby Suggs, holy, Sojourner Truth, and Harriet Tubman, would have been unimaginable.

The move away from the plantation and the development of denominational theologies brought an orthodoxy—borrowed from Euro-American theologies—that opposed Black women's spiritual leadership. Early nineteenth-century Black women preachers resisted this trend. Most Black male church administrations responded to their resistance by adopting a policy that allowed a semantic and symbolic difference between men's preaching and women's preaching. In deciding that women could give exhortations—

but not preach—Black churches effectively barred women from the symbolic sphere of spiritual authority: the pulpit. For Stewart, Baby Suggs, holy, and other nineteenth-century Black women preachers, the question was not simply one of rights but of responsibility—responsibility conferred by both cultural tradition and the exigencies of life in Slavery-era America. Indeed, the readiness with which Stewart took her message from the inner sanctum of the church to the outer reaches of the city suggests that exegetical privilege was not her goal. Rather, as Nellie McKay has noted of Stewart's contemporaries, "they wanted their words to change the hearts of the men and women whom they reached" (140–41). In fact, Baby Suggs, holy, affirms this definition and vision of preaching as an assertion of transformative agency, explicitly differentiating it from hermeneutic performance: "she didn't deliver sermons or preach—insisting she was too ignorant for that—she *called* and the hearing heard" (177). Moreover, for nineteenth-century Black preachers—many of whom were illiterate—interpretive agency was neither text-based nor text-centered. Instead, interpretive agency was grounded in a lived awareness of, and connectedness to, God. Maria Stewart and Baby Suggs, holy, both claimed and enacted a spiritual authority and social agency sanctioned by their connectedness to God. This spiritual authority was the foundation on which these Black women based their preaching ministry, providing a model and vision of righteous agency to multiple constituencies.

The interconnectedness of male and female aspects of Deity in African cosmology may well account for Black women's undaunted conviction of their own entitlement to and capacity for spiritual leadership. More than the fact of access to spiritual leadership through the office of the priestess, the acceptance of the female aspects of Deity—whether in the recognition of the male-female nature of Deity, as in Mawu-Lisa, among the Fon; or in the existence of female archdivinity, as in Ala, the Earth goddess, in Igbo cosmology—sanctioned Black women's spiritual authority. According to Paris, "it is difficult to get a precise estimate of the extent of female imagery pertaining to the supreme deity in Africa because many African languages do not have gender-specific pronouns" (32–33). "Nevertheless," Paris notes, "various subdivinities are male, female, or androgynous. Female imagery with respect to the supreme deity and the reality of female subdivinities and their priestesses enhances the status of women in the sphere of religion. . . . Thus African cosmological thought not only demonstrates the limits of male authority but also provides considerable resources for the exercise of female authority" (33). Indeed, in "The Goddess Osun as a Paradigm for African Feminist Criticism," Diedre L. Bádéjò notes that "Power and femininity co-exist in Osun's orature" and that "mythical images and myriad roles of Osun and countless other African deities . . . traversed the Atlantic" (27). The existence of this cultural model meant that while enslaved Black women met few examples of women's spiritual authority in the sociocultural environment of Euro-America, they nevertheless brought to their early engagement with Christianity and to the formation of Afro-Christianity an indomitable sense of entitlement to and preparedness for such roles.

Then, as now, spirituality served an important ideological function in resisting the distorting epistemologies of "master-narratives." As Ashraf Rushdy notes of *Beloved*, for example, the text situates itself within a contestation over competing narratives about Slavery. By way of mediating this contestation, Rushdy claims, "the novel both remembers the victimization of the ex-slaves who are its protagonists and asserts the healing and wholeness that those protagonists carry with them in their communal lives" (575). It does that and much more. Read through the paradigm of growth, the novel also exposes the self-inflicted injuries of the enslavers, injuries that are psychospiritual, moral, and epistemological; and illuminates, even as it counteracts, the ramifications of that untreated malady for the extratextual community of contemporary U.S. Americans.

Authorizing the Speaking Subject

In her analysis of the women's movement in the Black Baptist Church in *Righteous Discontent,* historian Evelyn Brooks Higginbotham amply demonstrates "that women were crucial to broadening the public arm of the church and making it the most powerful institution of racial self-help in the African American community" (1) in the post-Reconstruction era. Higginbotham explains that "In the closed society of Jim Crow, the church afforded African Americans an interstitial space in which to critique and contest white America's racial domination. In addition, the church offered black women a forum through which to articulate a public discourse critical of women's subordination" (10). In this context, Higginbotham notes

Stewart's early leadership in articulating a vision of Black women as social activists and institution builders that would later be crucial to Black women of the club movement era: "It is conceivable that all were influenced by Stewart's speeches, since she lived to publish her collected works in 1879" (124). In these published essays and speeches, Maria Stewart exemplifies and authorizes the Black woman priestess as activist preaching a message of spiritual and social transformation.

Maria Stewart began her public speaking ministry at the age of twenty-seven, shortly after the death of her husband and following a conversion experience. Emancipation from conjugal constraint through widowhood may have been as important to Stewart's ministry as was the mandate received by conversion. Like Stewart, Jarena Lee felt called to preach but was barred from doing so until the death of her husband some six years later. The dimensions and direction of Stewart's conversion exemplify the pattern of conversion among African American women. In *Conversions and Visions in the Writings of African-American Women,* Kimberly Rae Connor notes that through conversion Black women cast off the "old man," that is, the definition of self(-worth) crafted by the dominant culture, and put on a "new man," a new and blessed identity in which the previously discredited aspects of personal identity—Blackness and womanhood—are sanctified as the basis for spiritual authority and service. Connor cites and concurs with theologian Hans Mol in describing conversion in the lives of Black women as a process that leads to a "sacralization of identity" (4). Moreover, "in their effort to reclaim the sacred qualities of their own identities," Connor argues, "these women reflect a sentiment of black religious experience that expresses, as Vincent Harding has said, 'self-love as a religious calling'" (4). As testimony to this calling to self-love, Stewart wrote, "Many think because your skins are tinged with a sable hue, that you are an inferior race of beings; but God does not consider you as such. He hath formed and fashioned you in his own glorious image, and hath bestowed upon you reason and strong powers of intellect" (29).

Describing her new spiritual commitment and the sacralized identity it conferred, in 1831 Stewart wrote, "[I] now possess that spirit of independence that, were I called upon, I would willingly sacrifice my life for the cause of God and my brethren" (29). Asserting the political dimension of her spiritual commitment Stewart noted that "Many will suffer for pleading the cause of oppressed Africa, and I shall glory in being one of her martyrs" (30). Her consciousness of a spiritual and cultural connectedness to African peoples marks one of the striking aspects of Stewart's preaching. And because this sense of kinship is so pronounced, it gives a distinct thematic configuration to Stewart's spiritual leadership. Stewart's preaching develops around three related themes: economic self-reliance, promises of divine assistance to oppressed Africans, and women's participatory and leadership rights. In addition, it provides a deconstructive theological and political analysis of the marginalization of African peoples and culture, and a program for transformation.

In "Religion and the Pure Principles of Morality, The Sure Foundation on Which We Must Build," the text that inaugurated her career as a preacher, Stewart repeatedly calls on her contemporaries to "promote ourselves and improve our own talents" (35). Her vision of Black women's empowerment is completely divorced from any assumption of, or interest in, White America's sympathy. Fully aware of the magnitude of racist oppression, she exhorts her readers, "let us make a mighty effort, and arise; and if no one will promote or respect us, let us promote and respect ourselves" (37). Her strategies for engaging the hearts of her audience include rhetorical challenges, followed by explicit directives. As an example, Stewart asks, "Shall it any longer be said of the daughters of Africa, they have no ambition, they have no force?" Her response: "By no means. Let every female heart become united, and let us raise a fund ourselves; and at the end of one year and a half, we might be able to lay the corner stone for the building of a High School, that the higher branches of knowledge might be enjoyed by us; and God would raise us up, and enough to aid us in our laudable designs" (37). Here and elsewhere, sociopolitical commentaries are expertly sutured into Stewart's religious appeals and her exhortations to self-reliance.

Although Stewart is generally regarded as simply a public speaker, not a preacher, the content and form of her addresses justify the designation of preacher. Stewart's written and oral addresses take the form of religious exhortations petitioning Black people to a christological standard of moral behavior, and to a degree of political, social, and economic analysis and self-reliance inextricably bound to the former. In her comprehensive introduction to Stewart's *Essays and Speeches,* Marilyn Richardson argues that, "Not only did she master the Afro-American idiom of thundering exhortation uniting spiritual and secular concerns, she was able early on to exercise that skill with equal success on the printed page and at the podium" (14). Richardson also notes Stewart's "command of such sophisticated techniques as the implied call-and-response cadence set in motion by sequential rhetorical questions; of anaphora, parataxis, and the shaping of imperative and periodic sentences; along with the powerful and affecting rhythms of her discourse" (14).[2] In one of her occasional apostrophes, to "ye great and mighty men of America, ye rich and powerful ones," Stewart displays her command of these oratorical techniques.

> You may kill, tyrannize, and oppress as much as you choose, until our cry shall come up before the throne of God; for I am firmly persuaded, that he will not suffer you to quell the proud, fearless and undaunted spirits of the Africans forever. . . . We will not come out against you with swords and staves, as against a thief; but *we will tell you* that our souls are fired with the same love of liberty and independence with which your souls are fired. *We will tell you* that too much of your blood flows in our veins, too much of your color in our skins, for us not to possess your spirits. *We will tell you* that it is our gold that clothes you in fine linen and purple, and causes you to fare sumptuously every day; and it is the blood of our fathers, and the tears of our brethren that have enriched your soils. AND WE CLAIM OUR RIGHTS. *We will tell you* that we are not afraid of them that kill the body, and after that can do no more. (40; emphasis added)

In the context of nineteenth-century Black women's spiritual texts, Maria Stewart's articulation of her passionate commitment to her cultural community is unusual. While other evangelical women preachers like Jarena Lee, Amanda Berry Smith, and Zilpha Elaw were clearly opposed to oppressive practices in all forms, their writings display a curious and steadfast silence on the political status of African Americans,[3] and about the political and cultural environment within the United States. But because "God alone . . . has inspired my heart to feel for Afric's woes," Stewart's preaching and writing provide extensive critiques of the political and social conditions in which African Americans lived. In "An Address Delivered at the African Masonic Hall" in 1833, Stewart unmasks the ostensible benevolence of the Colonization Society whose goal was to repatriate free Blacks to West Africa, noting that "if the colonizationists are the real friends to Africa,

let them expend the money which they collect in erecting a college to edu-
cate her injured sons in this land of gospel, light, and liberty" (61). In "Religion and the Pure Principles of Morality," she offers her own penetrating
critique of the racially motivated discrepancy in U.S. government foreign
policy, noting that while the "mighty men of America" rejoiced in the liberation struggles of the Poles, Greeks, and Catholics, they "have acknowledged all the nations of the earth, except Hayti" (39). And in her "defense of
African rights and liberty," Stewart delivers an astute analysis of the ways
in which the historical distribution of socioeconomic privilege has benefited Euro-Americans: "Had we as a people received one-half the early ad-
vantages the whites have received, I would defy the government of these
United States to deprive us any longer of our rights" (61). Stewart's exhortations—ranging beyond theological/religious issues—exemplify how an
ethos of connectedness generates a multithematic preaching.

During the early nineteenth century, there were few precedents for Stewart's multithematic preaching. Indeed, Stewart's friend and mentor David
Walker provides the single example of a Black preacher whose preaching
did not simply condemn Slavery but who passionately entreated Black people to self-reliance, to exercise their capacity for righteous agency, and to
take immediate steps to redress political, social, and economic oppression.
Walker's *Appeal* incurred the wrath of Whites and the dismay of some
Blacks. In fact, a record-breaking bounty was placed on his head, and many
of his contemporaries believed that he was assassinated—by poison—because of the analyses and recommendations put forward in that text. Stewart, a woman, inspired an even greater hostility among members of the
Black community, and, it appears, was essentially run out of town because
of the perception that her unladylike behavior in speaking in public and the
strident tone of her exhortations jeopardized the carefully cultivated image
free Blacks wanted to preserve. In several of the "Meditations" Stewart
wrote during this period, she discloses the pain inflicted by intense perse-
cution. This is particularly evident in the twelfth and thirteenth Meditation,
written shortly before, and closest to, her departure from Boston. "Bless all
my friends and benefactors," she wrote. "[T]hose who have given me a cup
of cold water in thy name, the Lord reward them. Forgive all my enemies.
May I love them that hate me, and pray for them that despitefully use and
persecute me. Preserve me from slanderous tongues, O God, and let not my

good be evil spoken of" (46). In the penultimate and the final Meditation, Stewart reveals an inkling of how intensely she has suffered, writing, "Lord, when mine enemies multiplied themselves against me, then I cried unto thee in my trouble, and thou didst deliver me from all my distresses" (47), and declaring, "O, my soul, has not the voice of thy weeping ascended up before the throne of God?" (49).

In her comprehensive study of nineteenth-century African American women speakers and writers in the North, *"Doers of the Word"*, Carla Peterson comments on the tone reflected in Stewart's *Meditations,* arguing that "Stewart's prayers do not leave us with a sense of resolution, of 'the soul resting in God,' but rather with a vision of a restless, tormented individual" (63). In fact, the *Meditations* is in its expressive range strikingly similar to the Book of Psalms. Like several of the Psalms, Stewart's *Meditations* unveils the inner turmoil of the soul's cathartic confrontation with itself in the presence of the therapist God.[4] The inner peace that results from this outpouring manifests in the *lived* text of the speaker's replenished energies and renewed composure in confronting psychological and other assaults and comes *after* meditation. Some measure of this composure, this inner peace, can be discerned in "Mrs. Stewart's Farewell Address to Her Friends in the City of Boston":

> Yet, notwithstanding your prospects are thus fair and bright, I am about to leave you, perhaps never more to return. For I find it is no use for me as an individual to try to make myself useful among my color in this city. It was contempt for my moral and religious opinions in private that drove me thus before a [*sic*] public. Had experience more plainly shown me that it was the nature of man to crush his fellow, I should not have thought it so hard. Wherefore, my respected friends, let us no longer talk of prejudice, till prejudice becomes extinct at home. Let us no longer talk of opposition, till we cease to oppose our own. (70)

In this farewell address, Stewart offers a lengthy defense of the right of women to exercise spiritual and political leadership citing both historical and biblical precedents. Insightfully gauging the responsibility involved in women's spiritual leadership, Stewart tells her audience, "If such women as are here described have once existed, be no longer astonished then, my brethren and friends, that God at this eventful period should raise up your own females to strive, by their example both in public and private, to assist those who are endeavoring to stop the strong current of prejudice that flows so profusely against us at present" (69). The fact that this defense forms the larger part of her farewell address indicates Stewart's awareness that the opposition "at home" to her preaching was gender based.

Later texts by nineteenth-century Black women preachers, most prominently Jarena Lee, rearticulate Stewart's compelling defense of women's spiritual leadership.[5] Although Stewart did not have the communal support necessary to fulfill her vision of Black women exercising righteous and creative agency, Black women in the post-Slavery era would indeed unite to implement her vision of themselves as institution builders. Faced with the impenetrable closed-mindedness of her peers, Stewart, like other visionaries before and after, redirected her energies toward transmitting her vision to the next generation. As a teacher in New York, Baltimore, and Washington, D.C., Stewart had ample opportunity to teach and preach a message of economic self-reliance and women's participatory and leadership roles to scores of children, many of whom—as members of the educated elite—would undoubtedly become active participants in the Black women's club movement at the turn of the century. Indeed, like Baby Suggs, holy, Stewart's agency increased with death. Her last act of republishing her speeches and lectures a few months before her death in 1879 (at age seventy-six!) ensured the continuing availability and efficacy of her transformative vision for generations to come, effectively consolidating her ancestor role.

Like Stewart's, the public ministry of Baby Suggs, holy, begins after a conversion experience of sorts. In light of Connor's above-mentioned analysis of the joint theological and ideological aspects of conversion in Black women's lives, Baby Suggs's conversion can be traced to the moment she recognizes that her life belongs to herself and is sacred: "But suddenly she saw her hands and thought with a clarity as simple as it was dazzling, 'These hands belong to me. These *my* hands.'" (141). This epiphany, as her subsequent actions illustrate, has both spiritual and ideological ramifications.

Arriving in Cincinnati from a lifetime of enslavement in Carolina and Kentucky, Baby Suggs "decided that, because slave life had 'busted her legs, back, head, eyes, hands, kidneys, womb and tongue,' she had nothing left to make a living with but her heart—which she put to work at once" (87). "Accepting no title of honor before her name, but allowing a small caress after it, she became an unchurched preacher, one who visited pulpits and opened her great heart to those who could use it. In winter and fall she carried it to AME's and Baptists, Holinesses and Sanctifieds, the Church of the Redeemer and the Redeemed. Uncalled, unrobed, unanointed, she let her great heart beat in their presence" (87). In navigating these various denominational sites, Baby Suggs, holy, reveals the primary goal of her preaching: the re-collecting of a cultural/spiritual community distributed among various theological sites whose connectedness and self-definitions have been jeopardized by Slavery. In identifying her heart and humanity as the basic tools that support her spiritual authority and leadership, Morrison highlights and celebrates a model of empowerment that has long facilitated African American survival and informed the tradition of social activism. Like Baby Suggs, holy, Harriet Tubman's moral and military leadership was founded on these resources.

Shortly after its publication, Karla Holloway dubbed *Beloved* "a spiritual" in an analysis that focused on the novel's rhetorical and linguistic strategies. Holloway's article provides a nuanced interpretation of the ways in which, because of the author's decision to situate the novel within a mythological—and African—cosmology, "the potential of *Beloved* is freed from the dominance of a history that would submerge this story" (522). "This liberation," Holloway asserts, "is perhaps the most critical issue of Morrison's novel" (522). The re-creation of this cosmology and, with it, the deployment of spirituality has other significant effects. Through the depiction of Baby Suggs's spiritual agency, and the epistemology that undergirds it, the novel debunks "master-narratives" about enslaved Africans, their enslavers, and both their descendants that continue to (mis)inform public discourse.

Like most Slavery-era Black preachers, Baby Suggs, holy, could neither read nor write. As Albert Raboteau notes in *Slave Religion*, however, "Illiteracy proved less of an obstacle to knowledge of the Bible than might be thought, for biblical stories became part of the oral tradition of the slaves" (241). In claiming the responsibility and authority of spiritual leader/preacher, Baby Suggs's sole qualification is the vision of grace that came with the recognition that her heart was always already beating. Despite a lifetime of enslavement by Whites, *her* humanity was intact, her life holy, and wholly hers. The recognition of her own unimpaired humanity paves the way for the recovery of her interpretive authority and for a communally attentive expansion of her creative agency.

Baby Suggs's appearance is crucial to the novel's transformative ideology and agenda. Her multiple liberating roles are jointly shaped by African and Afro-Christian theological elements. Morrison's characterization of her displays several elements that suggest a christological context. The allusion to Christ, the Rock, in the description of Baby Suggs, holy, "situating herself on a huge flat-sided rock" is instructive. Her invitation to first "Let the children come!" resounds Jesus' statement, "Suffer little children to come unto me, and forbid them not." Like him, her body has been broken: "slave life had 'busted her legs, back, head, eyes, hands, kidneys, womb and tongue'" (87). Like him, she takes her message to "her own"—the Black people dispersed among various denominational sites.

Each phase of Baby Suggs's spiritual leadership has a theological aspect that is crucial to the novel's ideology: her role as preacher—in the Clearing; her quest for a liberating theodicy—in the keeping room; and her role as ancestor—after 1875. In the first of these roles, Morrison emphasizes the many ways in which the preaching of Baby Suggs, holy, exemplifies a chosen and self-conscious agency that is contiguous with the parameters of an African cosmology. While the preacher usually receives a "call" to the ministry, Baby Suggs "decided" to put her heart to work. In an incremental counterpoint to Christendom's rhetoric, her message rejects the assumption that Black people have "sinned" on the one hand, or that they are destined for some future glory, on the other hand. This depiction accords with and reinforces Paris's observation that "the vast majority of African Americans . . . placed the full and complete blame for slavery on the moral depravity of slaveowners" (46). In calling attention to what she did *not* say, Morrison accentuates Baby Suggs's rejection of Christendom's "explanation" of Black peoples' enslavement and oppression as either retributive or salvific. Instead, Baby Suggs's message details an enabling vision of survival and reveals aspects of divinity—capacity for creative/righteous agency— within the self that promote healing, survival, growth. Her sermon in the Clearing elaborates on these themes.

"Here," she said, "in this here place, we flesh; flesh that weeps, laughs; flesh that dances on bare feet in grass. Love it. Love it hard. Yonder they do not love your flesh. They despise it. They don't love your eyes; they'd just as soon pick em out. No more do they love the skin on your back. Yonder they flay it. And O my people they do not love your hands. Those they only use, tie, bind, chop off and leave empty. Love your hands! Love them. . . . and the beat and beating heart, love that too. More than eyes or feet. More than lungs that have yet to draw free air. More than your life-holding womb and your life-giving private parts, hear me now, love your heart. For this is the prize. (88–89)

This sermon provides a detailed analysis of the self-hatred oppression generates. More important, the deconstructive discourse within it illustrates the importance of interpretive autonomy to the Black community's psychospiritual and ideological well-being. Baby Suggs's sermon rejects and replaces the definitions that prevail in public discourse outside "the Veil" with a set of transformative definitions. Without the intellectual autonomy to craft their own definitions of their experiences and needs, survival in the post-Slavery context would still be endangered. In assisting her people in loving, collecting, and connecting the dismembered/unremembered parts of themselves, she exhibits her leadership role in preaching a liberating theology and in constructing a spiritually based liberating epistemology essential to their sociopolitical survival.

As her sermon in the Clearing demonstrates, Baby Suggs's ministry centers on the enactment of ritualized healing performances whose core elements are epistemological. Theophus Smith's insights on ritual clarifies the significance of the novel's reliance on this strategy. In *Conjuring Culture: Biblical Formations of Black America*, Smith defines ritual as "social practices in which the creative impulse to pattern reality results in a repetitive structuring of human action" (56). As Smith explains: "rituals are intended to be transformative more than representational. They are instrumental: focusing upon the 'means to' rather than the 'meaning of' transformed versions of reality. So understood, rituals need not be limited to religious performances but can also include secular transformations" (57). Smith's description of ritual's transformative instrumentality points to the ways in which these performances support the structuring of social formations. The social formation that Baby Suggs's healing rituals and their implicit ideology seek to (re)construct is cultural/spiritual kinship. They are, clearly, a primary vehicle for transforming the dismemberment precipitated by Slavery. Significantly, several features of an African spiritual cosmology appear in these ritualized "calls." Among other things, Baby Suggs' instruction to "Cry . . . For the living and the dead" attests to the unbroken kinship between the living and the dead. The ethos of interconnectedness is also discernible in the reconfiguration of a multidimensional subjectivity with which the healing ritual ends. "*It started that way: laughing children, dancing men, crying women and then it got mixed up. Women stopped crying and danced; men sat down and cried; children danced, women laughed, children cried until, exhausted and riven, all and each lay about the Clearing damp and gasping for breath.* In the silence that followed, Baby Suggs, holy, offered up to them her great big heart" (87–88; emphasis added). The pivotal event in this ritual is the rotation of roles—participatory *and* observational—that enables women, children, and men to become whole through experiencing and embracing the many dimensions of their full humanity.

Black Women (Pro)claiming Righteous Agency

Although preaching is a primary aspect of Baby Suggs's spiritual authority, she embraces other responsibilities in the Cincinnati Black community and has other functions in the novel. In fact, her quest for a liberating theodicy precipitates a more expansive vision of Black women proclaiming righteous agency. This quest begins when Sethe's former enslaver attempts to re-enslave her and the four grandchildren. The event culminates a lifetime of abuses by Whites and overshadows her creative agency to such an extent that Baby Suggs, holy, is forced to confront the ubiquitous manifestation of evil—reaching to her very door—despite the existence of God, despite her own attempts at righteous intervention.

While Baby Suggs may not have known of the lengthy duration or extensive geography of Slavery, by 1855 she had endured and/or witnessed a barrage of violations committed by Whites. The cumulative weight of these violations is so heavy that, after this last event, "Baby Suggs, holy, believed she had lied. There was no grace—imaginary or real—and no sunlit dance in a Clearing could change that. Her faith, her love, her imagination and her great big old heart began to collapse twenty-eight days after her daughter-in-law arrived" (89). "The whitefolks had tired her out at last" (180). The magnitude of the abuses she has witnessed forces Baby Suggs, holy, to withdraw to the keeping room "to consider what in the world was harmless" (181).

In the context of a social environment characterized by a system of violence predicated on a color/racial hierarchy, Baby Suggs's extended meditation on color—"the only thing in the universe that was harmless"— is deeply ironic. The question behind Baby Suggs's quest for a liberating theodicy is not, Why must I suffer? Instead, Baby Suggs questions the potency and extensiveness of "evil," given its apparent ability to defeat her attempts at creative agency. The theodicy that this meditation enables her to formulate is both subversive and liberating.

> Except for an occasional request for color she said practically nothing— until the afternoon of the last day of her life when she got out of bed, skipped slowly to the door of the keeping room and announced to Sethe and Denver the lesson she had learned from her sixty years a slave and ten years free: that there was no bad luck in the world but white people. "They don't know when to stop," she said, and returned to her bed, pulled up the quilt and left them to hold that thought forever. (104)

Baby Suggs's meditation on "color" parallels, and reflects, Morrison's commitment to what she describes, in the essay "Home," as the "manageable, doable, modern human activity" of constructing "a-world-in-which-race-does-not-matter" by "eliminating the potency of racist constructs in language" (4–5). Among its many critical insights, Baby Suggs's theodicy rejects and dismantles color/race as a category intrinsically denoting good or evil. While color/race has been used to construct a hierarchy of dominance, color itself, and itself alone in the universe, is "harmless." This view rejects the equation of "Whiteness" with goodness—and the right to dominate, and the equation of "Blackness" with evil—and a predestination to be oppressed. And while it may appear that this theodicy simply reverses the poles of an untenable hierarchy, it is important to note that Baby Suggs does not equate "Whiteness" with "evil" but attributes agency to White people for the unrelenting violence directed toward herself and other Black people. While theodicy is generally understood as a vindication of Deity (righteous agency) in view of the existence of (a metaphysical) evil (oppressive agency), Baby Suggs's theodicy regards racist violence and violations as manifestations of a *human* capacity for, and tendency toward, excess or a lack of (self-)moderation. Commenting on their understanding of Slavery's evil, Paris states that "African Americans' unequivocal designation of humans as the cause of their misery is wholly commensurate with the traditional African view of evil" (46). "In traditional African religions," Paris explains, "evil is thought to have its origin in human wrongdoing, which in turn causes some form of imbalance to occur between the human community and the realm of the spirit. . . . Consequently, in the face of suffering . . . priests and all concerned expend much energy investigating the circumstances in search of the human causative factor" (45).[6]

For Baby Suggs, holy, both good and evil are defined in epistemological terms: knowing, and not knowing, when to stop. Early in the novel, the narrator informs us that "Baby Suggs, holy, didn't approve of extra. 'Everything depends on knowing how much,' she said, and 'Good is knowing when to stop'" (87). In recognizing the pattern of White racist excesses as the result of an epistemological and, therefore, moral deficiency, she redefines and rediscovers expanded parameters for exercising righteous agency. If her White contemporaries cannot—because of a deep-rooted and debilitating socialization—determine when to stop, someone else can and must embrace that responsibility. This understanding of racist violence and violations terminates her suspension "between the nastiness of life and the meanness of the dead" (1–2). Coming at the end of an extended meditation on color, Baby Suggs's theodicy liberates her, enables her to reclaim her creative agency and to resume both her spiritual leadership and her progress toward a righteous equilibrium of interdependent relationships in the realm of the ancestors. And it is this ancestor role that propels the recuperative direction of the plot.

Although Baby Suggs, holy, has no embodied role for most of the novel, her role as ancestor is central to the lives of the Black people in the novel and to the novel's development as a whole. Consistent with this ancestor role, we learn—at the start of the novel—that her capacity for creative agency is not reduced, but in fact increases, with death. When, for example, the baby ghost fails to appear at Sethe and Denver's bidding, Denver concludes that her grandmother "must be stopping it" (4). In her ancestor role, she makes several transformative interventions.

First, she outfits Beloved with shoes needed for the journey of intercession to free Sethe, Paul D, and the entire Cincinnati Black community from the stagnation in which they are trapped because of their fear of remembering and the failure to utilize their own transformative and righteous agency, beginning with the community's failure to protect Sethe from School-teacher. The help needed to free Sethe and others is announced and antici-pated in Denver's vision: "The dress and her mother looked like two friendly grown-up women—one (the dress) helping out the other" (29). Beloved's new shoes are the authenticating symbol of her connection to the ancestor, Baby Suggs, holy. In fact, Beloved's cathartic presence both facilitates and exemplifies a recovery and release that emanates from Baby Suggs's theod-icy with its emphasis on *epistemological* intervention that undermines and transforms "evil."

In her second transformative intervention as ancestor, Baby Suggs, holy, counsels her granddaughter, Denver, on the relationship between knowl-edge and action, epistemology and agency. After questioning her knowl-edge of the abuses suffered by her ancestors, Baby Suggs directs Denver to "Know it, and go on out the yard" (244). For Denver, Janie, Ella, and each of the participants involved in the novel's multifaceted resolution, it is know-ing that it is time to end their various acts of omission that prompts specific interventions that release them from pain, regret, and longing.

Baby Suggs's theodicy, her third intervention, launches an extratextual agenda for transformation. The many challenges facing characters in the novel mirror challenges in the contemporary United States. Of these, none is perhaps as daunting as the challenge to resist and dismantle the mecha-nism for inflicting epistemological debilitation that is Slavery's primary legacy. As Wahneema Lubiano notes in the introductory essay to *The House that Race Built:*

> The idea of race and the operation of racism are the best friends that the economic and political elite have in the United States. They are the means by which a state and a political economy largely inimical to most of the U.S. citizenry achieve the consent of the governed. They act as a distorting prism that allows that citizenry to imagine itself functioning as a moral and just people while ignoring the widespread devastation directed at black Americans particularly, but at a much larger number of people gen-erally. . . . the operation of racism is so thoroughgoing that even those indi-

viduals who are its objects are not exempt from thinking about the world through its prism. (vii)

As defined in Lubiano's analysis, the "distorting prism"—the collective racism of U.S. society—is a heteronomous principle that was crucial to the maintenance of Slavery. It ensured, and ensures still, that working-class Whites will consent to economic and social policies that are harmful to themselves because they perceived these policies as having restricted application—to Blacks only.[7] Yet, in an economy in which Blacks were forced to work without wages, workers' rights—including the right to a livable wage—were similarly abrogated for Whites, as Amy Denver's experience indicates. While Lubiano's analysis points to the ways in which economic and sociopolitical well-being is jeopardized by the interpretive debilitation this "distorted prism" inflicts, Baby Suggs's theodicy points to the fact that moral agency is impaired when interpretive competence is destroyed. Through Baby Suggs's agency, Morrison is able to fashion a narrative resolution in which this process is reversed.

In their essay, "*Jazz* . . . On 'The Site of Memory,'" Judylyn Ryan and Estella Conwill Májozo point to what they call "the striking concept of social ethics" in Morrison's fiction. They note that "Morrison takes great pains to imagine and depict the re-fashioned social relationships resulting from the characters' expanded interpretive capacity" (150). "[M]oral agency," they argue, "increases with interpretive agency. As the characters learn to interpret their own motivations and actions, they are able to construct more wholesome patterns of interacting" (150). This process holds true for the community in *Beloved*. The ancestor, Baby Suggs, holy, preaches two sermons—one in the Clearing, the other in the keeping room—that contain analyses of contemporary crises and a vision of transformation that Morrison's readers are called to consider. Baby Suggs's definition of racist violations as an epistemological deficiency—"not knowing when [or why] to stop"—casts new light on contemporary attempts to dismantle the Civil Rights agenda and thereby reverse the nation's progress toward a veritable democracy. Viewed through the novel's discursive lenses, these acts demonstrate that a persistent weakening of the citizenry's ways of knowing and sources of knowledge continues to undermine the nation's development.

Like Maria Stewart, Baby Suggs, holy, displayed an approach to spiritual authority, within the framework of Afro-Christianity, informed by an ethos of (inter)connectedness and derived from an African cosmology. This ethos of (inter)connectedness engendered a connectedness and commitment to cultural/spiritual kin, and a vision of women's responsibility and capacity for creative agency. It informed and inspired their spiritual and sociopolitical visions. It also fueled the determination with which these Black women contested gender, race, and class-based restrictions on the exercise of creative/righteous agency and enabled them to define, embrace, and fulfill responsibilities consistent with the paradigm of growth.

Bearing Life-Force

Zora Neale Hurston, Ama Ata Aidoo, and Ntozake Shange

> And when my training was over
> they circled my waist with pumpkin seeds
> and dried okra, a traveler's jigida
> and sold me to the traders
> all my weapons within me.
> I was sent, tell that to history.
>
> —Lorna Goodison, "Nanny"

The focus of this chapter is a logical extension of the previous chapter's exploration of the sources and definitions of authority in Black women's lives. Here, however, the focus is two-pronged. First, I look at the communal roles and responsibilities of spiritually empowered Black women. Second, I examine the ways in which spiritual empowerment forms an integral part of the definition of womanhood in Black women's art.

Black Women's Political Vision and Leadership

In the poem "Nanny" from which the epigraph above is excerpted, Lorna Goodison pays tribute to the only woman among Jamaica's seven national heroes. In eighteenth-century Jamaica, Nanny organized an army of maroons and was such a successful military strategist that the British were eventually forced to negotiate a peace treaty recognizing the sovereignty of the maroon community. A native of Ghana, Nanny's capture was orchestrated with the explicit intention of sending someone from the continent with the inner resources to assist "New World" Africans in envisioning possibilities for negotiating their enslavement. Goodison's artistic representation of her training for political leadership emphasizes Nanny's spiritual apprenticeship and points to the ways in which the Black woman's spiritual vision and righteous agency are directed toward a broad range of responsibilities. The speaker's prophetic conclusion that "When your sorrow obscures the skies / other women like me will rise" (43) recalls those many Black women who embrace their responsibility for group preservation by combining political and spiritual leadership.

Goodison's tribute to Nanny and to other Black women like her assumes particular significance in light of Paris's observation that "African societies have had priestesses and prophetesses from time immemorial" (107). By way of differentiating between the roles of priest/ess and prophet/ess, in his discussion of religious authorities in *African Religions: Symbols, Ritual, and Community*, Benjamin Ray asserts that the "the distinctive mark of a prophet is his inspired sociopolitical leadership, while the distinctive mark of a priest is his ritual and symbolic authority" (116). The role of priestess is not always separable from that of prophetess since both are mediators between humans and the spirit realm, between humans and God, divinities, and ancestors. Ray also notes that: "The main task of a priest is to sustain and renew the life of the community he serves. Often the priest contains within himself the life-force which he seeks to mediate to his people" (116). By extension, one can posit that what distinguishes the priestess is the willingness to become the sacrifice offered on behalf of spiritual/cultural community. The priestess does not simply *prepare* the sacrifice but carries within herself the life-force that must be distributed to the community.

Viewed in this light, Baby Suggs, holy, and Maria W. Stewart both fulfill dual roles of preacher and priestess. Nevertheless, the typical depiction of the Black woman priestess does not present her in a religious office. Instead, Black women writers and filmmakers typically present the priestess in a range of secular roles as wife, midwife, mother, grandmother, artist, activist, warrior. Works such as Joanne Grant's *Fundi: The Ella Baker Story* (1981), Toni Cade Bambara's *The Salt Eaters* (1983), Erna Brodber's *Myal* (1988), and Ayoka Chenzira's *Zajota and the Boogie Spirit* (1989) depict Black women priestesses/ prophetesses fulfilling a variety of roles and initiating various transformative rituals. These roles coalesce in the priestess's sociopolitical leadership, which is linked to the community's quest for self-definition and direction, particularly in the midst of crisis and change. Frequently perceived as liminal, the priestess symbolizes Black women's illicit, self-styled, and veritable agency. As priestess, the Black woman exercises righteous/creative agency, mediates between cultural/spiritual community, its oppressors, and divinities and/or ancestors, and consciously presents her vision, her voice, her knowledge, her memory, and her art as offerings designed to strengthen the life-force of her community.

While bearing life-force in the role of priestess/prophetess is a significant theme and responsibility in Black women's literary and cinematic art, this role does not go unopposed. Indeed, early works that feature an explicit presentation of the Black woman as priestess frequently depict characters who face tremendous opposition in their attempt to distribute the life-force they bear through political leadership. Conditions of crisis and change are an additional hazard for the priestess since she is most likely to be opposed and/or unsupported in her development during such periods. Zora Neale Hurston's *Moses: Man of the Mountain* (1939) and Ama Ata Aidoo's *Anowa* (1970) both depict the Black woman priestess in a narrative and sociopolitical environment marked by crisis. In both works, the priestess encounters considerable opposition in fulfilling this responsibility, with significant consequences for her community. On the one hand, this crisis seems to call forth and release the priestess's agency and resourcefulness. On the other, the community's disorientation presents a unique challenge to the priestess's agency.

Since its publication in 1939, Hurston's third novel, *Moses: Man of the Mountain,* has been the victim of both critical misreadings and neglect. Blyden Jackson's introduction to the 1984 edition typifies critical evaluations of the novel. As he reads it, the novel "does not deviate by one essential whit from the same story as it is told in the Bible" (xv). Jackson's claim that "Hurston's folklore everywhere happily transports Hurston's readers to a position from which every Jew in Goshen is converted into an American Negro and every Egyptian in Old Pharaoh's Egypt into a white in the America where Hurston's folk Negroes live" (xv–xvi) belies the deliberateness of Hurston's re-creation of an Egyptian Moses. More recently, Deborah McDowell's foreword to the 1991 HarperCollins edition of the novel has provided a compelling analysis of the novel's "parallel lines of typology" (xvi). Still, McDowell rates the novel as "badly flawed." Neither Jackson's reading nor McDowell's claim does justice to the novel's rhetorical and ideological complexity. Far from being allegorical or flawed, *Moses* is a complex narrative that performs theory about the status and future direction of African

American liberation discourses, in which the Black woman priestess plays a central role. Hurston's seemingly gratuitous revision of Moses's cultural identity signals this direction and design.

The political design of Hurston's re-presentation of the Hebrew exodus from enslavement in Egypt appears in the African diaspora contextualization provided in the author's introduction to the novel. There Hurston identifies the "children of Africa" scattered "all across Africa, America, [and] the West Indies" as the community to which her Moses belongs, and unlike the protagonist of the biblical narrative, Hurston's Moses is indeed African— an offspring of the Egyptian monarch. In *Moses,* Hurston offers a glimpse of a precursor model for a Black liberation theology, one that is culturally informed, one in which the liminal position assigned to the Black woman priestess constitutes a telling critique of the post-Emancipation—and, prophetically, the post–civil rights—Black political vision.

While African American political vision is not monolithic, a major strand has been and continues to be both informed by biblical interpretation and dominated by denominational figures. Rev. Jesse Jackson and Rev. Al Sharpton—both former Democratic presidential candidates, in 1984 and 2004, respectively—are contemporary examples. Understanding the evolution of this conjunction of ideology and theology, particularly in relation to the crisis experienced during the 1960s, casts new light on Hurston's project. As theologian James Cone notes in "Black Theology as Liberation Theology," the development of Black liberation theology in the 1960s arose from a desire on the part of young Black clergymen to reconcile their agreement with the political analysis of American racism articulated by the Black Power movement with their commitment to Christianity, which the movement disdained as "the white man's religion" (182). Cone recalls that "Black preachers, in their struggle to be Christian *and* support Black power, had to develop a theology that was distinctly Black and also accountable to our faith." Specifically, they "wanted to show that Black power and the gospel were identical and that both focused on the politics of liberation" (182). This led to a reexamination of the nationalist and christological critiques of American racism by nineteenth-century Black male leaders such as Nat Turner, David Walker, Henry Highland Garnet, and Alexander Crummell, who all imagined God concerned for the sociopolitical condition of Black people and attuned to their racial/cultural experiences and conditions.

Reevaluating the writings of these nineteenth-century Black men, "Black theologians and preachers of the 1960s began to realize that they were not the first in the attempt to find theological meaning in Blackness and the gospel" (183). They concluded that God was concerned with the racial oppression of Black people, and that sociopolitical liberation and cultural liberation were both sanctioned by Jesus's ministry. This theological interpretation was summarized in the statement "Jesus is Black" (189). It is significant that in looking back to nineteenth-century predecessors to formulate a liberation theology for the twentieth century, no attention was directed toward extant writings by Black women like Stewart. Predictably, the movement did not address the question of gender oppression.

Like other liberation theologies, Black theology regards Jesus as both a revolutionary and liberator. Nevertheless, Moses has a distinct role in African American liberation discourse in both folk and formal contexts. As Paris explains: "as with all captive peoples uprooted from their respective homelands, African slaves gradually adopted many relevant ancestors of their captors which, in this situation, turned out be various biblical personages who eventually function for them as surrogate ancestral protectors. Thus, the inclusion of Moses, Joshua, Daniel, Mary, Jonah, or Paul in their spirituals was tantamount to granting them membership in the African realm of spirit" (57). Significantly, the "relevant ancestors" of their enslavers that enslaved Africans chose to adopt were biblical figures and *not* European or Euro-American political figures.

The adoption of biblical ancestors (including Moses) and the appropriation of the exodus motif were radical in their autonomous transformation of the oppressor's intended tool of submission into an expression of covert rebellion.[1] Enslaved Africans responded to the use of the Bible to sanction Slavery by *not* refuting its authority or openly challenging the power structure that manipulated it and thereby jeopardizing the effectiveness of any challenge. Instead, they chose to uphold the Bible's authority, reading into it another message, another theme. Consequently, Christendom's allegation of biblical sanction for slavery did not produce the intended response of passive submission, or passive waiting for the coming of God's chosen deliverer. To the contrary, the development of the Underground Railroad with its focus on self-emancipation—spearheaded by the symbolic leadership of Harriet Tubman-cum-"Moses"—demonstrates the enslaved Africans' view of Moses's actively subversive role. As historian Albert Raboteau concludes, "Revolutionary interpretations of the Bible by such slaves as [Denmark] Vesey and [Nat] Turner were proof to American slaveholders that slave Christianity could become a double-edged sword" (290).

The long history of appropriating biblical figures and using these to perform typological readings of Black people's experiences in the United States entered a new phase with the 1960s conception and articulation of a Black Christ. At least two decades before the formal beginning of a Black liberation theology, however, Zora Neale Hurston makes a significant theological, ideological, and theoretical gesture in conceptualizing a deliverer as culturally and theologically Black/African. While her focus on Moses as deliverer reflects his centrality to African American cosmology and liberation discourse, Hurston does not emphasize the typological significance of the Exodus story. Rather, she reconceptualizes a liberation narrative centered on Moses, who is theorized and theologized as culturally Black.

Several details attest to the complexity of Hurston's narrative project. Although the novel consciously manipulates the historical nexus between the Exodus theme and African American experience, it does not limit itself to that construction. Apart from the general themes of slavery, emancipation, and exodus, several major elements of Hurston's novel are not featured in the biblical narrative. For example, unlike the biblical protagonist, Hurston's Moses is not a foundling who is simply more familiar with his adoptive (Egyptian) culture than with his actual Hebrew roots. Instead, Hurston's representation of Moses's Egyptian identity privileges an African cultural identity (shared with the extratextual "Hebrews"/African Americans). And while the Hebrews in Hurston's novel are not recast as Egyptians, they are clearly portrayed as Black/African American through speech inflections, experience, and gesture.

As the title suggests, *Moses* does not focus on a Black woman protagonist. In fact, Miriam is figuratively and literally overshadowed by the titular protagonist. Nevertheless, the novel offers important insights into the communal role and responsibility of the Black woman priestess. Her presence in the novel illuminates Hurston's theological and ideological intentions in recasting the biblical plot.

Hurston reveals Miriam's inventiveness—a primary aspect of her priestess role—and remythologizes Moses's cultural identity in the same narrative gesture. Miriam first displays signs of her priestess role as Moses's narrative progenitor. As Hurston describes it, Miriam fell asleep while watching to see what would become of the baby brother who had been placed in a waterproof basket on the Nile. When she awoke, "The child and basket were gone, that was all. And she had not the least idea of where he had gone, nor how" (40). When she returns home, "Seeing her frenzied mother searching for something with which to strike her made Miriam come alive inside more thoroughly than she ever had done before in her life and suddenly an explanation flashed across her brain" (44). And thus was born the "myth" of her brother's Egyptian adoption. Significantly, there is no new baby at Pharaoh's palace to substantiate Miriam's "explanation." Nevertheless, Hurston reports that "Others conceived and added details at their pleasure and the legends grew like grass" (51).

While Miriam's "explanation" arises from an impulse to preserve herself, it is also part of a much larger psychological impulse within her cultural community. Through the aperture she creates, the community taps into a large narrative reservoir from which they reaffirm their humanity and their claim to full human rights by fashioning a kinship/human connection between themselves and their oppressors.

Consistent with his revised identity, Hurston's (and Miriam's) Moses develops a liberating vision long before he accepts the "call" to spiritual and political leadership on behalf of the enslaved Hebrews. Indeed, this vision precipitates his initial departure from Pharaoh's court. The narrator describes him as someone "wishing for a country he had never seen. He was seeing visions of a nation he had never heard of where there would be more equality of opportunity and less difference between top and bottom" (75). Prompted by his vision of a just society, Moses relinquishes his privileged position and "crosses over."

> Moses had crossed over. He was not in Egypt. He had crossed over and now he was not an Egyptian. He had crossed over. The short sword at his thigh had a jeweled hilt but he had crossed over and so it was no longer the sign of his high birth and power. He had crossed over, so he sat down on a rock near the seashore to rest himself. He had crossed over so he was not of the house of Pharaoh. He did not own a palace because he had crossed over. He did not have an Ethiopian Princess for a wife. He had crossed over. He

did not have enemies to strain against his strength and power. He had crossed over. He was subject to no law except the laws of tooth and talon. He had crossed over. The sun who was his friend and ancestor in Egypt was arrogant and bitter in Asia. He had crossed over. He felt as empty as a post hole for he was none of the things he once had been. He was a man sitting on a rock. He had crossed over. (103–4)

In the lyrical repetition of the phrase "He had crossed over," Hurston literally pours out the previous content and signification of the Moses concept. This passage both manifests and encapsulates Hurston's narrative project: to overturn the concept, leaving it empty—but *full* of potential—ready for a new investment that is facilitated by Moses's "new" cultural, theological, and political investiture. In the twelfth and final repetition, therefore, the reader is keenly aware that this protagonist, sign, concept is about to receive a new post and mission, despite his/its seeming desolation. "He felt as empty as a post hole for he was none of the things he once had been. He had crossed over."

In subsequently accepting the call to liberate the Hebrews, Moses displays his commitment to dismantling a "slave holding" society and race-based hierarchies of privilege. Moses's strategy centers on developing a religious ideology that would enable the Hebrews to rediscover and reclaim their own expropriated creative agency. This strategy is consistent with the parameters of traditional African religion. There, too, the revelation of their connection to powerful creative agencies—God and lesser divinities—is crucial to the process of empowering people to recognize and exercise their capacity for creative agency.

Despite the merits of his strategy for liberation, Moses's program is considerably weakened by his failure to fully assess the psychologically damaging effects of enslavement. More important, his failure to examine the goals of liberation from multiple perspectives and, specifically, from the perspective of the most oppressed, and his opposition to Miriam's leadership role severely compromise the scope of his liberation theology. The narrator states that "Immediately after his arrival in Goshen he told Aaron to summon the Elders of the tribes to meet him, and anyone else of influence. When they came, Moses was surprised to find a woman among them" (134). In Miriam, the liberation goals of women and the poor are conjoined.

Through Moses's treatment of Miriam, Hurston points to the limitations of a liberation theology that seeks to transform only one aspect of oppression. Through Miriam, Hurston critiques Moses's one-dimensional liberation theology and political vision.[2] In so doing, she offers a penetrating analysis of the ways in which intracommunal opposition to Black women's spiritual, intellectual, and political leadership impedes development.

Hurston's depiction of the priestess/prophetess Miriam, and of the ways in which her cultural, spiritual, and sociopolitical authority is discredited by Moses forms part of a comprehensive critique of gender(ed) relations and oppression that unfolds in several of her works. In her first novel, *Jonah's Gourd Vine* (1934), and in *Their Eyes Were Watching God* (1937), the relationships between Lucy and John Pearson, and between Janie and each of her three husbands, respectively, provide similar analyses of empowered women dominated by men whose success they help create. Hurston's exploration of the relationship between the priestess/prophetess Miriam and the prophet Moses is a bold step toward eliminating what Paula Giddings has called "the last taboo." In the essay so titled, written in response to (Black) public reaction to Anita Hill's testimony during the 1991 confirmation hearings for then Supreme Court nominee Clarence Thomas, Giddings notes the continuing refusal among African Americans—men, mostly, but also women—"to disclose not only a gender but a sexual discourse unmediated by the question of racism" (442). What this means is that today, as in the pre–civil rights era, liberation discourses within the African American political constituency are reluctant to acknowledge or to commit to transforming gender/sexual oppression of Black women by Black men. *Moses* both highlights that omission and transcends it. Indeed, Hurston displays her commitment to the paradigm of growth by her willingness to expose and explore intracommunal attitudes and behaviors that are endangering.

Moses's disposition toward, and relationship with, Miriam is not an isolated instance of personal antagonism. Rather, his treatment of Miriam forms part of an extensive pattern of radically differing attitudes toward men and women. The contrast between his relationship with his father-in-law, Jethro, and his relationship with his wife, Zipporah, is instructive. The "little comforts and delights with Zipporah" (255) do not compare with the "long exchange of thoughts with Jethro" (255). Moses regards Jethro, not his daughter, as his intellectual and spiritual counterpart. Moses's interactions with both Zipporah and Miriam reveal an inability to see women as having an equal humanity, with equal capacities. His view of Miriam is founded on a sexualized definition of womanhood: "She was a woman, but he never had been able to quite think of her as such. What with her lack of female beauty and female attractions, and her loveless life with one end sunk in slavery and the other twisted and snarled in freedom" (265).

Moses's condescension toward Miriam—his inability to recognize or respect her humanity or gendered and class-informed experience as a poor Black woman—exposes the limitations of his prophetic vision, a vision that devalues and endangers connectedness. Because Moses does not view women as having the same complex humanity that he assumes for himself, Jethro, Joshua, and other males, he cannot and does not consider the meaning or dimensions of liberation for Black women. Consequently, the redistribution of opportunity and resources that emancipation promised never fully materializes because he sees no urgent reason to dismantle gender and class hierarchies. His blindness delays—and perhaps jeopardizes—the community's post-Slavery recovery.

Predictably, Miriam does not have the stature with which Moses is endowed in the novel. Although the novel provides only a limited depiction of her service to the community, their complete acceptance of her status as an elder and leader in Israel suggests that she has a proven record of sociopolitical and spiritual leadership. In fact, Moses testifies to the importance of her political leadership in his eulogy. Through this speech, "The young ones were told what the old ones had forgotten—all about those days back in Egypt when the house of the prophetess Miriam was the meeting place of all those who were willing to work for freedom. How she had gathered folks together by two and threes and changed weakness into resolution" (265). This history suggests that Moses's opposition to Miriam's spiritual and sociopolitical leadership is at odds with prevailing cultural values. His decision to tolerate Miriam's presence—not participation—because "She would be useful in handling the women" (135) is also at odds with the prevailing ethos of interconnectedness. Frustrated at being stymied in her priestess role, Miriam is keenly aware that the class structures (and definitions) that restricted her human agency in slavery are being rebuilt, instead of dismantled, under Moses's regime. "Miriam stood off at a short distance from the elaborate tent being put up for the exclusive use of Mrs. Moses and her saliva turned to venom in her mouth. She went up closer to finger the royal linen that Moses had brought out of Egypt for his wife. Then, as before, she looked down at her rough clothing and work-twisted feet and hands and she became aware of class" (221).

Miriam's fate encapsulates the fate of the Black woman in the post-Emancipation/post-colonial era, who—under the aegis of a new patriarchy—lost the culturally sanctioned political power she held within African societies and even within enslaved Black communities. As Anthonia Kalu has noted, Slavery and colonialism installed a new European paradigm that confounded traditional models of leadership by denying the Black woman's right and responsibility to participate. In "Those Left Out in the Rain: African Literary Theory and the Re-invention of the African Woman," Kalu notes that "the western-style classroom and church removed the African woman from the scene of invention and participation during a significant transitional moment in Africa's history on both sides of the Atlantic" (89).[3] Prior to this exclusion, Kalu notes, women's participation in political decision-making spheres in precolonial Africa was culturally sanctioned. As Miriam recalls, "You see, I was a prophetess back in Egypt and I had power, that is what the people told me, anyhow" (263). Moses's vehement opposition to Miriam's involvement in the leadership sphere marks the beginning of a change that jeopardizes the status of women and thereby the well-being of the community. Although Kalu identifies "the western-style classroom and church" as the sites on which this disenfranchisement took place, Miriam's (and Anowa's) experience indicate that the disenfranchisement of the Black woman occurred in other venues. Kalu's insistence on the urgent need to reinsert the African woman in the construction of development analyses and initiatives concurs with Hurston's analysis of Moses's failed liberation agenda.

In Moses's private reflections, Hurston provides a detailed description of Miriam's agency and of his awareness of the ways in which this agency facilitated and contributed to his own political ascent. Although he views her as an inadvertent auxiliary to his own achievement, Miriam's influence on Moses's life illustrates that the vision of interconnectedness persists even in relationships that are hegemonic.

He thought how the threads of his life had gotten tangled with the threads of this homely slave woman. He wondered if she had not been born if he would have been standing there in the desert of Zin. In fact, he wondered if the Exodus would have taken place at all. How? If she had not come to the palace gates to ask for him and to claim him as a brother, would he have left Egypt as he did? He doubted it. He never would have known Jethro, nor loved Zipporah, nor known the shiny mountain, nor led out a nation with a high hand, nor suffered as he had done and was doomed to keep on doing. A mighty thing had happened in the world through the stumblings of a woman who couldn't see where she was going. (265–66)

The differences between Moses's and Miriam's objectives and strategies coincide with the distinction theologian Delores Williams makes between the "liberation tradition of African-American biblical appropriation" and the "survival/quality-of-life tradition of African-American biblical appropriation." In *Sisters in the Wilderness: The Challenge of Womanist God-Talk,* Williams notes that while the former is more "male-centered" and concerned with the figure of the liberator, the latter is "female-centered" and, as the example of the biblical Hagar illustrates, concerned with "survival and . . . [the] development of an appropriate quality of life" strategy.[4] Hurston's representation of Miriam's role corroborates Williams's conception of the "female-centered," "survival/quality-of-life tradition." Moreover, the account of events generated through Miriam's actions demonstrates that while her public career was restricted by Moses's opposition, her creative agency was not reduced by that denial. In fact, she plays a vital role in Hurston's deconstructionist analysis of the limitations of liberation theologies and political strategies that persistently disregard and suppress the creative agency and responsibility of the Black priestess.

The Priestess Stabilizing Community

Like Hurston's novel, Ama Ata Aidoo's play *Anowa* offers important insights into the role and political vision of the Black priestess. Published in 1970 and set in West Africa in the late nineteenth century, *Anowa* portrays a society grappling with the legacy of Slavery and with renewed European capitalist interest in Africa. This, we know, culminated in 1885 with the "Scramble for Africa" at a Berlin conference table where slices of the continental pie were divided among Britain, France, Belgium, Italy, Portugal, Germany, and other European nations. The play, however, is set in the 1870s,

> a little less than thirty years
> [since the time] When the lords of our Houses
> Signed that piece of paper—
> The Bond of 1844 they call it—
> Binding us to the white men
> Who came from beyond the horizon (68)

As the Ghanaian poet, statesman, and scholar Kofi Awoonor explains, "For nearly two hundred years [prior], British power manifested itself solely through . . . forts and trading stations managed by the British trading firms" (74). The signing of "the Bond of 1844 was the consolidation of British colonial power in the Gold Coast. It provided the basis for the ultimate and unambiguous declaration of the Gold Coast as a Crown Colony in 1874" (83), marking the "movement from European trading posts to colonial possessions" (73).[5]

In *Anowa*, Aidoo presents us with a society not only in transition but one in crisis. The conversation between the Old Man and the Old Woman that forms the prologue outlines the dimensions of this crisis. Among other things, we learn that the local armies have become ineffective, local rulers have conspired with European traders and colonial administrators in defrauding the people of their wealth, and that Kofi Ako—to whom, we later learn, Anowa is married—is among those who have collaborated with the Europeans. In relaying these details, the Old Man alludes to Slavery and its contribution to the crisis:

> there is a bigger crime
> We have inherited from the clans incorporate
> Of which, lest we forget when the time does come,
> Those forts standing at the door
> Of the great ocean shall remind our children
> And the sea bear witness (66)

Almost as an aside, they mention the puzzling behavior of Anowa in refusing her many suitors. Anowa is introduced as a beautiful but spoiled and intractable girl. The prologue ends with a terse warning from the Old Woman (who, in subsequent appearances, constantly maligns Anowa) that "the gods will surely punish Abena Badua for refusing to let a born priestess dance!" (68). This is the first of several references to Anowa's obvious calling as a priestess and to the fact that this unfulfilled responsibility will generate tragic consequences. Since Kofi's financial success comes after his marriage to Anowa, in the second and third acts of the play, the prologue contextualizes the crisis that gradually unfolds in the course of the drama.

The insertion of Anowa's story in this politically charged dramatic framework indicates Aidoo's interest in exploring interlocking aspects of a social crisis brought on by a repressed consciousness of Slavery, an uncritical embrace of European capitalism, the restriction of women's creative agency in marriage, and an unprecedented opposition to the priestess's participation—events and attitudes that endanger the community's survival and growth. Toward that end, the play, organized in three acts, provides short vignettes of three consecutive phases in the life of the titular character, Anowa: her life before marriage, her life as a new wife, and her life as a repudiated wife.

Aidoo's analysis of the ideological and spiritual crisis in which Anowa and Kofi are embroiled outlines both its continental and New World dimensions. In the stage directions following Anowa's narration of the dream that signals her calling to the priesshood, Aidoo writes, "Then suddenly, the voices of an unseen, wearied multitude begin to sing 'Swing Low, Sweet Chariot'" (107). This description, with the pointed reference to the signature composition among African American spirituals, summons the presence of cultural kin dispersed by Slavery. While this event is not part of Anowa's dream, it suggests the diasporic proportions and significance of her vision and bridges the physical and ideological distance between events that are assumed to be restricted to one Atlantic coast or another.[6]

This, however, is the second explicit reference to the diasporic dimensions of the play's analysis. In the instructions on costumes in the production notes, Aidoo writes that "Anything African will do as long as a certain consistency is followed" (61). On the one hand, these instructions call attention to the blueprint shared by diverse cultural nationalities. More important, however, they underscore the relevance—throughout the diaspora—of the play's exploration of economic and political agendas and of the ways in which they can derail and undermine cultural, spiritual, and philosophical priorities. The name of the titular protagonist itself expresses Aidoo's diaspora focus. As theologian Mercy Amba Oduyoye explains in *Daughters of Anowa: African Women and Patriarchy,* Anowa is "the mythical woman, prophet, and priest whose life of daring, suffering, and determination is reflected in the continent of Africa. It is this that leads me to name Anowa Africa's ancestress" (6).

The ostensible cause of Anowa's not being apprenticed to become a priestess is her mother, Badua, who repeatedly voices her objection to "turn[ing] my only daughter into a dancer priestess" (71). Badua wants her daughter "To be a human woman" (72) rather than a priestess because "a priestess lives too much in her own and other people's minds" (72), and because priestesses "become too much like the gods they interpret" (71). While her mother's opposition poses a significant obstacle, this does not fully explain why Anowa does not seek an apprenticeship after her marriage to Kofi.

In many African societies, and certainly among the Akan, the priest(ess)-hood is not restricted to unmarried persons, and many initiates begin their training after marriage. Nevertheless, the various conversations in the play about Anowa's unfulfilled calling reveal a great deal about the signs, functions, and training of the priestess. We are told that "from a very small age, she had the hot eyes and nimble feet of one born to dance for the gods" (80). The sign of her calling also appears in her dream about Slavery after which "there was talk of apprenticing me to a priestess" (107). The dream/ vision indicates that more than the calling to be a mere *medium,* Anowa has access to ways of knowing, the sign of a greater calling, the calling of a *priestess.* We learn that priestesses are respected as healers and that Badua "consult[ed] them over and over again when [she] could not get a single child from [her] womb to live beyond one day" (71). We observe Anowa's attempt to find an alternative outlet for her creative and mediational powers in choosing Kofi—the watery cassava male, and perhaps the suitor with the least capacity for creative agency—so that she can "help him do something with his life" (77–78). We witness Kofi's increasing discomfort at her discernment, her uncanny ability to divine his secret intentions and covert actions.

The relationship between Anowa and Kofi is the symbolic terrain in which the conflict of contradictory objectives plaguing this community is acted out. Kofi Ako is impressed by the model of economic success that the European traders represent, and he seeks to emulate them. Anowa, however, wants to strike a balance between the structural readjustments caused by the European presence, and personal and communal responsibilities pertaining to an ethos of interconnectedness. The conflict between Anowa and Kofi over which economic philosophy and direction to pursue mirrors a larger conflict within the cultural community. Like Anowa, other members of the society who hold a critical view of the capitalist model are disdained and ostracized. Anowa's dream/vision and her subsequent conversations with Kofi about the purchase of slaves and the pursuit of leisure underscore the issue at stake in this crisis.

As presented in *Anowa*, the imitation of a Western capitalist model has economic, social, spiritual, and ideological consequences for African peoples. Unlike precolonial African societies that defined and measured wealth in terms of the increase of life-force, capitalism measures wealth in terms of the increase of leisure. Indeed, in the capitalist model, life-force—symbolized by Kofi's "birth seeds"—is diminished as it is exchanged for leisure-as-wealth. As exemplified by the institutions of feudalism and Slavery, the development of a leisure class requires the maintenance of a serf/slave class. The leisure class's exemption from its portion of life-sustaining labor is procured by the creation of a slave class whose sole activity consists of diverse forms of service. The interconnectedness of human community guarantees that the "blessing" of the leisure class will constitute the "curse" of the working class. In his pioneering study *How Europe Underdeveloped Africa*, Walter Rodney first identified this pattern, noting that the creation of the wealth of Europe in the seventeenth, eighteenth, and nineteenth centuries was procured from the impoverishment of Africa.[7] Both instances of the economic and sociopolitical imbalance violate the tenets of African cosmology that privilege the preservation and/or restoration of a *righteous equilibrium* of interdependent relationships, as outlined in chapter 1. The philosophical goals of this cosmology are attained through a distinct set of economic and social relations. As Oduyoye notes: "African society is organized in such a way that all able-bodied persons work almost as soon as they can walk. When they can no longer walk, they still function as a source of wisdom and as the storehouse of the collective memory of the family" (194). Kofi's vision of wealth involves no commitment to creativity or to strengthening the family, clan, or community, through the redistribution of wealth. Indeed, Kofi's (pro)creative agency, and the creative agency of his wife, are suspended in accordance with the goals of this new (European) cultural, spiritual, and ideological paradigm.

Given the broad sociopolitical ramifications of Kofi's vision of wealth, Anowa's marriage to him can be seen as a spiritual intervention toward modifying his economic policies to coincide with an African cultural and spiritual cosmology. This would account for why Anowa does not seek a formal apprenticeship. Her role in the marriage is largely mediational, challenging and exposing the spiritually and socially harmful effects of his adopted ideology and economic agenda. At the moment of impasse between them, for example, Anowa recalls the dream of Slavery. This historical subtext magnifies the implications of Kofi's capitalist agenda and leisure lifestyle.

> That night, I woke up screaming hot; my body burning and sweating from a horrible dream. I dreamt that I was a big, big woman. And from my insides were huge holes out of which poured men, women and children. And the sea was boiling hot and steaming. And as it boiled, it threw out many, many giant lobsters, boiled lobsters, each of whom as it fell turned into a man or woman, but keeping its lobster head and claws. And they rushed to where I sat and seized the men and women as they poured out of me, and they tore them apart, and dashed them to the ground and stamped upon them. And from their huge courtyards, the women ground my men and women and children on mountains of stone. But there was never a cry or a murmur; only a bursting, as of a ripe tomato or a swollen pod. And everything went on and on and on. (106)

Anowa's discursive agency—in challenging, interrogating, and exposing socioeconomic and political choices—suggests that the role and functions of the priestess can and do evolve to fit changing circumstances. Despite the limited success of her mediational efforts in the world of the play, Aidoo's depiction of Anowa's agency holds even greater significance as an attempt to unveil the historical origins of contemporary crises and to prompt a reevaluation of "development" initiatives in light of the spiritual, socioeconomic, and political liabilities of Kofi's economic agenda. Given the relevance of this analysis to contemporary situations outside the play, Anowa's success must be measured in terms of the ideological analysis to which her psychospiritual vision contributes.

Like Hurston's Miriam, Anowa is ousted from the very sphere in which her mediational agency is most urgently needed and traditionally sanctioned. Kofi's repudiation of Anowa's vision is as much a repudiation of a specific spiritual vision as it is a repudiation of her assertiveness as a woman claiming both spiritual and sociopolitical authority, and intellectual autonomy. In her conversation with the portrait of Queen Victoria, Anowa provides a gender analysis of her own predicament.

> *Hei,* sister, I hear you are a queen. Maybe in spite of the strange look of you, you are a human woman, too, eh? How is it with you over there? Do you sometimes feel like I feel, that you should not have been born? Nana. . . won't you answer? . . . I hear in other lands a woman is nothing. And they let her know this from the day of her birth. But here, O my spirit mother, they let a girl grow up as she pleases until she is married. And then she is like any woman anywhere: in order for her man to be a man, she must not think, she must not talk. (112)

Despite the fact that Queen Victoria clearly symbolizes the imperialist/capitalist apparatus unleashing new dangers in the society, Anowa recognizes her specific identity as a gendered (and ambivalent) symbol of female political authority. For Anowa, her muteness is as compelling as her authority.

While Miriam receives *posthumous* tribute for her spiritual and sociopolitical leadership, Anowa's fate appears quite bleak. In *Black Women, Writing and Identity,* Carole Boyce Davies argues that Anowa's confinement—and displacement—in the "Big House" that Kofi acquires "becomes an external reference for the entrenchment of colonial power and male dominance" (61). Davies also notes that her "exit from the play is a tragedy of historical closure for women" (61) since it suggests the triumph of gender-based prescriptions. Yet, if as Oduyoye argues, Anowa is indeed "Africa's ancestor" and not just progenitor of a female genealogy, the implications of the play's denouement cannot be read as gender restricted. They extend, naturally, to the continental/diaspora community she represents. In fact, Anowa is not alone in being confined and displaced in the "Big House." So, too, are the servants, especially the twin boy and girl who represent the future; so, too, is Kofi. Although Kofi's colonialist privilege opposes and restricts Anowa's creative agency, this is a self-endangering privilege. What matters then is not simply who is confined within the "Big House." Rather, as Kalu's analysis suggests, what matters is that it has replaced former shelters and has become the new paradigm structuring sociocultural and political relationships. Yet, in her choice of a specific mode for Anowa's exit—suicide by drowning—Aidoo encodes possibilities for a liberating resolution.

While suicide is typically interpreted as a narrative and ontological "dead-end," the strikingly high incidence of suicide by drowning among enslaved/displaced Africans throughout the Slavery era supports an alternative reading of the play's ending. Throughout the continent, African societies have deeply rooted taboos against suicide. In light of the severe sanctions against suicide, the frequency with which enslaved Africans nevertheless embraced death by drowning suggests the possibility of a special dispensation. Surviving narratives of African captives who "walked on water" or "swam" back to Africa—popularized for contemporary readers in Paule Marshall's *Praisesong for the Widow* and the legend of Igbo Landing—indicate that drowning was viewed, if not as a triumph, then at least as an avenue of return. While Marshall's novel states that the Igbos "just kept walking right on out over the river" (38), in Julie Dash's *Daughters of the Dust,* two truths about the Igbos emerge. Bilal Muhammed, a ten-year-old eyewitness at the time, states that the Igbos walked in the water with chains and irons, and "they ain't never come up." Eula, on the other hand, repeats Marshall's account, confirming that they walked back home. In describing the significance of this event in her film, Dash recalls that

> in my research, I found that almost every Sea Island has a little inlet, or a little area where the people say, "This is Ibo Landing. This is where it happened." And so, why is it that on every little island—and there are so many places—people say, "This is actually Ibo Landing"? It's because that message is so strong, so powerful, so sustaining to the tradition of resistance, by any means possible, that every Gullah community embraces this myth. (30)

Despite Bilal's eyewitness testimony, the camera affirms Eula's account in treating the viewer to the spectacle of Eli walking on water to meet the ancestral figure floating off Igbo Landing. There is, however, no necessary conflict between the two accounts. The Igbos drowned themselves, and, in embracing this choice, they combined their own creative agency with the water's agency as a conduit for the spirit and walked home. For them, and for Anowa, this was not historical closure but a rerouting toward a future of continuing agency, as exemplified by this priestess's narrative longevity.

The Priestess as a Model of Womanhood

In the character Indigo, the epicenter of her novel *Sassafrass, Cypress, and Indigo* (1982), Ntozake Shange provides one of the most enabling portraits, in literature or film, of the Black woman bearing life-force. Celebrating the resourcefulness and agency of the priestess is, however, just one of several responsibilities Shange takes on in this novel. Through this simple coming-of-age narrative, set in the early seventies, Shange examines the choices facing young Black women, exposes the hidden dangers they are likely to encounter, reveals the devastation they may experience, charts paths to re-covery from emotional and physical abuse, and identifies the resources and strategies—art, ancestors, spirituality, and sisterhood—that can assist them in moving from woundedness to wholeness.

In the title of her earlier, and most renowned work, the choreopoem *For Colored Girls Who Have Considered Suicide . . .* (1975), Shange expressed her vision of the work of art as an offering designed to strengthen and increase the life-force among young Black women. In the introduction to the chore-opoem, she writes, "i am offering these to you as what i've received from this world so far" (xvi). *Sassafrass, Cypress, and Indigo* is informed by a sim-ilar commitment to sharing received knowledge. As a resource and mecha-nism for growth, spirituality informs every aspect of the novel, from its multigeneric structure, to its depiction of a female kinship network an-chored by the mother, Hilda Effania, to its characterization of the priestess figure, Indigo. In fact, the most resonant line of *For Colored Girls . . .* —"i found god in myself / & i loved her / i loved her fiercely"—becomes the dominant theme in *Sassafrass, Cypress, and Indigo* as it charts the lives of the three sisters journeying into womanhood. Through the figure of the priestess, the novel redefines an empowered Black womanhood as it ex-plores the interior world of "a woman who knows her magic," "a woman in charge of her powers," a "woman [who] is a consort of the spirits."

Unlike Hurston's *Moses* and Aidoo's *Anowa*, this novel's concern with celebrating the priestess's mediational agency—manifested in her vision, voice, knowledge, and art—appears in its opening salutation, which immediately positions Indigo in an affirming narrative environment. "Where there is a woman there is magic. If there is a moon falling from her mouth, she is a woman who knows her magic, who can share or not share her powers. A woman with a moon falling from her mouth, roses between her legs and tiaras of Spanish moss, this woman is a consort of the spirits" (3). While Miriam and Anowa are positioned within narrative environments marked by crisis and change, Indigo's world is relatively stable. Nevertheless, in noting that "There wasn't enough for Indigo in the world she'd been born to" (4), Shange characterizes her social environment as deficient. For Indigo, as for African Americans at large in the post–civil rights era, there still isn't an adequate range of economic, political, artistic, and psychological resources. Indigo's response to this shortage—"she made up what she needed. What she thought the black people needed" (4)—reveals a creative agency already attuned to individual and collective needs. Although, at age twelve, she is only a woman-child, and not yet a woman, this display of compensatory agency already signals Indigo's calling to the role and office of the priestess.

Unlike her two older sisters, Sassafrass and Cypress, who are set adrift from their cultural moorings by the educational opportunities that become available to Black students in the post–civil rights era, particularly in the North, Indigo remains rooted in the knowledge of village ancestors undergirded by an intense spiritual self-consciousness. "When her father died," the narrator notes, "Indigo had decided it was the spirit of things that mattered. The humans come and go" (8). Ancestors—both living and deceased—people Indigo's world. Indeed, in its representation of the village elders who nurture Indigo, the novel exemplifies what Morrison has identified in "Rootedness" as a primary feature of Black literature. That is, the sustaining presence of the "advising, benevolent, protective, wise Black ancestor." "Extending its theological usage in African religion/culture to designate the community of *deceased* elders who continue to fulfill sustaining roles in the lives of their descendants," Ryan and Májozo explain, "Morrison uses the term 'ancestor' to designate *living* elders with a similar responsibility and capacity" (136). In "City Limits, Village Values," Morrison notes that one of the distinctive features of Black literature is the presence of an ancestor who is crucial to the moral and spiritual development of the characters and to their (strategies for) survival. Indigo's development into an empowered womanhood and into her full capacity as priestess conforms to this pattern since it is assisted by Mrs. Yancy, Uncle John, Sister Mary Louise, and culminates with her apprenticeship to Aunt Haydee.

The contrast between the absence of such ancestors in the lives of Miriam[8] and Anowa and their ubiquitous presence in Shange's novel underscores one of the primary factors that account for Indigo's success in her priestess role. Not only is Indigo's development assisted by these ancestors, but her relationship with each constitutes an apprenticeship of sorts. In fact, Shange's portrait of Indigo's apprenticeship and connection to these village elders bears a strong resemblance to Marshall's description of Avey's early apprenticeship to Aunt Cuney in *Praisesong for the Widow*. In both instances, the deliberateness with which the ancestor engages the child suggests a conscious preparation for a future "mission." As Avey later recalls of Aunt Cuney's role in her life:

> She had laid claim to [her] for a month each summer from the time she was seven. Before she was seven! Before she had been born even! There was the story of how she had sent word months before her birth that it would be a girl and she was to be called after her grandmother who had come to her in a dream with the news . . . and then as soon as she turned seven had ordered her father to bring and deposit her every August in Tatem, which he had done over her mother's unceasing objections. (42)

Through this apprenticeship, centered—like Indigo's—around storytelling/communal histories, "the old woman had entrusted her with a mission she couldn't even name yet had felt duty-bound to fulfill" (42). Although it takes Avey several years to discern her mission, the parallel between her own and Indigo's apprenticeship accentuates the significance of early training and initiation.

In her interactions with village elders, Indigo is presented with situations that call forth the life-force within her. Some of the strategies that these ancestors use to assist Indigo's development include storytelling, performing rituals, and providing cultural and artistic resources. As an example, one of Indigo's favorite and seemingly casual pastimes is visiting the old women in the community and listening to their stories. The narrator notes that "Old ladies loved for Indigo and Company to pass by. They would give her home-made butter cookies or gingerbread. They offered teas and chocolates, as well as the Scriptures and the legends of their lives. . . . Indigo listened to their tales, the short and long ones, with a mind to make herself a doll whose story that was or who could have helped out" (7–8). These experiences prepare Indigo for the priestess role and, perhaps more important, for Black womanhood. As the novel demonstrates, the storytelling and the doll-making form part of an intergenerational discourse about Black women's lives, one that subsequently becomes an important resource for survival. The compensatory attitude with which Indigo engages the women's stories, the first expression of her mediational agency, extends beyond this interaction to inform her childhood creative activities: "Indigo had made every kind of friend she wanted. African dolls filled with cotton root bark, so they'd have no more slave children. Jamaican dolls in red turbans, bodies formed with comfrey leaves because they'd had to work on Caribbean and American plantations and their bodies must ache and be sore. Then there were the mammy dolls that Indigo labored over for months" (6). In the engagement with the past she encounters through storytelling, Indigo's creative agency is given purpose and direction. In fact, historical consciousness shapes the trajectory of Indigo's mediational role. In its focus on the priestess, the novel explores the myriad uses of power, including its inventive, compensatory, protective, expressive, transformative, liberating, connective, and epistemological functions.

Indigo's journey into womanhood stands in radical counterpoint to that of her two sisters whose experiences more closely reflect the challenges confronting (educated) young Black women in the post–civil rights, post–Black Power, postfeminist era. While Indigo remains rooted (but not sequestered) in the South, her sisters' experiences outside the South—Sassafrass's on the West coast, Cypress's on the East—run the gamut of contemporary scenarios. Sassafrass's relationship with Mitch is one of several (potentially) abusive relationships in the novel. The relationships between Mabel and Prettyman, Hilda Effania and Albert, and Cypress and Idrina are not equally abusive, or abusive in the same way. Nevertheless, they are all marked by an undercurrent of dominance. In her relationship with Mitch (and his friends), Sassafrass encounters the multiple dangers of a nationalist, misogynistic, self-destructive anger. In Cypress's journey, Shange examines both professional and personal relationships. She explores the different environments available to professional Black women artists and the ideologies that shape those environments.

In its unmasking of the flaws behind idealized liberation ideologies, the novel displays its most autonomous stance. The reactive posture that required—in an earlier period—an uncritical (and therefore self-endangering) solidarity with Black people, Black men, Black women, or all women has yielded to a proactive stance that prizes cultural and gender distinctiveness without romanticizing those communities, or jeopardizing growth. As such, the novel's depiction of the misogyny that makes the dance company psychologically inhospitable toward Black women is as significant as its depiction of the culturally affirming repertoire of the Kushites Returned. Similarly, its exposure of the predatory attitudes of some of the women is as instructive as its depiction of the self-affirmation and self-discovery Cypress achieves in Azure Bosom and in the lesbian community.

The journeys of the three sisters are important to Shange's goal of providing instructions—in the form of maps, charts, recipes, formulas—about specific areas of women's lives. In their lives, the novel provides its most extensive mapping—maps depicting and celebrating the changing configurations of Black women's lives; maps that reveal the dangers, possibilities, and, above all else, the resources and the strategies through which creative/righteous agency can be (re)claimed and/or (re)directed. This concern informs the multigeneric structure of the novel, which includes letters (from Hilda Effania to each of her three daughters), recipes, formulas for blessings, purging evil, healing oneself, and so on.

Although the South functions as a ritual ground that sustains Indigo's development, Shange does not idealize this landscape. There are dangers in the southern environment. As Hilda Effania cautions her daughter: "Little boys don't come chasing after you for nothing good. White men roam these parts with evil in their blood, and every single thought they have about a colored woman is dangerous" (22). Some hints of these dangers can be traced in Indigo's first encounter with Spats and Crunch. "There was something moving up her leg, something that was not supposed to be there. Indigo looked down, lost a little fear, just a twig. How was a twig going up & down the inside of her leg, tickling her. . . . Indigo looked cautiously behind her where two brown-skinned boys leaned over Sister Mary Louise's fence"

(37). The novel provides a more extensive representation of southern dangers in Indigo's encounter with the pharmacist, Mr. Lucas. His assault, the narrator makes clear, is not random. Rather, his is a pointed assault prompted by his view of a dispossessed and subordinate womanhood as normative: "Mr. Lucas took a step toward Indigo, like he was looking for the woman in her. . . . Every once in a while, he saw a woman with something he wanted. Something she shouldn't have. He didn't know what it was, an irreverence, an insolence, like the bitch thought she owned the moon" (28–29).

What Indigo has, what Mr. Lucas believes she and other women should not have, is an empowered self-definition. In describing Indigo's response to this assault, Shange provides the first of several guidelines on how to identify, negotiate, and recover from destructive onslaughts. First, we note that although she is perhaps too young to fully recognize the danger, "Indigo heard somebody talking to her" (29). The "somebody" alerting her to the danger, we later learn, is the fiddle that carried/carries the voices of the ancestors. Not only does the fiddle alert her to the danger, it also assists her in escaping Mr. Lucas's pursuit. "The fiddle was knocking all kinds of personal hygiene products off shelves," creating an obstacle course for "Mr. Lucas behind her, lumbering, quiet" (29). Given her extensive conversations with the old women in the community, the "somebody talking to her" also refers to Indigo's own well-developed inner consciousness nurtured by a participatory listening to other women's life stories. The ritual she creates—"To Rid Oneself of the Scent of Evil"—in the aftermath of this assault is transformative in each of its stages. The first stage eliminates the very likely danger of denial and repression: "Though it may cause some emotional disruptions, stand absolutely still & repeat the offender's name till you are overwhelmed with the memory of your encounter" (30). The second stage affirms her being: "Take two deep slow breaths, on a 7 count." The third stage enacts discursive, epistemological control through naming: "Then, waving your arms & hands all about you, so your atmosphere may again be clean, say the name of the offender softly." The fourth stage extends the benefit of the third stage to others. That is to say, this naming as an act of self-affirmation and discursive control affirms other women's experiences: "Each time blowing your own breath into the world that we may all benefit from your renewal."

While the narrator attributes Indigo's cultural/spiritual vision to "the South in her," the distinctiveness of her character depends on both the South in her and her being in the South. Of the three sisters, she alone never travels outside the South. In fact, the trajectory of her journey is "southerly" —not in spatial terms but in cultural and historical terms—as she travels from Charleston to Difuskie for her apprenticeship with Aunt Haydee, the healer. Her choice affirms the sustaining elements of that sociocultural milieu, elements that can play an even more important role in negotiating the challenges her sisters and other Black women confront today. In that sense, Indigo's journey coincides with and prefigures the trajectory of Paule Marshall's *Praisesong for the Widow,* Gloria Naylor's *Mama Day,* Julie Dash's *Daughters of the Dust,* and other Black women's texts in which "the South" serves as a proxy for another, more ancient territory upon which to ground an empowered self. More than is true of her sisters, it is her vision—and *not* just her experiences—that instructs and stabilizes the community of readers. In its extended focus on the woman-child Indigo, the novel demonstrates that an empowered womanhood is rooted in an empowered girlhood, and that both are sustained by the gifts and the foundation that ancestors provide.

Reversing Dispossession

Black Women's Cinema

From the moment that Africans were brought to the Americas and made slaves, we lost much more than our freedom. We lost control of our image. Film and television have been crucial in this legacy of loss, our loss of name and culture, for Hollywood has the power to rewrite, redefine and recreate history, culture, religion and politics. Hollywood has the power of the spoken word and the visual image and all sounds and dreams.

—ALILE SHARON LARKIN, "Black Women Film-makers Defining Ourselves"

This chapter provides a second introduction to the study by, first of all, reviewing the history of Hollywood filmmaking and its psychosocial impact on U.S. Americans as an important context for examining the ideological goals shaping Black women's cinema. Here, I discuss how Black women filmmakers use cinema as a vehicle for expanding the social text and its positioning of human subjects. Specifically, I argue that one of the most important concerns shared by Black women filmmakers is a concern for the ways in which national history is constructed—off-screen as well as on-screen. I show how this concern is connected to a broader commitment to democracy and to the rights to representation and participation it endorses. The chapter begins with an examination of the connection between how national histories are constructed and how roles/characterization are assigned to various communities. This discussion paves the way for an analysis of Julie Dash's *Illusions* in which I explore her attempt to redefine the terms for Black women's participation in both national history and national cinema—in front of and behind the camera.

Black Women Re-casting History

In the chapter epigraph, filmmaker Alile Sharon Larkin points to the prominent role of film and television in a pattern of dispossession that began with Slavery. In using their art form to reverse this history of dispossession, Black women filmmakers frequently return to the past in order to reinscribe the history of Black women's agency as a basis for constructing future agency. The past—its predicaments and possibilities—is, therefore, a recurring focus in Black women's films. Typically, the character's engagement with an empowering ancestral gaze frames the representation of the past. Maya Angelou's *Down in the Delta*, Julie Dash's *Daughters of the Dust*, Zeinabu irene Davis's *Compensation*, Euzhan Palcy's *Sugar Cane Alley*, and Yvonne Welbon's *Remembering Wei Yi-Fang, Remembering Myself* all exemplify this narrative focus.

The decisiveness and frequency with which Black women artists engage the past is striking given that this past is usually saturated with experiences of loss. For these filmmakers, this is no cursory "stroll down memory lane." Rather, it is a calculated return to sites of oppression from which, paradoxically, mechanisms of self-empowerment are retrieved. This narrative pattern expresses a view of the past that coincides with art historian John Berger's description of its functional and enabling character. In *Ways of Seeing*, Berger observes that "the past is not for living in. It is a well of conclusions from which we draw in order to act" (11). Berger's assessment underscores the direction in which transformative agency is channeled through the encounter with the past. Yet, his view of the past as a resource that increases (future) agency contrasts sharply with popular cultural sensibilities. Far from seeking to extrapolate usable "conclusions" or readings from the "well" or text of the past, our most persistent desire is for an uncritical immersion in an aesthetically anesthetized[1] past in which to experience moments of pleasure rarely available to our ancestors. This is not to suggest that the past held no joy for those who lived it but that the audio-visual stimuli prompting our vicarious pleasure are categorically different from their lived stimuli.

Apart from its opposition to our most prevalent disposition toward the past, Berger's description of the past as a "well" suggests that it can be utilized as a resource from and by which future agency can be refilled, perhaps limitlessly. This view of the past as a resource shapes Black women's film narratives. Their goal is not simply to provide "correct" versions of the past. Rather, they return to sites of oppression in an attempt to reinscribe their own empowered self-definitions erased from the official text of national history. This involves the reinscription of self-definitions encoded in memory, orature, and other art forms. These cinematic interventions are designed to reshape the future. Or, more precisely, *our* futures. That is, the many futures that viewers will chart—individually and collectively—because of their expanded ability to generate new readings. In their frequent engagement with the past, Black women filmmakers extend the role of priestess, enabling viewers to reverse dispossession by positioning them to reclaim their own interpretive agency.

The film that most fully illustrates this process and that, as the subsequent analysis will demonstrate, functions as a manifesto for Black women filmmakers, is Julie Dash's *Illusions. Illusions* exemplifies the many dimensions of Black women's commitment to the paradigm of growth, especially their commitment to interrogating and revising "master narratives" and the "preferred readings" of history they sustain. It also reflects their commitment to revisiting ancestral texts and retrieving the alternative readings they encode. To understand this dual focus, however, one needs to examine the ways in which national history functions as an epistemology and an ideology, functions most clearly displayed in Hollywood narratives, functions consistent with Joseph Campbell's monomyth.

"Monomyth" is the term coined by Campbell to designate the unvarying pattern to which the diversity and abundance of myths—from different cultures, different regions, and different centuries—irrevocably conform. In his classic analysis of myth, *The Hero with a Thousand Faces,* Campbell notes that "it will be always the one, shape shifting yet marvelously constant story that we find, together with a challengingly persistent suggestion of more remaining to be experienced than will ever be known or told" (3). Campbell also points to myth's resemblance to dreams, a connection based on what he sees as its involuntary composition. Like dreams, he notes, myths emerge from the inner recesses of the human psyche, a fact that partially explains their transcultural and transhistorical constancy.

Myth has generally been viewed as outside of, if not opposed to, the category of history. Indeed, in popular parlance, "myth" denotes a distorted historical narrative. Yet anthropologists have pointed to myth as a mode of historicity that fulfills an important social function. In "The Role of Myth," Joanna Overing observes that myth supplies knowledge of why things are the way they are within a particular social universe. Myth has power both to explain and to explain away. In that sense, Overing notes, myth can also productively inform social theory. Overing's view of myth as a mode of historicity, when combined with Campbell's view of myth as a product of the psyche, can enable us to uncover certain aspects of the national psyche if we consider national history as myth. In fact, the concept of the monomyth can be used to provide new insight on the genre of national history.

Like myths, national histories conform to a monomythic structure with identifiable formal elements and narrate an unvarying "adventure" of nationhood, to borrow Campbell's term. This typically begins with a "call to adventure"—what Vladimir Propp calls an "initiating situation"—involving a founding patriarch (Sundiata of Mali, the biblical Abraham and Moses, George Washington, Mshaka, Lenin, Mao, Castro, Nkrumah, Lumumba, and others) inspired with a new vision. Other structural and thematic features include the confrontation of threats—domestic and foreign—which the hero overcomes with the aid of helpers, and "temporary" set-backs in the "adventure." Despite surface variations, therefore, national history is remarkably constant; its monomythic constitution points to the ubiquity of the "adventure" of nationhood.

While Campbell's analysis views this constancy as the workings of the collective psyche, Etienne Balibar attributes it to historiography. He regards the crafting of national history as a politically motivated project—one contingent upon "presentation." The "identical pattern," in his view, is a construction resulting from the "prejudices of various historians." In "The Nation Form: History and Ideology," he writes:

> The history of nations, beginning with our own, is always already presented to us in the form of a narrative which attributes to these entities the continuity of a subject. The formation of the nation thus appears as the fulfillment of a "project" stretching over centuries, in which there are different stages and moments of coming to self-awareness, which the preju-

dices of the various historians will portray as more or less decisive . . . but which, in any case, all fit into an identical pattern: that of the self-manifestation of the national personality. (86)

Propp, one of the premier structural theorists, offers a different view. Discussing, in *Morphology of the Folktale,* the transcultural constancy of folktales, Propp notes:

> The historian, inexperienced in morphological problems, will not see a resemblance where one actually exists; he will omit coincidences which are important to him, but which he does not notice. And conversely, where a similarity is perceived, a specialist in morphology will be able to demonstrate that compared phenomena are completely heteronomous. (16)

Propp's analysis supports Campbell's view of national formation (nationhood) as an always already scripted "adventure," a script as informed by psychological processes as it is by ideological ones. While I concur with Balibar's analysis of the ways in which ideologically motivated choices by historians shape the construction of national histories, I view this as evidence of their involvement and/or investment in those histories.

In their discussion titled "The Imperial Imaginary" in *Unthinking Eurocentrism,* Ella Shohat and Robert Stam make a similar observation. They refer to Hayden White's concept of "master tropes" that shape historical discourse and, in that sense, are closer to Etienne Balibar in identifying the ideological construction of historical narratives. While the two views are not antithetical, my analysis focuses on the involuntary construction of these narratives as a transcultural, transhistorical product of the psyche. In my analysis of Hollywood film "history," I follow Campbell's and Propp's models in examining national history as a genre whose monomythic constitution is not simply the creation of historians but a reflection of (latent) psychological desires motivating the manifestation (and self-representation) of national personality, of which historians are, inevitably, a part.

Although national histories conform to an unvarying pattern, specific versions can collide without disrupting the monomythic structure. For example, the same agents that are designated "helpers" in one national history can be cast as "villains" in another, as are the Soviets in Cuban and U.S. national history, respectively. Likewise, "villains" can be recast as "helpers" as have the Russians in the U.S.-led "War on Terrorism." Moreover, like dreams and myths, national histories express the latent content of the collective psyche, which can display signs of repression, displacement, projection, denial, and other defense mechanisms. As such, national history can be "read" in ways parallel to both dreams and myths. It can provide useful insights even (or especially) when its content is obviously distorted. As an expression of the national psyche, it represents a distinct mode of historicity and a distinct epistemology; one, therefore, requiring a distinct interpretive approach. Our task is to interrogate specific histories for what they reveal of the nation's desires, fears, anxieties, guilt—the complex baggage of the psyche. Understanding the monomyth of national history, specifically the U.S. version, in terms of its casting of roles, is key to deciphering Julie Dash's objectives in recasting the genre in *Illusions*.

In U.S. national history, the threat to the nation-subject's progress is alternately represented as domestic (Native Americans, the landscape, the climate, the weather) or foreign (the British, the Japanese, the Germans, the Soviets, the Cubans, the Chinese, the Koreans, the Arabs), with immigrants representing a convenient conflation of both aspects. Despite their prominent role in the development of the nation, neither version allowed or required the distinct casting of African Americans.

Throughout the Slavery era, enslaved Africans were expunged from the national "we" in versions of U.S. national history featuring a foreign threat and were erased in versions focusing on a domestic threat. During this period, Africans in the United States were cast as "the rescued," a group uniquely indebted to the nation. This positioning represents one of the first signs of rupture in the genre. The logical demands of narrative dictate that the recipient of help be viewed as the subject/hero(ine) of his/her own adventure, whose progress is assisted by helpers. In the U.S. version of national history, however, the casting of Africans as the rescued permanently denies them a subject position in their own "adventure." This casting is similar to that of Friday in Daniel Defoe's *Robinson Crusoe* (1719). While Crusoe is himself rescued from numerous dangers and assisted in resuming the narrative progression of his adventure as its subject, Defoe and Crusoe conspire to permanently exile Friday from his own adventure by "rescuing" him.[2] Friday is both dispossessed and exiled, developments that simultaneously terminate his (narrative) subjectivity. The fact that his own original name is never mentioned or recalled—even when he is temporarily re-united with his father—signals and reinforces the absolute erasure of sub-jectivity.

Friday's encounter with Crusoe reassigns him to an object position that prefigures the position assigned to enslaved Africans. This narrative reposi-tioning within the text of U.S. national history points to a concerted act of collective repression. As novelist and essayist Ralph Ellison described it in "The Shadow and the Act": "The problem, arising in a democracy that holds all men as created equal, was a highly moral one: democratic ideals had to be squared with anti-Negro practices. One answer was to *deny* the Negro's humanity—a pattern set long before 1915" (276). In denying Black people's humanity, in assigning them to the role of indebtedness, the nation denied knowledge of, and culpability for, the undemocratic treatment of Africans. In a parallel gesture of repression aimed at preserving the purity of its own self-representation, "race" was deployed to malign the image of African peoples throughout Western society, and eventually throughout the world. This ideology recast Black people as lacking in humanity, cultural achieve-ments, history, and other common human capacities; it concurrently posited a definition of White people as civilized, advanced, superior, intelli-gent, moral, rational, and uniquely endowed with the highest cultural and human capacities. The maneuver—a classic display of projection—estab-lished a binary system of racial characteristics that assigned positive/con-structive capacities to Whites and negative/destructive capacities to Blacks and inscribed the reciprocal nexus of ideological whiteness and ideological blackness. It thereby created a morphological rationale for the oppression of Blacks, recasting it as the benevolent guardianship of a people desper-ately in need of, and yet incapable of, civilization. In sum, it denied Black people's intellectual and ethical independence and elided their capacity for righteous/creative agency.

More than other forms, the U.S. national history projected on-screen represents a particularly virulent expression of the genre as it articulates and disseminates authorized versions—what Stuart Hall calls "preferred readings"—of how things are and the reasons why they are the way they are. Taken as a whole, Hollywood films clearly exemplify Campbell's concept of the monomyth. Despite the multiplicity of titles, settings, and characters, these film plots all repeat one "marvelously constant story." Moreover,

Overing's summation of myth's social function in supplying morphological explanations of the world as it is, is more patently true for the national history projected on-screen. In constructing its monomyth, Hollywood cinema assigns an irresistible logic and meaning to every sociocultural practice and event.

Of the many aspects of Hollywood's role as a distributor of the text of national history, one—its monocultural casting of national history—has particular significance for our understanding of Dash's reformulation of the genre in *Illusions*. At first glance, this seems contradictory. If the monomyth is, by definition, *trans*cultural, it can hardly be accused of being simultaneously *mono*cultural. The contradiction, however, is easily resolved. What can and should vary in the monomyth—as folktale or national history—is not the plot but the assignment of roles. That is to say that while, for example, the adventure of the feudal landlord may have the same monomythic elements as that of the peasant, each occupies a unique subjectivity and plays a distinct role in their particular adventure. For example, while the landlord (or U.S. American) may cast himself as the heroic dragon slayer (or defender of democracy) in his own myth/history, he is likely to be cast as villain (or enemy of democracy) in the peasant's (or Puerto Rican's) "adventure."

The rotation of roles is a variation that both disrupts and preserves the monomyth. It preserves it by maintaining the constancy of plot—the progression of the "adventure." It disrupts it by recasting traditionally designated helpers as villains, for example. Despite the fixed parameters of the monomyth, such variations in casting can allow a multiplicity of meanings to emerge from the text of national history. Conversely, it is the fixed casting of roles that depletes the text. The fixed assignment of roles imposes one static meaning. When filmmaker Alile Sharon Larkin notes that, as a consequence of Slavery, African people lost control of their image, this can be understood not simply as a repositioning within a different geopolitical history but as a recasting of their role in the text of U.S. national history, a recasting frequently inscribed as "structured absence." Yet, if a *democracy of narrative participation* is a narrative option under official dictatorships, it is—as African Americans have long insisted—an imperative in a multicultural democracy.

As the subsequent analysis of *Illusions* will demonstrate, versions of the national monomyth that accommodate a casting of African Americans as subjects of their own "adventure" need not mimic the gesture of erasure with regard to Euro-Americans. In fact, to do so would be to subscribe to the tenets of the paradigm of resistance. A recasting of roles can occur without changing the plot. To date, however, such a rotation has not occurred in versions of U.S. national history. To the contrary, D. W. Griffith's *The Birth of a Nation* (1915) provided the script for, and debut casting of, African Americans in a distinctly new role, the role of threat.

The erasure of Black peoples' subjectivity, and with it, their culture and history, received added impetus in the ideologically charged literary and cinematic productions of the post-Reconstruction era. These provided "proof" for the late nineteenth-century claim that Blacks had reverted to their "native savagery" following the removal of Slavery's "civilizing" influence. As Angela Davis explains, new racial stereotypes that would have been politically and economically damaging for White enslavers became politically expedient in the post-Reconstruction era: "In the immediate aftermath of the Civil War, the menacing specter of the Black rapist had not yet appeared on the historical scene. But lynchings, reserved during slavery for the white abolitionists, were proving to be a valuable political weapon. Before lynching could be consolidated as a popularly accepted institution, however, its savagery and its horrors had to be convincingly justified" (184). Davis concludes that "The institution of lynching . . . complemented by the continued rape of Black women, became an essential ingredient of the postwar strategy of racist terror. In this way the brutal exploitation of Black labor was guaranteed, and after the betrayal of Reconstruction, the political domination of the Black people as a whole was assured" (184–85).

Griffith's updated national history, *Birth of a Nation,* was *the* event that unveiled a new casting of old stereotypes to legitimate the practice of domination in the post-Slavery context. This, at a time when racist violations and violence against African Americans were at an all-time high and would culminate with the "Red Summer" of 1919.[3] A supreme instance of projection—in both cinematic and psychological terms—the film, as Morrison describes it in *Birth of a Nation'hood,* "gathered up and solidified post–Civil War America's assumptions of and desires for white supremacy" (xxvii).

Here, Morrison accurately gauges the nation's psychological desires and the strategies of repression, displacement, projection, and denial that allowed these desires and their (continuing) opposition to democratic principles to remain undetected, unexamined, and untransformed.

Outing the Self

Of the many commitments Julie Dash embraces in *Illusions*, the most significant is her commitment to exploring and expanding the narrative responsibilities of democracy. Dash foregrounds her critique of the construction of "democracy" and "history" in Hollywood with the opening reference to Ellison, her voice-over narrator grappling with the problem of how to mount "an attack upon Hollywood" for its role in perpetuating undemocratic representational practices that endorse White supremacist ideologies. Given Hollywood's role not as originator but as imitator/distributor, and its operation not by action but by means of illusion/projection, how does one successfully challenge its hegemony, reverse or curtail its disabling effects? Dash deciphers and answers Ellison's riddle by providing a film manifesto that unmasks the "state power" projected through Hollywood cinema, even as it makes use of classic cinema conventions.

Illusions begins with a long shot of an Oscar statuette glimmering in the dark, and a female voice-over echoing Ralph Ellison's 1949 essay, "The Shadow and the Act": "To direct an attack upon Hollywood would indeed be to confuse portrayal with action, image with reality. In the beginning was not the shadow, but the act, and the province of Hollywood is not action but illusion." We then see a montage of documentary footage from World War II, followed by visuals of a film studio over which is superimposed the title: "Hollywood 1942." Dash thereby opens with three separate registers that together make up the complex narration of this film: the disembodied female narrator, who blends the voice of the subsequent film's main character, Mignon Duprée (Lonette McKee), with the thoughts and assertions of its director (Dash); documentary film footage clearly referencing history, the "act" to which the voice-over refers, and its illusory shadow on film; and finally, Hollywood in 1942, the industry producing such "illusions." In order to get at the complexity of this structure, I take "Hollywood 1942" to signal the beginning of a film within the overall film titled *Illusions*.

The film "Hollywood 1942" begins with a male voice-over identified as that of a character, Lieutenant Bedsford (Ned Bellamy), dictating a communiqué to his secretary. The subsequent story focuses on a light-complexioned Black woman, Mignon Duprée, who passes for White and is employed as a producer at National Studios. Events in the film within the film unfold during the course of a single day at the Studios, where Lieutenant Bedsford is stationed as a consultant on behalf of the Office of War Information, and where Ester Jeeter (Rosanne Katon), a Black singer, finds occasional employment providing the vocal accompaniment to the visual performances of White female movie stars, such as Lila Grant (Gaye Kruger). The main order of business for the day is trying to avert a financial disaster following a technical mishap that has left the audio reel for Grant's latest film out of sync with the video reel. Since Grant is on tour with the USO, Mignon is given the task of turning this technical disaster into a "top money-maker." This precipitates her encounter with Ester, who is hired to rerecord the sound for Grant's performance.

Although *Illusions* focuses on the Black woman *passing*, this is not its only trope. Equally important to its analyses are the tropes of *(un)masking,*

Esther (Rosanne Katon) in the recording studio in *Illusions.* Courtesy of Women Make Movies.

closeting, and *outing.* The film's fluctuation between the tropes of *closeting* and *outing* parallels its oscillation between masking and manifesting, between mask and manifesto. Indeed, in its exploration of these discursive valences, *Illusions* functions as a manifesto that unmasks the role of "state power" in underwriting Hollywood narratives, deposes the White male gaze that dominates film spectatorship as well as genre and production conventions, and offers a view of what I call a *democracy of narrative participation.* This term enhances the discursive and theoretical potential of the word/ concept *democracy,* whose original impetus—as articulated in the U.S. Declaration of Independence—was human rights and, linked to this, the rights to representation and participation. While these rights have been given extensive consideration in relation to structures of governance and electoral processes, Dash's film manifesto demonstrates that a genuine commitment to democracy requires, among other things, representation and participation in national cinema and national history.

As the film progresses, we observe Mignon's efforts to persuade National Studios chief C. J. Forrester (Jack Radar) that the public is ready for a new type of film narrative, one that deals with the war's effects on the average citizen; her commitment to ensuring proper working conditions and a just remuneration for Ester; her struggles to balance her identity in and responsibility to the Black and national publics with her role and responsibility in the (ideologically) White world of "Hollywood 1942"; and her attempts to avoid Bedsford's unwelcome sexual pursuit. Two related events prompt a somewhat unexpected resolution. Mignon's conversations with Ester allow her to fully evaluate the self-censorship imposed by her masked identity. Shortly thereafter, Mignon's Black identity is unmasked, which forces a declaration of her own counterhegemonic vision of, and role in, the filmmaking industry. The film's ending discloses the "autobiographical" design in *Illusions* when Mignon, ventriloquating Dash, proclaims her new determination to "use the power of the motion picture."

While *Illusions* does not fuse the identity of the actual filmmaker (Dash) and the fictional filmmaker and narrator (Mignon), the closing scene consolidates the internal and the external signification of the narrative. It reveals the parallel visions and concerns of the filmmaker *within* the film and the filmmaker *outside* the film. Indeed, in tracing the process of Mignon's transformation from simply desiring change to consciously pursuing it, the film both critiques the Black woman filmmaker's assigned position within that arena and formulates a public declaration of her intentions: to "stay right here and fight" because there are "many stories to be told and many battles to begin.'" Thus, Mignon's closing declaration of her interest in those stories whose inclusion promotes a more democratic cinematic praxis, and of the importance of the ideology embedded within historical representation, prefigures the theoretical direction taken in other works by Dash (including *Daughters of the Dust*), and by other Black women filmmakers, most notably Yvonne Welbon and Cheryl Dunye. Like *Illusions,* Welbon's *Remembering Wei Yi-Fang, Remembering Myself* (1995) and Dunye's *The Watermelon Woman* (1996) both retheorize the dialogic relationship between the past and the present as it influences the space of Black women's creativity. In their fashioning of narrative techniques, these Black women filmmakers illustrate the relevance of Barbara Christian's concept of narrative theorizing to the analysis of African American *cinematic* narratives.

In "The Race for Theory," Christian dismantles the divide between theory and performance, suggesting that in works by Black women artists, theory is performed. *Illusions* performs theories about Black women's position in the filmmaking industry by exploring their various roles as musical props, disembodied voices, and would-be producers. Like other Black women artists, Dash's theorizing unfolds through the use of narrative techniques that underscore the collaboration between the artist and her protagonist, and that enables the former to simultaneously occupy several discursive positions. Prominent among these techniques is her use of the vocabulary of silence.

Toni Morrison's analysis of the critical content of Black women's silence and their discursive relationship to "civilization" clarifies its significance as an expressive modality in Black women's art. In "A Knowing So Deep," Morrison evaluates Black women's silence as a meaningful—in fact, eloquent—discourse, undergirded by an epistemological standpoint that has the potential to challenge, expose, and nullify hegemonic discourses: "In your silence, enforced or chosen, lay not only eloquence but discourse so devastating that 'civilization' could not risk engaging in it lest it lose the ground it stomped" (230). This assessment sheds light on Dash's choice of discursive strategy—her effective deployment of a preexisting hegemonic silence for a liberating project. In *Illusions,* Dash provides a filmic rendition of the vocabularies of silence. She strategically manipulates the hegemonic institutional silence on the treatment of racial minorities through a seemingly casual framing of shots that gesture toward another subtext—at the margins—in the form of studio posters, such as the one for the 1941 musical *The Chocolate Soldier*. Given this film's focus on a Russian soldier, its placement here signifies on the absence of film narratives about Black/ "Chocolate" soldiers. Such shots provide tellingly ironic commentary on undemocratic practices in "Hollywood 1942." In enunciating the marginalized analyses of various communities of the silenced and the silent, Dash—like other Black women artists—reveals the discursive power of silence, and the interpretive and epistemological agency of those communities.

Given its ideological objectives and its reliance on silence, *Illusions* does not (need to) assign Black subjects to an ahistorical prominence in "Hollywood 1942." In fact, despite Dash's highly touted casting of Mignon Duprée as a "studio executive," her executive status is still subject to gender and other ideological restrictions. Although she exerts some influence in her negotiations over Ester's wages, Mignon does not—as one might wish or expect—have the power to approve film projects dealing with new topics.[4] However, while her *executive* power is limited, the power she claims and shares with the camera is not. Mignon's discursive agency enables her to assist the camera by exposing, and interrogating, the regime of *closeting* responsible for both the pattern of "structured absences" and her own recourse to *passing* in "Hollywood 1942." In fact, Dash's exploration of *passing* is designed to reveal its relation to the systemic failures of democracy, and not the psychological failure of a single alienated consciousness.

In U.S. cinema, *passing* is usually the narrative trope chosen for a frantic flight away from blackness, and from the social, economic, and political subordination reserved for racial minorities. Films such as *Imitation of Life* (1934) and *Pinky* (1949) depict *passing* as a (futile) means of escape from what the central characters (initially) perceive as a disabling identity and of accessing otherwise restricted socioeconomic opportunities. Making the assumption that *passing* is the film's primary trope, Saidiya Hartman and Farah Griffin argue, in "Are You as Colored as that Negro?," that "the climax of Julie Dash's *Illusions* occurs when the white Lt. Bedford [*sic*] exposes the racial identity of the beautiful passing heroine Mignon" (362). In fact, however, the climax in this encounter is not Bedsford's exposure of Mignon's racial identity but Mignon's *outing* of herself.

The film registers its lack of interest in Bedsford's exposure through the fact that it generates no penalties, sanctions, or other adverse consequences for Mignon. To the contrary, the event culminates with Mignon moving to occupy the studio chief's chair. Dash also diminishes the significance of Bedsford's discovery by allowing Mignon to *out* herself in an earlier phone conversation with her mother. In fact, Dash has Mignon progressively *out* herself through the photo of her fiancé, her speech inflection, her gestures, and a gaze that invites Ester's and the viewer's discovery. Dash's decision to film Mignon's conversation with her mother as a de facto soliloquy, without the standard shot/reverse shot, heightens its importance as a declarative event. By themselves, Mignon's words express this declaration only in part. The scene's full meaning emerges through the silent vocabulary of the mise-en-scène and camera work. Pointedly avoiding a close-up of Mignon's face, the camera notices, then slowly zooms in on a small sign pasted to the wall of the phone booth that reads, "I am *so* an American!" Here, Dash employs (and inverts) the discursive symbol and space of the closet (the phone booth) for a formal *outing* of Mignon's Black identity and her political vision, while affirming and insisting on the citizenship and participatory entitlements these would otherwise preclude.

In her astute reading of the *passing* narrative in film and literature in *Not Just Race, Not Just Gender,* Valerie Smith describes it as a genre that "manipulates spectatorial allegiances" by designating the *passing* individual's implicit desire for social equality as a betrayal of her/his race. Smith's observation that these narratives are "sites where anti-racist and white supremacist ideologies converge" reveals a key motive for Dash's revision of the genre—to undo or refashion the terms and effects of this convergence (36). In particular, Dash's characterization of Mignon Duprée follows a very different trajectory than typically occurs in *passing* narratives in films by White directors. Here, Dash re-presents *passing* as a strategy for accessing power *on behalf of* various constituencies, including Black people, Black women, Native Americans, *and* White boys. Unlike standard cinematic representations of the *passing* individual who suspends or severs her/his group affiliation and who hides her/his connection to Black people as a shameful secret, Mignon maintains important emotional, cultural, and sociopolitical connections to family members and to other Black people. This depiction is an original and compelling variation on the motif of *passing* that can be read as an exploration of the *closeting* that occurs when Blacks and other racial minorities gain admittance to "ideologically White" institutions.

Being *closeted* is traditionally regarded as a self-selected positioning on the part of those individuals who lack the safety, support, consciousness, or courage to claim an Othered, discredited, marked identity. As a corollary to this, *coming out* typically signals a voluntary and conscious self-disclosure, while *outing* is typically understood as the intentional (and politically motivated) disclosure of someone else's Othered identity. In *Illusions,* Dash offers a more expansive way of understanding *closeting* and the act of *outing* the self.

Although the vocabulary of *closeting* and *outing* is almost exclusively applied to lesbian, gay, and bisexual experience, these terms can apply more broadly to a range of subaltern subjectivities. In a monological (and therefore undemocratic) social order, identities, experiences, choices, and commitments beyond the single "preferred" option are always already Othered, excluded, marked, closeted. (Here, I use the term "preferred" in the sense that Stuart Hall uses it to mean endorsed by, and supportive of, hegemonic interests.) To the extent that the single "preferred" option is assumed to represent "everyone," being closeted—having one's identity, experience, choice, or commitment excluded—is never self-initiated. Rather, being closeted is a preassigned subject positioning. In response to this a priori assignment, one can acquiesce, remain in the closet, and try to *pass;* or one can covertly resist and *mask* within the closet; or one can openly resist and *out* oneself by an explicit and *contra* declaration.

As a presumably transparent and overdetermined subjectivity, race— and specifically "non-whiteness"—is thought to be incommensurate with the discursive valence of the closet. As Eve Sedgwick argues in *Epistemology of the Closet,* "Racism . . . is based on a stigma that is visible in all but exceptional cases" (75). While Sedgwick's analysis is generally accurate, racism can and does generate a structure of relationships, as well as determine the terms of participation, in ways that constitute a form of *closeting.* Underlying the admittance of racial minorities to "ideologically White"[5] institutions is the assumption that they share the same goals, desires, and belief as traditional members, and that despite continuing group vulnerability to the ravages of White supremacy, individuals admitted will make no fundamental challenges to the institution. Thus, unless it commits to redefining itself, an "ideologically White" institution that admits racial minorities implicitly *closets* them by its a priori expectation that they will and must embrace the same concerns, interests, attitudes, priorities, and agenda as those held by its traditional members, even as it "welcomes" them! Tiger Woods's early career on the PGA tour is instructive.

When Woods, whose mother is Asian American and whose father is African American, won his first Masters' tournament in 1997, he was given the customary honor of selecting the menu for the following year's Champions' Dinner. Senior PGA golfer "Fuzzy" Zoeller's warning that he had better not select "fried chicken . . . or collard greens or whatever the hell they serve" did not simply disparage traditional African American cuisine but also implicitly cautioned that in granting him admittance to this "ideologically White" institution, the professional golf community expected Woods to uphold and not challenge or transform its traditional identity and behavior. His "race," not his particular cultural experiences, values, commitments, choices, perspectives, would suffice to indicate that this sports institution was now transformed and more inclusive. While *closeting* Woods, the institution used his racially marked presence to mask what James Scott calls its "hidden transcript" (xii)—its continuing investment in the institutional attitudes, behavior, and agenda ostensibly disavowed by his admittance. Woods's response to Zoeller's warning—he selected hamburgers—can be read as a de facto decision to *pass* by acquiescing to the institution's simultaneous welcoming and *closeting* of him.

By contrast, the campaign strategy used by Barbara Jordan (1936–96), the first African American elected to the Texas state senate (1966–72) since Reconstruction, and who later served in the U.S. Congress (1972–78), provides a good example of *masking* within the closet of race. When Jordan first ran for public office, she made a conscious decision not to include photos of herself in campaign ads. Given the intensity of anti-Black racism, Jordan chose to *mask* behind the "preferred reading" of her name as "White" to assist voters in seeing her candidacy in terms of the political issues at stake and not solely in terms of race. In her subsequent actions as a legislator, Jordan clearly demonstrated that her political vision was shaped by an awareness of Black women's history and that she had no interest in *masking* as a strategy for participating in the ideologically White institutions of the Texas state senate and the U.S. Congress.

The monological expectations that motivate the *closeting* of racial minorities can persist even in progressive settings, as Audre Lorde's critique of 1980s White feminist attitudes indicates. In "Age, Race, Class, and Sex," Lorde observed that: "By and large within the women's movement today, white women focus upon their oppression as women and ignore differences of race, sexual preference, class, and age. There is a pretense to a homogeneity of experience covered by the word *sisterhood* that does not in fact exist" (116). Significantly, *Illusions* was produced at the very moment that Lorde and other Black feminists were interrogating and rejecting many of the monological assumptions underlying White feminist praxis. Expectations of, and demands for, a homogeneity of experience, perspective, style, and commitment function as a mode of *closeting* against which Black women artists have vigorously asserted themselves.

Outing the self is thus an important act of self-definition and self-empowerment for Black women artists. In the early years of her literary career, for example, Nobel laureate Toni Morrison was adamant in rejecting the *closeting* implicit in evaluations that her writing was "like" the single/"preferred" model of literary greatness—White men. In an interview with literary critic Nellie McKay, she insisted:

> I am not *like* James Joyce; I am not *like* Thomas Hardy; I am not *like* Faulkner. I am not *like* in that sense. I do not have objections to being compared to such extraordinarily gifted and facile writers, but it does leave me sort of hanging there when I know that my effort is to be like something that has probably only been fully expressed perhaps in music, or in some other culture-gen that survives almost in isolation because the community manages to hold on to it. (426)

In this interview and in numerous other interviews and essays, Morrison made a concerted effort to *out* herself in order to create discursive and social space for her literary performance to be received on its own *cultural* terms. Of her many nonfiction works, the essay "Rootedness: The Ancestor as Foundation" offers perhaps the most extensive articulation of the cultural paradigm informing her literary vision. With the film *Illusions,* Dash creates a comparable vehicle for *outing* herself as a Black feminist film-maker and for articulating her own distinct cultural vision and cultural commitments, commitments consistent with the paradigm of growth.

Although Mignon does not initially reject the closeted position to which she is assigned, she does envision changes in both the film industry and the larger society after, and because of, the war. As she explains in the phone conversation with her mother, "I want to be part of that change. If they don't change in this industry . . . Well, I don't think they're going to change at all." Mignon's interest in participating in change reflects a characterization that conforms more precisely to the trope of *masking* than to the trope of *passing*. Indeed, Dash redefines *passing* as a form of *masking*.

As both an African American cultural strategy and an artistic trope, *masking* involves the deliberate projection of a duplicitous external illusion in order to conceal a different internal reality that, if it were known, would jeopardize the individual's or group's survival or well-being. Its development and deployment by African Americans invariably coincided with situations that were patently undemocratic, and that were shaped by cultural and political hierarchies beginning with Slavery, and as existed, for example, in "Hollywood 1942" and other spheres of American public life. As a discursive strategy fashioned for a *mixed* social milieu, it insulates (necessary) communications from discovery in the presence of hostile and powerful others. A form of cultural literacy, *masking* involves the encoding and decoding of meaning so that two or more layers of signification are simultaneously available to culturally literate or knowledgeable recipients. While the mask functions as a double-voiced or polyvocal signifier for the culturally literate, for those not versed in the tradition it is a reassuringly transparent and univocal signifier. As a form of literacy, *masking* requires and encourages participants in the discursive community to develop an interpretive praxis that seeks meaning beyond surface levels of signification or, more specifically, that seeks *additional* levels of signification in any communication event. It presupposes—but does not guarantee—that outsiders will not detect secondary/subtextual communications, and that knowledgeable/intended recipients will.

In creating a protagonist who initially *masks* in the ideologically White world of the film industry in order to access power on behalf of various constituencies, Dash reveals her interest in exploring the strategies and consequences involved in adopting a counterhegemonic stance and *outing* the self in such a setting, and *not* the mythic ambivalence of a racially ambiguous persona. Mignon's encounter with Ester and her final confrontation with Lt. Bedsford mark the two phases of her self-*outing.* Her conversation with Ester initiates this process. As a first step, Mignon acknowledges the side-effects of *masking:* that her "mask" has atrophied, has become, in essence, a univocal/monological signifier because of her inability to define and implement autonomous objectives, and that *masking,* as a prolonged stance, inevitably perpetuates the censorship of the closet. This conversation therefore serves as the catalyst for Mignon's recognition of her own shadow role in "Hollywood 1942" and her formulation of a plan to "take action," by facilitating self-exposure, self-interrogation, self-recognition. The event demonstrates the importance of Black women's discourse to Black women's psychological and professional well-being.

In Ester's presence, Mignon is able to confront the reality of her own liminal presence and the risk to her psychological health from her acquiescence to the ideological demands of being closeted. She later asserts that her conversation with Ester helped her to "see beyond the shadows dancing on a white wall . . . to define what I had already come to know and to take action without fearing." The statement suggests the extent to which the absence of like-minded colleagues denied her the opportunity to engage in a critical dialogue about her experience, her actual role, and her potential agency within this hegemonic environment. Dash's depiction of the dialogue between the two women exemplifies Patricia Hill Collins's observation that: "While domination may be inevitable as a social fact, it is unlikely to be hegemonic as an ideology within that social space where Black women speak freely. This realm of relatively safe discourse, however narrow, is a necessary condition for Black women's resistance" (95).

Mignon's completes the process of *outing* herself in her final encounter with Lt. Bedsford. In this *outing,* she critiques and repudiates the socially and psychologically debilitating practices of the filmmaking industry and announces her intention to become a participant in that industry. As she sits in the studio chief's chair, her dialogue becomes a voice-over soliloquy that speaks back to the voice that opened *Illusions.* That is, it projects Mignon's declaration out of the narrative of "Hollywood 1942" and into the present of 1982, the year Dash made the film. The portrayal of Mignon's fear and loss of vision identifies and negotiates one of the many dangers confronting Black women *closeted* in the contemporary filmmaking industry. In creating a protagonist for whom being closeted undermines the potential social benefits of entry into and participation in this ideologically White institution, Dash suggests that claiming transformative agency requires an *outing* of the self. The film transcends the Black woman's isolation by imagining and engaging a community of women filmmakers and by exemplifying the type of critical praxis that would enable them to define and pursue a self-empowering vision. As Mignon acknowledges in her soliloquy, the conversation with Ester rekindled her confidence in her ability to "use the power of the motion picture" to design and develop the liberating transformations she envisions despite—and also because of—her awareness of the ways in which the cinema's culturally hegemonic practices endanger the national public.

Unmasking "State Power"

In its attention to the responsibilities of democracy, *Illusions* claims for itself the status of, and functions as, a manifesto.[6] As a manifesto, *Illusions* demonstrates Dash's counterhegemonic vision through its redefinition of the narrative (and ethical) responsibilities of democracy, as well as its explicit critiques of failures. The film also demonstrates her ability to refashion classic Hollywood cinema conventions to advance new and transformative objectives. In this regard, Janet Lyon's analysis of the manifesto as a form that "exposes the broken promises of modernity" (3) is especially useful for interpreting Dash's film exploration of the broken promises of U.S. democracy. In *Manifestoes: Provocations of the Modern,* Lyon asserts that the manifesto "makes itself intelligible to the dominant order through a logic that presumes the efficacy of modern democratic ideals" (3). Thus, like other manifestoes, *Illusions* employs a rhetorical strategy that "promulgates the very discourses it critiques." Significantly, Dash's critique of Hollywood filmmaking practices is wholly dependent on the logic of "modern democratic ideals." The emphasis throughout the film is on the ethical, sociopolitical, representational, and narrative imperatives of democracy.

Not only does *Illusions* conform to Lyon's description of the manifesto's discursive dynamic, but it also advances what Sidonie Smith identifies, in

"Autobiographical Manifestoes," as the "six constituent aspects of manifesto": "to appropriate/contest sovereignty"; "to bring to light, to make manifest"; "to announce publicly"; "to perform publicly"; "to speak as one of a group, to speak for a group"; and "to speak to the future" (435–38). The significance of the film's function as an autobiographical manifesto is suggested by Smith's observation that "Through the manifesto, the autobiographical subject confronts the ghost of the identity assigned her by the old sovereign subject" (435–36). For Mignon, perhaps the ghost of an identity reappropriated and made manifest by Dash, that assigned identity/position is in the closet. Through the manifesto, Smith continues, "the autobiographer purposefully locates herself as a subject leaving behind the object status to which cultural identities have confined her" (436). Although *Illusions* cannot be considered "autobiographical" in the sense of recounting individual experience, it both constitutes and is informed by Black women's (collective) social biography. The parallel between Mignon's and Dash's visions recalls Jacqueline Bobo's comment in "Black Women's Films" that a "[c]ongruence between the personal histories of filmmaker and subject is a predominant feature of Black women's biographical documentaries" (9). According to Bobo, the Black woman filmmaker's focus on this congruence is meant to "illustrate how both filmmaker and artist have overcome obstacles to create art that is meaningful for Black audiences" (9).

As a manifesto, *Illusions* can also be compared to other declarative texts by Black women filmmakers that explicitly announce a set of aims while rejecting the closet in favor of a formal *outing* of the self within the field of filmmaking. Alile Sharon Larkin's essay "Black Women Filmmakers Defining Ourselves" (1988), Zeinabu irene Davis's essay, "Woman with a Mission" (1991), and Cheryl Dunye's *The Watermelon Woman* (1996) are obvious examples.[7] The affinities among these self-declarative texts are largely occasioned by the ubiquity of contemporary *closeting* regimes. Like *Illusions*, Larkin's and Davis's essays and Dunye's feature film also challenge U.S. history and Hollywood filmmaking as a precondition for enacting a Black feminist film praxis. Paving the way for this later work, *Illusions* critiques the ways in which these twin sites of oppression support what Wahneema Lubiano describes in *The House That Race Built* as "a profound violation of the spirit of democracy" (vii). At the same time, it reaffirms and reinscribes Black women's (future) agency on those very sites by inverting and rede-

Lt. Bedsford (Ralph Bellamy) and Mignon (Lonette McKee) face off in
Illusions. Courtesy of Women Make Movies.

ploying classic cinema conventions. In so doing, Dash reveals that U.S.
democracy, like the film project the Black woman producer Mignon must
work to salvage, is an illusion whose sound reel (its rhetorical claims) is out
of sync with its video reel (its ongoing institutional practices).

While there are many sites of contestation in *Illusions,* the central conflict enacted on screen is between Mignon Duprée and Lieutenant Bedsford
in their respective functions as narrators. Mignon, the initially disembodied
female narrator who opens *Illusions* and then "finds" her voice through the
story of her character in "Hollywood 1942," faces off in the final scene with
Lt. Bedsford, the disembodied male narrator who opens "Hollywood 1942"
and whose voice and authority are progressively contested and overridden
by hers. This conflict between Mignon and Bedsford serves several purposes. First, it confirms Dash's interest in exploring the role of what Lubiano
calls "state power"—which Bedsford, the military consultant, represents—
in "ideological warfare" against the national public. Lubiano cites Timothy
Mitchell's definition in identifying the "state" in "state power" as both the
system of formal government and the "'common ideological and cultural
construct [that] occurs not merely as a subjective belief, incorporated in the

thinking and action of individuals [but] represented and reproduced in visible everyday forms'" (327). According to Lubiano, "state power" includes "the actual workings of the executive branch of the government" as well as "the ways that the national public reproduce[s] state concerns and interests" (327).

Applied to the context of "Hollywood 1942," "state power" includes Lieutenant Bedsford's specific role as propaganda consultant on behalf of the government—as articulated in his communiqués—as well as subsequent reproductions of "state concerns and interests" by National Studios. In having Mignon explode, not to the studio chief but to Lieutenant Bedsford, "Your scissors and your paste methods have eliminated my participation in the history of this country and the influence of that screen cannot be overestimated," Dash levels her critique at the state power in whose service Hollywood filmmaking is deployed.

Illusions further unmasks the role of state power in the construction of Hollywood versions of U.S. national history by interrogating the relationship between film illusion and the illusion of democracy. It thereby takes on the manifesto's primary function as precursor text and catalyst for the revision of national history because it insists on an interrogation and recasting of assigned roles. As Lyon notes, manifestoes do not dismantle the discourse; they participate in and expand it. In Bedsford's communiqué at the beginning of "Hollywood 1942," he lauds the fact that with "its manpower and vast material resources . . . the motion picture industry is privileged to stand in the very forefront of the united American endeavor" to "meet the totalitarian challenge to the democratic way of life." Coupled with Bedsford's comments about the "motion picture's essentiality" and its "broad sphere of service to the war," the war movie images seen in the beginning of the film underscore the relationship between the war machine and the Hollywood machine. These images point to the ideological function of Hollywood filmmaking and unmask the many battlefronts on which the motion picture industry wages ideological warfare.

Dash's critique of Hollywood's role as a primary distributor of national history is pointedly set at "National Studios." Her objective is not (simply) to debunk "preferred readings" of "Hollywood 1942," this pivotal chapter in the "adventure" of U.S. nationhood. Rather, she exposes patterns of denial, projection, displacement, and rationalization, and the latent desires—psychological and ideological—that undergird them. Through its intratext, *Illusions* positions itself within the genre of national history in order to disrupt this history's monocultural hegemony. Thus, even as it appears to conform to them, *Illusions* exposes and challenges several trends in Hollywood cinema that together erase Black people's social presence and/or sanction their subordinate social status. As an example, Dash casts only two Black characters and no Native American characters in the film. While the film does not violate contemporary Hollywood filmmaking formulas in terms of racial casting, it succeeds in filling the parameters that this casting establishes with both the illusion and the "truth" it negates. African Americans and Native Americans aren't simply absent from "Hollywood 1942" and the narratives produced there. Rather, as testimony to Lyon's claim that "the manifesto marks the gap between democratic ideals and modern political practice" (3), their absence is marked and interrogated throughout the film.

While Hollywood films have traditionally permitted the controlled "presence" of a few Black actors as supporting props more than human subjects, *Illusions* exposes the presence of Blacks not as screen stars but as *workers:* the janitor glimpsed in the opening sequence, and the singer/day-laborer Ester, who is barred from union membership and its benefits and protections. By exposing the undemocratic treatment of Black subjects in "Hollywood 1942," *Illusions* reveals both the mechanism by which "structured absences" occur and the *motivations* behind these absences. Moreover, in revealing both the African American and the Native American contributions to the war "on behalf of a democracy which does not even exist at home," the film simultaneously unmasks "the ideology of whiteness" and manifests the paradoxical truth of a "united American endeavor" in World War II. For National Studios to depict African American and Native American participation in this war "on behalf of democracy" would be to link, imagistically, the undemocratic treatment of Europeans under Nazi occupation and the undemocratic treatment of non-White peoples in White America. Such a thematic montage would constitute an unprecedented critique of the contradictions between the nation's foundational vision of human equality and its equally foundational practice of inequality. In simultaneously referencing African American and Native American participation in the war and the deliberate erasure of those contributions, *Illusions* invites such a critique with Mignon's outburst: "We are overseas defending some kind of a democracy that doesn't exist at home. Let's make a film about *that*, Lieutenant!"

The film exposes the complex mechanisms used to ensure the (visual) illusion of cultural homogeneity—executive decisions that mandate the dismissal of narratives about Native American radio operators as "mumbo jumbo," despite a U.S. Office of War Information (OWI) bulletin lauding their strategic importance since they can "send and receive messages in a code the enemy is unable to break"—and the erasure of conflict, even when that conflict is as benign as the struggle of "the average [White] citizen" to come to terms with the effects of the war. These mechanisms ensure that the patriotism and participation of Black and Native American soldiers are expunged; and that the devastating "effects of war on the average [White] person" are censored in favor of "upbeat" narratives glamorizing the heroism of the "[White] boy next door." And, most important, they endorse the commodification of Black culture through the parodic appropriation of Black dance and musical forms and the widespread use of disembodied Black voices that "pass" for White. (The negotiations over Ester's salary remind us that her vocal talents—packaged as White—are in "great demand.") The movies produced by this machinery create a monolithic narrative whose primary goal is to uphold the illusion of a culturally homogeneous, uncontested, and already attained democracy.

Deposing the White Male Gaze

In addition to facilitating an exploration of the ways in which "state power" is channeled through Hollywood, Dash structures Mignon's contestation with Lt. Bedsford to depose the classic cinematic gaze—the White male gaze. Through this contestation—announced in their competing roles as frame narrators—the film deposes his gaze sexually, ideologically, psychologically, and cinematically.

In her analysis of the ways in which Black people have traditionally resisted the White male gaze, bell hooks states that "The 'gaze' has been and is a site of resistance for colonized black people globally." Yet, hooks notes, "Critical, interrogating black looks were mainly concerned with issues of race and racism. . . . They were rarely concerned with gender" (117–18). hooks's assessment suggests some of the ways in which Dash's Black feminist gaze is unusual. First, contrary to the precepts of classic Hollywood cinema, the gaze and face that Mignon regards—almost longingly—is Ester's. In the essay "Oppositional Gaze," hooks observes that "The bond between [Mignon] and the young black woman singer Ester Jeeter is affirmed by caring gestures of affirmation, often expressed by eye-to-eye contact, the direct unmediated gaze of recognition" (129). Ester's gaze humanizes Mignon by registering her full identity and by questioning her actual motives for being in the film industry. Its most visible effects are psychological and ideological. Under the scrutiny of the Black female gaze, Mignon achieves critical self-consciousness. By contrast, Bedsford, the would-be suitor, does not achieve the centrality or suave persona that the classic cinematic gaze usually confers. His sexual attitude, and the gaze which informs it, are discredited by Dash through her protagonist. Mignon's rejection of Bedsford's gaze is total. In their first on-screen encounter, she tells him, "I'm not interested in you, or anything you have to say." His sheepish response, "I'm not the enemy," is deeply ironic. The camera's framing of the "blonde bombshell"—Forrester's secretary—further attests to Dash's deconstruction of the White male gaze. Although her provocatively hip-swinging walk is meant for the consumption of the White male gaze, the camera relegates that reaction to the periphery. Instead, it frames a reaction shot of Mignon's and Ester's laughter at the "bombshell's" swish. While this laughter exposes the performance, it also attests to Ester's and Mignon's shared ways of reading that, based on common experiences, constitute a shared epistemology.

Dash's portrayal of the demeanor of the "blonde bombshell" and other White women employed at National Studios also critiques the construction of White women by the White male gaze. As aspiring copies of the glamorized, objectified, and infantilized screen star Lila Grant, the women internalize and reproduce the definition of womanhood posited by Grant's screen image as being whose performance of self must be shaped for a phallocentric gaze. While it is possible to read the spectacle of a languid Grant intravenously feeding on Ester through the sound apparatus as parasitic, this event also reveals the enlivening potential of Black women's voices.

Second, while the White male gaze—Forrester's and Bedsford's—ignores the war's impact on the society at large, Mignon acknowledges its psychologically damaging effects on "little boys" and "on the average citizen." That is to say, the Black female gaze notes and exposes the ways in which the White male gaze endangers *White males* through the packaging of film narratives that glamorize war while suppressing the truth about the psychological trauma it inflicts.

Dash's depiction of Mignon's attentiveness to the psychological needs of White male viewers is indicative of the expansive social vision arising from the ethos of interconnectedness. Her exposure of the ways in which the White male gaze endangers constituencies privileged by race and gender is consistent with the broad commitment to human community it fosters. Like the filmmaker outside the film, Mignon recognizes that representations that are damaging or otherwise endangering to one constituency are likely to be equally so for other communities, though in different and perhaps less obvious ways. As a prime example of antihuman art, it was clear from the outset that D. W. Griffith's *The Birth of a Nation* disfigured the image of Black peoples. What was perhaps not so clear was the equally profound though distinct manner in which it disfigured White audiences under the guise of entertainment. Mignon's concern with the ways in which White communities are endangered by film entertainment supports a larger critique of antihuman art. As Griffith's film so clearly illustrates, antihuman art has won awards and prizes, been lauded, celebrated, enthroned—in fact, enshrined—in print, celluloid, academic curricula, archives, and libraries, not to mention museums and art galleries, throughout the globe; has sustained careers, hierarchies of power, oppressive regimes, and extended scholarly discussions, while frequently encouraging and making it possible for individuals and societies to remain committed to, and comfortable with, private and public behaviors well below the full humanity of which they were eminently capable.

In her reading of *Illusions*, hooks claims that "the film does not indicate whether . . . Mignon will make Hollywood films that subvert and transform the genre or whether she will simply assimilate and perpetuate the norm" (129). While one might question Mignon's (although not Dash's) ability to develop the cinematic *strategies* to support a transformative vision, hooks's question about Mignon's *intentions* is perhaps based on an assumption that Mignon shares the ambivalent and assimilationist stance of the traditional *passing* protagonist. In fact, *Illusions* provides extensive evidence of the transformative vision of Mignon's Black feminist gaze. A constant theme in Mignon's conversations with Forrester is the need for a type of representation that would respond therapeutically to the psychological needs of a country experiencing the losses of war: "We should be the first studio to give the public situations and characters that they can recognize as part of their own lives."

In staging its deposition of the White male gaze, *Illusions* uses many of the stylistic elements of film noir, a genre prominent in the 1940s. Through the use of black-and-white cinematography, low-key (and low-budget)[8] lighting, mirrors, and the glass paneled door through which silhouettes appear, the mise-en-scène conveys a sense of repressed consciousness in the ubiquitous presence of shadows. Since noir techniques are frequently used to suggest psychological dualism or conflict, one might assume that Dash's usage of these techniques in her film must refer to Mignon's psychological state as a Black woman *passing* for White. These cannot, however, be assigned to Mignon since she displays no signs of conflict about her identity or her commitment to her cultural community. Instead, they mirror the conflict between Hollywood's—and the nation's—assertion of democratic ideals, and its undemocratic representational practices.

The place, Hollywood 1942, as character, is unmasked through these film noir techniques. Dash's use of noir techniques to portray the institutional setting as a determinant of actions and options constitutes a form of what Toni Cade Bambara calls "spatial narration." As I discuss in chapter 5, Bambara describes spatial narration as a discursive strategy for exploring institutional causes. She notes that the exploration of space coincides with and supports the rejection of a related film ideology, one that emphasizes individual/psychological causes rather than systemic or institutional/ideological ones. By contrast, the exploration of space in independent Black filmmaking supports a representation of space as context—institutional context—in addition to deconstructing domination ideologies. Ester's emergence from the darkness of the recording studio and Bedsford's unexpected emergence from the shadows with two cups in his extended hands (as Mignon's moves to get coffee for herself and Ester) are typical examples of this emphatically shadowed mise-en-scène. Sometimes, as in the case of the footage in which Lila Grant gives her first performance—the shadows have distinct shapes. In that scene, the shadows of the White actors mimicking instrumental performers symbolically represent the Black musical foundations of this White entertainment product. In sum, these techniques are used to represent Black people's hidden contribution to Hollywood, to the progress of the nation-subject, and the hidden collusion of "state power" in underwriting Hollywood narratives.

The film's third and most significant strategy for dismantling the White male gaze is Dash's construction of Mignon's and her own discursive agency. Over the course of the film, Mignon's voice and ideological analysis move from a marginal space, that of a disembodied female narrator implicitly positioned outside the dominant narrative and sociopolitical text, to one where she is directly involved in the film text of "Hollywood 1942." This progression, this transformation of the status of her voice, both challenges and subsumes Bedsford's voice and his authority.

In *Illusions*, Dash does more than expose the illusions behind Hollywood filmmaking. The title shot of an unraveled film reel bearing the word "Illusions" acknowledges that *all* filmmaking is a projection of illusions. That judgment applies to Dash's own work as much as it applies to Hollywood filmmaking. For example, when Ester performs to match the lip movements of the White actress on screen in the studio, a carefully timed extreme close-up of Rosanne Katon reveals that she too is lip-syncing, and that *Illusions* too is a projection. Dash's decision to have Katon lip-sync to a recording of jazz great Ella Fitzgerald attests to the deliberateness of this gesture. This exposure of the filmmaker's/camera's discursive agency is emblematized in a series of alternating shots in the recording studio. A triple montage captures Ester singing in the dimly lit studio, the projection of the White actress, and the mirror image of the White technicians manipulating vocal/visual illusions, under the metacritical gaze of the Black woman producer.

The anachronistic turn of events that follow the disclosure of Mignon's identity provides another occasion for Dash's unmasking of the film's construction. Bedsford's expected denigration of Mignon is "limited" to a comment that "You're not the same person you were this morning." Given his prior sexual interest in Mignon and the sociopolitical context of the 1940s, the expected avenue for plot development would be a depiction of new jeopardies concomitant with the disclosure of her identity as a Black woman.[9] Instead, the discussion between the two adversaries centers on the political implications of Mignon's role as a Black woman with executive status in an industry whose power is literally mightier than the sword. Although Bedsford hastens to tell her, in a pre-McCarthyist gesture, "Nothing's changed here. Nothing's changed except you," Mignon assures him that "From now on I'm here for the same reasons that you are." While it unveils the filmmaker's discursive agency, this denouement also affirms Mignon's and Dash's future agency. The closing shot of a Black woman in the director's chair dissolves the frame and moves the action out of "Hollywood 1942" to 1982 and beyond.

Dash's self-conscious unmasking of the film's construction serves several purposes. These and other similar metacritical devices prevent the viewer from becoming solipsistically immersed in the world of the film. They disturb. In so doing, they remind us that "Ester" is an actress portraying an event, and that this too—but from a different ideological position—is not "reality." Recognizing that the filmmaker is not concerned with creating/maintaining the illusion of reality, the viewer is able to consider other possible objectives and motivations behind filmmaking. New interpretive possibilities, a different kind of "truth" emerges from the viewer's awareness of how persons and events are *positioned* on-screen and why. In fact, the deliberate exposure of the film's illusions allows the viewer to see the portrayal not as transparent "reality" but as negotiated "truth." Dash suggests that there are modes of representation that—because they do not acknowledge themselves to be representations—prevent the exercise of interpretive agency and foster the misleading equation of fact and truth, portrayal and reality.

The narrator's (and Ellison's) observation that "The province of Hollywood is not action" can be understood to mean that Hollywood denies the viewer agency, the ability to take action. A subsequent exchange between Ester and Mignon accentuates this critique of Hollywood filmmaking. Explaining her interest in making movies, Mignon confides: "I overheard a producer talking, blasting a movie critic, he said, 'History is not what really happened, even if it's written in a book. The real history, the history that most people will remember and believe in is what they see on the silver screen.' . . . I wanted to be where history is being made." *Illusions,* then, remakes "Hollywood 1942." Moreover, in exposing the negation and restructuring of not only the African American presence but also the Native American presence, Dash signals her feminist commitment—in this and other works—to breaking out of the confinement of a binary analysis of racist discourse to reveal multiple constituencies affected by, and implicated in, the practice of cultural hegemony.

Illusions accomplishes several important goals. As a manifesto, alternating among the discourses of history, logic, and prophecy, it recasts African American and Native American contributions to U.S. national history, as well as Black women's *vocal* contribution to American film history; measures the cost and terms of that participation; imagines expanded roles and greater agency for Black women in film; facilitates Black women's self-empowerment through film; and, in encouraging new modes of critical viewing, provides a new paradigm for constructing interpretive agency. In its depiction of the vision orienting Mignon's future film praxis, the film speaks for and to a community of Black feminist filmmakers. It asserts that, whether in front of or behind the camera, a Black woman in Hollywood is likely to be welcomed as a new prop, assigned a position of illusory agency, and *closeted* in a new form of ideological and cultural invisibility, unless a historicized consciousness leads her to *out* herself by fully enunciating her presence, position, and potential on the battlefield. Through such independent self-representation, however, Black women filmmakers can engage cinema not only as a site of struggle but also as a site of transformation on which to redefine and enact the narrative responsibilities of democracy.

5

Renewing Self-Possession

Euzhan Palcy, Julie Dash, and Maureen Blackwood

As independent Black women film-makers, we actively create new definitions of ourselves within every genre, redefining damaging stereotypes. . . . We hope that with our films we can help create a new world, by speaking in our own voice and defining ourselves. We hope to do this, one film at a time, one screening at a time, to change minds, widen perspectives and destroy the fear of difference.

—ALILE SHARON LARKIN, "Black Women Filmmakers Defining Ourselves"

This chapter offers analyses of three Black women's films—Euzhan Palcy's *Sugar Cane Alley,* Dash's *Daughters of the Dust,* and Maureen Blackwood's *Home Away from Home.* It examines the ways in which these works celebrate Black women's creative agency by the camera's intimate explorations of the unvoiced analyses that determine Black women's strategies for stabilizing the development of their children and grandchildren. It extends the analysis begun in chapter 4 by demonstrating how artistic choices made in both characterization and narrative construction enable viewers to forge new self-definitions, achieve greater autonomy, and become more competent interpreters. As I demonstrate, the distinctiveness of each film's ideological project is suggested by the new genre category each (implicitly) claims for itself—whether "organic musical," "speculative fiction," or "new silent film."

Re-framing Postmodern Black Subjects

In addition to establishing the critical, ideological, and aesthetic parameters within which Black women's cinema can be understood, *Illusions* points to an agenda aimed not simply at reversing dispossession but more broadly at renewing self-possession by privileging the psychological needs of Black viewers. This requires a restoration of those possessions—voice, narrative control, interpretive competence and autonomy, historical consciousness, and self-consciousness—that have been expropriated. It also requires reestablishing conditions and relationships expressive of an ethos of interconnectedness, consistent with the paradigm of growth. Thus, for Black women artists, cinema is an expanded channel for fulfilling the priestess's responsibility for group preservation.

Given the degree to which the multiple dimensions of this project have been shaped by destabilizing historical events, renewing self-possession is inextricably connected to a Black postmodernist agenda. In "The Postmodern Rag," Wahneema Lubiano argues that we might "consider Black American postmodernism not only as a moment when modernism's intellectual and cultural hegemony is at least being questioned but as a general epistemological standpoint for foregrounding what has been left out of larger discourses, a consideration of certain kinds of differences, and the reasons for their absences from those larger discourses" (94). Here, Lubiano challenges mainstream definitions that "universalize" postmodernism. She notes that in linking postmodernism to "*twentieth*-century horrors," scholars "pass over the sixteenth through nineteenth centuries' European and Euro-American genocide of the indigenous American population and slavery." In calling for a more culturally and historically nuanced description of postmodernism's relation to Black communities, Lubiano's analysis accentuates the two most prominent objectives that shape Black women's films— to provide complex and comprehensive representations of postmodern Black subjects in relation to both old and new destabilizing events, and to construct "new" epistemological standpoints. Despite the daunting financial and distribution challenges they face, their self-appointed task is nothing less than to interrogate and destabilize the authority of, and definitions encoded within, various master-narratives, and to construct expanded readings and representations through the paradigm of growth. These representations are carefully crafted to reflect an ethos of interconnectedness and to affirm a democracy of narrative participation by fully framing human subjects.

In light of Larkin's analysis of the role of film and television in exacerbating the dispossession and thereby the destabilization that characterizes Black postmodernity, renewing self-possession is perhaps an inevitable goal for Black women filmmakers. Since dispossession results in both a loss

Filmmaker Maureen Blackwood and camera crew on the set of *Home Away from Home.* Courtesy of Women Make Movies.

of control over self-representation and a loss of interpretive agency, renewing self-possession logically entails restoring both dimensions. As advanced within the Black women's films in this study, renewing self-possession involves two related constituencies. On the one hand, it focuses on the characters whose control of their images and self-definitions is restored. On the other hand, renewing self-possession focuses on, and extends to, viewers—especially, but not exclusively, Black people/women viewers. Both processes are assisted by a (narrative) reliance on spirituality.

Euzhan Palcy's *Sugar Cane Alley* (1984) exemplifies this joint approach to renewing self-possession. It illustrates the concern of Black women's cinema with redefining images of Black women/people, and with expanding the viewer's interpretive competence by constructing a new cinematic epistemology. According to Black film studies pioneer Clyde Taylor in "Paths of Enlightenment," "All important black expression carries the burden of changing the world's mind, upending received wisdom, reformulating knowledge—not only a body of material, but the very categories through which we know or don't know." Taylor also asserts that the most enabling Black films "will burn and erase synapses clogged with stereotypical thinking, sclerotic Occidentalisms, and backward social mythologies, even while they are being replaced with beings unanticipated by the conventional spectator's consciousness" (127). Taylor's assessment emphasizes the epistemological goals to which Palcy aspires. Through the use of innovative film and narrative techniques, Palcy pursues these goals while constructing a new film genre—one that I dub an *organic* musical.[1]

Set in a neo-plantation Black community in the 1930s, *Sugar Cane Alley* presents a simple narrative about a young boy's coming-of-age in Martinique and is widely touted as one of a small handful of Caribbean films. "For the public at large," writes novelist Maryse Condé, "Caribbean cinema, all islands and origins combined, revolves around two films . . . the Jamaican film *The Harder They Come* . . . [and] the Martiniquan film *Sugarcane Alley*" (371). At the same time, however, the film has come in for some harsh criticism from Condé, who insists that it "did not offer Caribbean people a first realistic glimpse of themselves" (375), presumably because the events and issues depicted in the film's 1930s setting are not contemporaneous with, and therefore relevant to, the 1980s, the period in which it was released. Condé's criticism disregards the importance of historical and historicized self-representation and seems to argue that only contemporary representations can be "realistic" or enabling. Yet, as the previous analyses of *Beloved, Illusions,* and *Anowa* illustrate, historical representation provides an important mechanism for self-discovery. In his reading of the cinematic choices that support this process, Alain Ménil notes that, in viewing *Sugar Cane Alley,* the community "recognized itself"—"Half of the population of Martinique and Guadeloupe . . . came to see themselves" (154)—because "Palcy deliberately chose to talk about the Antilles from the inside, to talk about its convulsions from the point of view of the convulsion" (162). Telling the story "from inside" is one of many strategies designed to promote self-recognition and thereby renew self-possession.

Several devices contribute to the restoration of Black people's self-possession both within the film-text (as film subjects) and in the world in which the film is situated (as film viewers). The presence of a narrator who is part of the story he tells, and the internal positioning of the camera, are two devices Palcy uses to allow the community's story to emerge from *within.* Second, the depiction of Black people's cultural and psychospiritual autonomy amid socioeconomically debilitating circumstances creates an enabling view of Black people as fully human subjects. In addition, the depiction of the intracommunal functions of Black music and singing traditions fosters the creation of an *organic* musical, one in which Black people are not musical props, one in which Black music is not mere entertainment. Instead, the film reveals the ideological, psychological, and spiritual functions these traditions serve. Moreover, in revealing Black people's life "within the veil," the film discloses another cultural paradigm, one that transcends the limitations of the Eurocentric model enshrined in the education system. And finally, the central focus on the relationship between Ma Tine (Darling Légitimus) and her grandson, José (Garry Cadenat), provides a close-up of the intergenerational transfer of self-possession that empowers film subjects and film viewers alike.

One of the primary strategies that Palcy uses to construct and revise images of Black people is an internal positioning of the camera-narrator and the character-narrator. Hollywood films—whether fiction or documentaries—typically narrate Black people's lives, histories, and struggles from a detached and external distance. Ménil notes that this tendency is particularly egregious in Western representations of Caribbean peoples. Prior to

Palcy's film, Ménil argues, cinematic representation tended to exoticize the Caribbean since "the great majority of films cannot see in the Antilles anything other than arboreal debauchery, a journalistic synthesis of the three 'S's' (*sea, sex,* and *sun*), unable as they are, to detect in the islands [or its peoples] any measure of complexity or depth."[2] In these films, the external narrative position signals the narrator's/camera's/filmmaker's distanced and superior relationship to the Black subjects. This positioning reflects and perpetuates the view of Black peoples as both alien and inferior.

In *Sugar Cane Alley,* by contrast, the character-narrator and the camera-narrator are positioned as participants within the story they narrate. Given the structure of Zobel's plot, José's positioning within the narrative is not surprising. What is surprising and significant is Palcy's refusal of the prescribed external positioning of the camera-narrator in favor of a positioning that announces the camera's identification with, and affirmation of, the gaze of its Black subjects. The sequence in which the children crowd into Ma Tine's hut to evade the overseer's gaze provides an early example of this positioning. Unlike conventional cinema, the camera-narrator does not endorse or participate in the overseer's surveillance of these Black subjects. Instead, the camera-narrator enters the hut with the children, and—with them—peeps out at the overseer riding by on horseback. Although he is on horseback, the overseer does not occupy a visually dominant position. Instead, he is shot on the same plane as the children. In this and other scenes, Palcy avoids high-angle shots of the children by using a hand-held camera.[3] In doing so, she preserves the children's visual autonomy and does not symbolically diminish their subjectivity.

Although "based on" Joseph Zobel's novel *Rue Cases-Nègres* (1950), *Sugar Cane Alley* features several important innovations in its depiction of the community's struggle to unlock the many doors to freedom that remained steadfastly closed despite the formal emancipation of enslaved Black people in French colonies in 1848. The translation of the title *Rue Cases-Nègres* as *Sugar Cane Alley* and not as *Black Shack Alley,* the title used for English translations of the novel, matches the film's distinct ideological emphasis. The long takes and high-angle shots of the cane fields are used to spatially narrate the subtext of Slavery, and its reincarnation in the "plantation model" that determines choices and shapes relationships in this community. By revising the plot to accentuate the theme of resistance to oppression and to dramatize the spirit of resilience and cultural autonomy in this Black community, Palcy provides more than a mere "adaptation." As an example, she replaces the duo of José's mother and grandmother in the novel with a single parental figure, the grandmother, Ma Tine, to intensify the film's artistic and ideological effect.

One of Palcy's many innovations is to rework the narrative to highlight the overlay of an African cosmology. José's view of Africa as the "home" of the dead is one of several indications of this cosmology. In the scene that introduces Léopold's father, we see that the children are taught a Catholic theology that includes a definition of Heaven and Hell as the home of the dead.[4] Despite his exposure to this catechism, José confidently asserts that the deceased elders have gone to Africa. This type of assertion, Paris notes, was quite characteristic for enslaved Africans: "In many and varied ways, their belief in ancestral spirits was kept alive, and most believed that their souls would return to Africa after death, where they would be reunited with their ancestors" (57). Bobo's analysis in "Black Women's Films" of the intention behind such allusions in Black women's films clarifies its function here as well. "Africa is not only a historical construct for political reference and import," writes Bobo, "but also a metaphorical construct of ontological inquiry and cultural identification" (23).

Another technique Palcy uses to develop the film's analysis is to foreground those events in the life of the villagers that attest to the persistence of the "plantation model." Scenes such as the one in which wages are disbursed on pay day, Ma Tine's visit to the "Overseer's Office" to register José for school, and Mr. Médouze's (Douta Seck) storytelling and history lesson indicate that Palcy's narrative is not, in fact, dedicated to what Condé describes as "the dream of a nicely idealized society, still peasant, where, if the master's lesson were welllearned [sic], the individual could still become a petitbourgeois" (375). Rather, in giving these events narrative prominence, Palcy allows the film's political analysis to emerge from within the community being represented.

Sugar Cane Alley revises the entire cast of what Toni Morrison calls "Africanist personae"—the "mammy," the "pickaninny," the "old uncle," the "tragic mulatto," the "buck," and "Sapphire"—by relocating Black characters in a culturally autonomous environment. As Morrison defines it, the term "Africanist personae" provides a more complex insight on stereotypes by identifying "the entire range of views, assumptions, readings, and mis-readings that accompany Eurocentric learning"—that is, "master narra-tives"—about African peoples.[5] The outlines of these stereotypes are dis-cernible in Ma Tine's buxom figure, in the children's scant clothing, in Mr. Médouze's advanced age and his role as storyteller, in the paternal rejection experienced by José's biracial school friend, Léopold, and in Julien Twelve-Toes's intimidating physical size, respectively. And while the film does not include an outline of the stereotypically promiscuous Black female, Car-men—the man with a woman's name who has "lots of girlfriends," and who is also a sex toy for his White female employer—represents a cross-gen-dered "Sapphire" of sorts. Given the historical intractability of these stereo-types, Palcy takes enormous risks in this effort at redefining and re-present-ing Black personhood.

In the attempt to rectify racist distortions of Black personhood, Black artists have frequently employed the strategy of creating model Black char-acters from whom all resemblances to Black people—mythic or real—have been expunged. Historically, this has involved a visual dissociation from the dual signs of Black people's "inferiority": poverty and "low," that is, Black, culture. In a daring and ideologically affirmative move, Palcy retains these signs and historicizes them to illuminate their contextual significance. Poor Black people in *Sugar Cane Alley* are unapologetically poor and Black. If there is a tragedy in poverty, the film suggests, it is not that it diminishes the villagers' humanity or their creative abilities, but that they are relentlessly defrauded of the wealth they produce. If the communal traditions of Black people are unsanctioned, they nevertheless retain their capacity to en-hance the social, psychological, and spiritual life of the villagers. In fact, by repositioning this cast of characters within their own cultural environment, Palcy undermines the authority of racist representations. Her revision of the "mammy" image through the portrayal of Ma Tine is instructive.

As Collins notes, the "mammy" stereotype is not only buxom and moth-erly, but she "embodied the faithful domestic servant, with an infinite ca-pacity for nurturing White children, while neglecting her own. She symbol-izes the ideal relationship between Whites and Blacks, and within the Black family was likely to indoctrinate her own children into a similar demeanor of subservience toward Whites" (71). When positioned within Black house-holds/families, the image of the Black woman was vulnerable to another distorted representation as the matriarch. The matriarch, Collins explains, is portrayed as overly aggressive and is essentially a "failed mammy." She behaves in ways that are deemed pathological. For instance, her independence is represented and defined as domineering, that is, "castrating." Although these definitions have been reiterated by numerous scholars, Angela Davis identifies E. Franklin Frazier's *The Negro Family* (1939) as the work that first proffered these defaming narratives.[6] Palcy's characterization of Ma Tine must negotiate the double jeopardy of these narratives, both of which are imprisoned in the paradigm of resistance.

Palcy subverts the distorted definitions of Black womanhood/motherhood by repositioning Ma Tine in two distinct ways. First, Ma Tine is repositioned within her own cultural community rather than within the White household. Second, Palcy resituates her within a more historically accurate work space—the cane/cotton/tobacco field—and not the domestic space in which Black women, especially older Black women, are typically positioned on screen.[7] Once she is thus repositioned, we are allowed a rare filmic gaze at the autonomy, consciousness, and vision of this Black mother and worker.

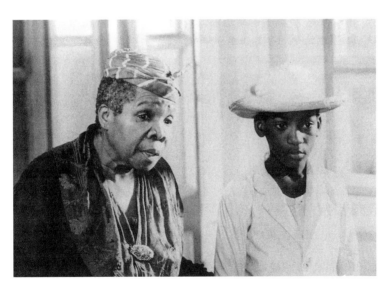

Ma Tine (Darling Légitimus) accompanies her grandson, José (Garry Cadenat), into town to register for school in *Sugar Cane Alley*. An Orions Classic Release. Courtesy of New Yorker Films.

Ma Tine's relationship with her grandson, José, provides the context for observing her autonomy, consciousness, and vision as she transfers these possessions to him. His responses to various challenges attest to her success in instilling an awareness of his human capacities and human rights. As an example, this awareness shapes his response to Mme. Léonce's attempt to condition him to accept a subordinate positioning. The chores that she reserves for him—washing dishes and shining shoes—are obvious reminders of the employment options reserved for Black people. José's defiant act of hurling two large rocks at the dishes is both an expression of his anger and an expression of his awareness—of his own human capacity for greater achievement and of his human right to do so. By not chastising him for the destruction of the dishes, Ma Tine affirms his response and models this attitude in her response to the minimal scholarship award. Dressed in her finery, viewers are treated to a display of fist-pumping defiance in her refusal to succumb to the intended discouragement of a scholarship allotment well below her expectations and a financial burden well above her means.

> MA TINE: They're wicked! One quarter scholarship! That's like giving nothing! They don't know I'm a fighting woman! I won't give up that one quarter scholarship! We going to move to Fort-de-France, and you're going to attend their school!

While the film is centered on the character-narrator José, he is not unique in his sense of self and of his rights. His playmates are equally self-aware, defiant, intelligent, resourceful, and self-loving. In fact, the film's most psychologically empowered subjects are the children; here, too, Palcy's redefinition of damaging stereotypes is apparent. Although the film bears some resemblance to the picaresque in its representation of the children, this resemblance does not privilege an entertainment objective. Rather, the emotional depth, complexity, and richness of the children's lives is crucial to the film's ideological objectives in re-presenting Black communities for Black audiences.

In her portrait of one of the children, José's friend Léopold, Palcy revises the stereotype of the "tragic mulatto." As in *Illusions*, Léopold's character represents a distinct variation on the portrayal of "mulatto"/biracial individuals. Léopold is neither alienated from his own cultural self-definition nor from his cultural community. Rather, his access to the inner working of the White world makes him more politically aware than his peers of the mechanisms by which Black people are subordinated.

Among *Sugar Cane Alley*'s most significant achievements is its interrogation of oppositional dichotomies and hierarchies of difference. It does so through the presentation of a Black cultural paradigm—articulated by Ma Tine and Mr. Médouze—that envisions a democracy of cultures in the interdependence of animate and inanimate beings. The village elder, Mr. Médouze, introduces this cultural paradigm in his instructions to José on the complementarity of fire and water. Following this lesson, José is able to explain the difference between "singing" and "cackling" in terms that reflect a democracy of cultural aesthetics. Instead of simplistically defining one sound as pleasant and the other as noise, as one might have expected, he identifies several sounds in the natural environment—the wheels of a cart, wind in the cane fields, and so on—as forms of singing.

In addition to introducing a distinct cultural philosophy, Médouze plays an important role in the film in challenging the schoolteacher's confident assertion that "learning is the key that opens the second door to our freedom." (Presumably official emancipation opened the first door.) His narration—of post-Emancipation developments in Martinique—provides an important counterpoint to the teacher's focus on education as an avenue for self-empowerment. Since his history lesson follows both the disbursement of meager wages on pay day and the shopping trip that exposes the St. Louis family's deepening poverty, this narrative montage underscores Mr. Médouze's role in exposing Slavery as an informing economic subtext. Historian Bridget Brereton concurs with Mr. Médouze's history lesson in describing the persistence of the "plantation model" as a structuring principle of economic, political, social, and cultural relations in the Caribbean. In "Society and Culture in the Caribbean," Brereton notes: "It is almost a truism that emancipation did not transform the nature of Caribbean societies, nor the fundamental patterns of race relations, nor the way power was held and exercised, nor even the values and attitudes that had most prestige. Because the plantation was still the most important unit in most of the islands, a rigid class/race stratification continued to exist, reinforced after 1838–48 by new divisions of race, religions, and language" (85). Médouze's narrative discloses the historical subtext that continues to operate in this social milieu. It disrupts the film's temporal linearity by suggesting that contemporary socioeconomic and political circumstances are part of a recurring pattern of oppression. In fact, by revising Zobel's novel to show that despite his obvious scholarly talent and diligence, education does not open the doors to opportunity for José, Palcy endorses Médouze's analysis and not the schoolteacher's hopeful expectation. Were it not for the high school teacher's (guilty) intervention in recommending him for a scholarship, José's fate would be no different from that of his equally deserving village playmates. The film suggests that while the forces that keep the doors closed are determined, organized, and powerful, the opening of the door—for this one child—is quite random.

Palcy also uses Médouze's history lesson to foreground the linkages between Africa in the past and Africa in the present. The music from the villagers' nighttime refreshings form a call-and-response dialogue with the text of Slavery narrated by Médouze. While his narrative expresses both a longing for Africa in their past and a perceived inability to imagine an avenue of return other than death, the music functions as a second voice that announces other possibilities, and that confirms the reality of Africa in their midst.

Another strategy Palcy uses to renew Black people's self-possession is the construction of an *organic* musical. In describing *Sugar Cane Alley* as an "organic musical" I refer to the frequency and spontaneity with which the villagers break into song and to the specific functions served by this singing. Two types of musical events appear in the film: spontaneous and ritualized. Both types of musical performances are important analytical vehicles and therapeutic mechanisms. The first example of spontaneous singing occurs when one of the workers—"Ti Coco"—is docked for stopping to urinate. The ballad his coworkers sing—in creole—allows them to voice their sympathy for him and to satirize the oppressive roles of Whites and their "mulatto"/biracial secondaries. The ritualized song and dance performances at the center of the nighttime festivities following the disbursement of wages are part of a cultural tradition of self-regeneration designed to heal the psychological wounds inflicted by economic and sociopolitical subordination. Similarly, the ritualized performances at the wake for Mr. Médouze allow the villagers to participate in a ritualized self-mockery that satirizes the life of a Black man in a White supremacist world. The spontaneous singing in the closing sequence is an expression of the villagers' protest against

Léopold's arrest and against the oppression of Black people, in Martinique, Guadeloupe, and elsewhere. In every instance, singing—as in the tradition of the spirituals and the blues—enables the villagers to acknowledge oppressive circumstances while facilitating a definite psychological and spiritual release and transcendence. Significantly, these musical performances are not aestheticized by nondiegetic instrumental enhancements. In choosing not to present these performances as entertainment commodities, Palcy allows them to retain their internal significance and positions viewers to understand this internal function.

In addition to representing an important survival strategy, Palcy's depiction of music as a collective and subversive discourse enables her to dismantle one of the most pernicious trends in mainstream cinema—the projection of a desire to be dominated onto members of subordinated groups, particularly at historical moments when progressive political movements have not yet gained mainstream acceptance. At such moments, mainstream films strategically "plant" and foreground one or more Black persons who are projected as deeply suspicious of, if not openly hostile toward, everyone and everything that challenges the status quo. By such representations, these films imply that Black people *like* things the way they are and would prefer that they did not change. In representing the collective articulation and endorsement of the sociopolitical analysis encoded in the villagers' songs, Palcy liberates the film's Black subjects from a history of imagistic defamation.

A Democracy of Narrative Participation

Of the films discussed in this study, none provides a more extensive representation of spirituality than does Julie Dash's *Daughters of the Dust.* Indeed, so pronounced is this aspect that most critical responses to the film have noted it of necessity. In "Daughters of the *Terreiros,*" for example, Clyde Taylor explores the film's complex theological structure in relation to Afro-Brazilian Candomblé.[8] And in "Reading the Signs, Empowering the Eye," Toni Cade Bambara offers a compelling analysis of the ways in which spirituality assists the film's pedagogical and ideological goals. Bambara notes that *Daughters of the Dust* "asks that the spectator honor multiple perspectives rather than depend on the 'official' story offered by a hero; it asks too that we note what particular compositions and framing mean in terms of human values" (133). "The reward," she concludes, "is an empowered eye" (133). My concern in discussing this film is not to repeat prior discussion of its spiritual elements but to expand upon those discussions by analyzing the ways in which an ethos of interconnectedness informs Dash's representation of this family crisis, her exploration of the family's "hidden" branches, her use of multiple narrators to construct a full portrait of the community, and the ways in which these choices both reflect and assist the film's commitment to a democracy of narrative participation.

The most extensive representation of spirituality in *Daughters of the Dust* is the ethos of interconnectedness reflected in its focus on the complex kinship matrix, the multiple temporal realms, the multiplicity of genres, and the migrating narrative consciousness that supports a democracy of narrative participation. Dash displays her commitment to a democracy of narrative participation by expanding the narrative parameters to include ancestors and the Unborn Child as well as the living; the Native American presence as well as African Americans; "sons of drum" as well as daughters of the dust; Yellow Mary and Trula as well as the heterosexual couples—Eli and Eula, the newlyweds, Iona and St. Julian, and Viola and Mr. Snead. Moreover, in relegating Eula's rapist, the lynchers, and their assaults to an off-screen existence, the film avoids an oppositional focus. It foregoes a discursive preoccupation with what "they" have done and follows this community's engagement with the question of what it must do to renew its development in accordance with the paradigm of growth.

Set in 1902 in the Sea Islands, *Daughters of the Dust* depicts a community—comprised of four generations of the Peazant family—struggling to cope with two related and paradoxical crises: the impending birth of the newest offspring whose mother, Eula (Alva Rogers), was raped by a White planter; and the impending departure of several family members for the mainland. Both events hold ambivalent potential. Should the unborn child be viewed as the sign and symbol of a violent past or the promise of a reinvigorating future? Should the mainland be viewed as the sign and symbol of the promised land or the site of struggle and perhaps exile? Should the past itself be viewed as an encumbrance from which to be unfettered or as a resource for renewing the future? If children are a renewal of self, how does one claim that renewal in the context of rape? If the future is a renewal of the past, what future can or should one renew given the violence that saturates this history?

Typically, these questions are posed as sociological interrogations. In *Daughters of the Dust,* however, Dash consciously frames them as spiritual interrogations. The real crisis, the film makes clear, is not a crisis of paternity or of migration. As Nana Peazant (Cora Lee Day) fears, and as both Eli's destruction of the bottle tree and Haagar's materialist longings confirm, the crisis involves a loss of faith, memory, vision, and connectedness. The forms of crisis within the Peazant family all involve a lack of connectedness. As an example, the lack of memory reflects and reinforces a disconnection of past from present, present from future. This disconnection generates other forms of disconnection as, for example, the family's rejection of the "ruint woman," Yellow Mary (Barbara O). The rejection of Yellow Mary reflects a disconnection of the families exposed branches from its "hidden" branches.

Significantly, Dash narrates the family's response to these crises so as to affirm an ethos of interconnectedness. The visual emphasis on *hand* contact throughout the film constitutes a cinematic rendering of this ethos. It appears in the ritual game of hand signals among the young men, in the image of the women on the beach superimposed in the cup of Nana Peazant's hands, and it culminates with the "hand" that Nana makes to guide her children as they go to a land that, she declares, will not be flowing with milk and honey. The talisman that Nana makes—comprised of both the Bible and emblems of an ancestral presence—forms a "hand" that is both a symbol of connectedness and a guide. By inviting her descendants to "kiss my hand. Take me where you go, I your strength," Nana Peazant defuses the crisis in the family by reminding all that their survival depends equally on the preservation of kinship ties and historical consciousness. As she insists, "There must be a bond, a connection between them who a go North and those who remain; between us on this side and those on the other side."

In addition to expressing an ethos of interconnectedness, the resolution of the crisis is carefully constructed to support a democracy of narrative participation. As illustrated in the analysis of Dash's earlier film, *Illusions,* the term *democracy of narrative participation* refers to a pattern of representation in which characters who would otherwise be considered "marginal" are allowed to occupy the narrative foreground. This cinematic approach reflects Dash's decision to deconstruct the binary casting of central and marginal characters consistent with the goal of depicting and establishing interdependent relationships. It informs the film's exposure of the family's "hidden" branches—the ancestors, the Unborn Child, and the lesbian. Significantly, Nana Peazant and Eula (Alva Rogers), the two figures who embrace the priestess's mediational role, collaborate in unveiling and embracing these hidden members. The affirming presence of the Unborn Child (Kai-Lynn Warren) is a direct result of Nana Peazant's spiritual intervention. The Unborn Child narrator informs us that "Nana prayed for help; I got there just in time." She resolves the crisis by convincing "my Daddy that I was his." Eula makes a similar intervention in seeking help from her own dead mother. As she explains to Yellow Mary, "My ma come to me last night. . . . she take me by the hand." Together these agents assist Eli (Adisa Anderson) in abandoning his frustration over a threatened and threatening *ownership* in favor of a renewed *kinship* with his child, his wife, and his ancestors. They remind the community of the many ways in which the past—through the ancestors—can invigorate the future.

Transforming Yellow Mary's status as a rejected/"hidden" member of the kinship matrix is also crucial to the resolution of crisis in the film. As Eula's closing monologue indicates, the family's disconnection from ancestors and their rejection of Yellow Mary are both prompted by the same impulse. Reclaiming and reaffirming kinship with Yellow Mary because as Eula sees it, "she a part o' we," reenacts the affirmation of kinship with the ancestors that facilitates a renewed self-possession.

Dash's construction of a democracy of narrative participation exemplifies the type of representational and discursive practices that a commitment to democracy requires and constitutes another expression of what Lubiano calls a Black postmodernist epistemology. As legal scholar and activist Lani Guinier notes: "Participation matters, after all. . . . Participation among and with others offers more than simple survival. It nourishes and reinforces both the individual and the community. . . . And democracy demands the ability to participate, the opportunity to act in close association with others, and the right to a hearing" (18). Significantly, the titular emphasis on women's experiences does not generate a marginalized male presence. The film is equally committed to representing the human complexity and supporting the narrative participation of Eli, Mr. Snead (Tommy

Yellow Mary (Barbara O), Nana Peazant (Cora Lee Day), and Eula (Alva Rogers) in *Daughters of the Dust.* Courtesy of Kino International.

Hicks), St. Julian Lastchild (M. Cochise Anderson), and other male figures. For example, by allowing St. Julian Lastchild to exercise the right of a discursive *self*-representation, the film enables him to emerge as a fully human subject. Instead of remaining simply a prop, *he reveals himself*—through the letter—as a man with a full and complex interior life, a man in love with a woman, a man who is perturbed by the rapid pace of out-migration and its impact on the lives of those left behind. And although the film focuses on the Peazant family, it pays a moving tribute to the Native American community for whom this land is ancestral home, a necessary gesture given the thematic centrality of ancestry. By expanding the narrative parameters, Dash exposes the complex emotional interdependence of "major" and "minor" characters. This democracy of narrative participation constitutes a new epistemological standpoint since it supports a very different—and more representative—construction of U.S. American society and history.

The expanded representation of diverse religious practices within this Gullah community is yet another way in which the film expresses an ethos of interconnectedness. In addition to its depiction of the types of agency provided or precluded by various forms of spirituality, *Daughters of the Dust* points to the danger arising from a rejection of spirituality expressed as materialism. Haagar's disdain for the past and her obsession with ownership—her naming of the daughters Myown and Iona, pronounced defiantly as "Iownher"—diverge sharply from the respect for the past and commitment to kinship that can be discerned to varying degrees in every form of spirituality. Although Haagar and Viola are visually positioned in opposition to Nana Peazant—each occupying a chair on either side of her—their two visions are radically different. While Haagar views Bilal as "nothing but a heathen," Viola grudgingly acknowledges her kinship with Bilal despite her disdain for his spiritual direction. And while all members of the family —including a reluctant Viola—accept and embrace Nana's "hand," Haagar's disavowal of the need for ancestral guidance is singular and cautionary.

Dash uses body language as a technique for enhancing the democracy of narrative participation. Beyond the centrality of hand contact in this film, Dash has described the use of body language in all of her works as an affirmation of its importance to Black culture. Her most innovative use of body language is in the development and depiction of the subplot involving the lesbian couple Yellow Mary and Trula. Yellow Mary's carriage throughout the film expresses a language of independence, as well as a language of intimacy, especially in the scenes on the beach. Dash's use of the silent vocabulary of body language—the language of embrace, touch, and gaze—to depict this relationship coincides with filmmaker Dawn Suggs's analysis of the importance of the language of silence to Black lesbian filmmakers. In an interview with Greg Tate, Suggs noted that "Silence is one of our languages too. Silence can be used in a very empowering way. Through your marginality you find different types of tools. In time our silence can be used very effectively."[9] The depiction of the Yellow Mary/Trula relationship exemplifies the effective use of the language of silence. That is to say, Dash's "visual subplot" underscores and makes use of a *preexisting,* societally imposed silence. Given the film's 1902 setting, to have allowed a verbal narration of this relationship would have misrepresented the discursive constraints on lesbian experience.

In addition to body language, Dash relies on several cinematic techniques to develop this subplot. In the early shots of their arrival, the mise-en-scène includes only Yellow Mary and Trula. The framed couple is subsequently replaced by a mise-en-scène composed of a shifting triangular configuration in which Yellow Mary is always positioned between Trula and Eula. In the tree scene, for example, Trula is positioned in the upper branches, Eula on the ground, and Yellow Mary midway between them, on the lower branches. When Yellow Mary begins to reconnect with her heritage, the three are no longer framed together. Instead, Trula is framed alone, on the periphery, or at a distance. The camera frequently crosscuts from scenes with Yellow Mary to reaction shots of Trula in which she displays her increasing anxiety at the crisis in their relationship as Yellow Mary moves progressively toward cultural and familial reconnection.

The language of independence suggested by Yellow Mary's carriage throughout the film, especially her poses on the fallen tree trunk, differs considerably from her body language, posture, and dress in the closing scene. Lavish white dress, white shoes, and white gloves are replaced by blue-flowered print dress; her open coiffure is reconfigured in two braids. At first glance, the transformation seems to indicate a reinscription of domesticity concomitant with her decision not to accompany her lover, Trula, to Nova Scotia. Read more carefully, however, the transposed body language signals Yellow Mary's recovery of the ease and familiarity of a nonperformative self-consciousness, an outward expression of the culturally autonomous self-possession she finds on Igbo Landing.

The existence of two distinct communities within the film—one comprised of those members of the family who "remain[ed] behind growing older, wiser, stronger"; another that went North, to find the "culture, education and wealth of the mainland" and perhaps to experience cultural alienation and amnesia—provides a narrative explanation for the complexity of contemporary diaspora attitudes *outside* the film. The filmmaker's role in

bridging the gap between these two constituencies and attitudes is prefig-
ured by Mr. Snead, the photographer, who reminds the Peazant clan posing
for a panoptic family photo, to "Look, look up and remember Igbo Landing." Mr. Snead's role is a proxy for, and resembles, the role of the film-
maker/artist as mediator/priestess. Significantly, technology is not one of
the forces contributing to the destabilization of this diaspora community.[10]
Like other Western artistic instruments—the saxophone and the novel, for
example—the camera is presented as a new technology that, if "saturated"
with a Black cultural ethos, can help counter the destabilization of postmodernity by facilitating a renewed self-possession.

Film and the Language of Self-Possession

As Dash's "narration" of the subplot of Yellow Mary and Trula's relationship
illustrates, a primary strategy used by Black women filmmakers to construct new patterns of looking involves deploying the discursive power of
silence. As discussed in chapter 4, Morrison's observation of the critical
content of Black women's silence and its discursive relationship to "civilization" underscores its significance as a vocabulary and expressive modality
in Black women's texts. In *Home Away from Home*, Afro-British filmmaker
Maureen Blackwood enunciates the analysis coded within this eloquent silence. The film does not simply deploy the silent vocabulary of the gaze to
narrate the plot. Rather, it constitutes a new "silent film." The absence of dialogue supports the development of a nonverbal audio aesthetic indicated
by the abundance and richness of environmental sounds, including the
prominent motif of overhead aircraft sounds used to signal exile. Unlike
early cinema, silence here is not driven by technological limitations. The
prominence of the soundscape accentuates Blackwood's enunciation and
exposure of the hidden transcripts embedded in ideologically and aesthetically motivated silences.

Home Away from Home tells the story of a Nigerian woman, Miriam
(Ellen Thomas), living in London, and her attempt to cope with the twin
crises of her own longing for home and the increasing alienation of her
daughter Fumi (Ashabi Asikawo). The film, set in the 1990s, opens with a
medium shot of commercial airplanes taking off from and landing at London's Heathrow Airport. We then see a woman, Miriam, looking longingly at

these departures and arrivals before she returns to her job at an airport café. Seeing a young woman proudly wearing an African outfit, Miriam is reminded of her own daughter's contrasting disdain.

Fumi's alienation has broad ramifications for the family. The shots of the children walking home from school visually enunciate her leadership. In each instance, she is in the lead position, with the younger siblings following in her wake. Her alienation and antagonism reverberate in the disruptive behavior of the younger siblings and in the turmoil within the household. To narrate these developments, Blackwood uses slow frame filming and amplified environmental sounds that call attention to events and underscore their meaning. As an example, Fumi's disdain for and rejection of her culture is narrated through the amplified sound of the rejected African cloth being hurled to the floor in slow motion. Likewise, the sound of the dish crashing to the floor and its contents scattering (again in slow motion) symbolize the emotional fracturing of Miriam's house.

Blackwood's portrait of Miriam illustrates how an ethos of interconnectedness and an awareness of her own creative agency can shape daily attitudes, actions, and interactions. Despite her obvious homesickness, Miriam cannot afford, and does not choose, to make a physical return home. And despite her teenage daughter's obvious hostility toward her, Miriam refuses to meet her in an oppositional mode. Instead, she redirects every new provocation. When, for example, Fumi turns up the volume on the radio, Miriam turns the channel to a dance beat and entreats her with enticing dance movements. As with her daughter, Miriam refuses to let her neighbors' antagonism compel her to adopt an oppositional stance or to distract her from her parental responsibilities. As a proactive gesture, she decides to build a mud hut in her London backyard.

Like Palcy's characterization of poor Black people in *Sugar Cane Alley,* Blackwood's deployment of the hut as a visual symbol of African cultural belonging is fraught with risk. In the imagistic vocabulary of Hollywood cinema, the hut is synonymous with uncivilized, undeveloped, and underdeveloped Africa. At the same time, however, works such as Langston Hughes's poem "The Negro Speaks of Rivers" provide another point of reference, defining the hut as familial, intimate, communal, ancestral space. Hughes's poem celebrates the transnational expanse and transhistorical breadth of the African diaspora experience by referencing its many associations with rivers. The speaker recalls, for example: "I built my hut by the Congo and it lulled me to sleep. / I looked upon the Nile and raised the pyramids above it." What emerges from the speaker's multiple geographic references is a sense of permanence, of a lasting and tranquil presence, summarized in the closing declaration, "My soul has grown deep as the rivers." Blackwood's depiction of the hut in *Home Away from Home* resounds this celebratory tone.

As a proactive strategy, Miriam's decision to build the hut generates three significant reactions. The construction of the hut reorients the younger children. Playfully involved in building it, the younger children are drawn away from Fumi's destabilized and destabilizing orbit and are reoriented in the mother's stable orbit as they participate in the reinvention of "home." The hut also intensifies Fumi's antagonism toward her mother. Like the African cloth given to her on her birthday, the hut, for Fumi, is a potent and unwelcome reminder of the family's cultural distinctiveness. For the neighbors, the building of the hut provides shocking confirmation of their deepest suspicions about this African family. It therefore intensifies their surveillance of Miriam's yard.

Although Morrison identifies silence as a discursive resource of Black women and other subordinated groups, Blackwood's film demonstrates that it has also become a hegemonic discursive weapon. In the post–civil rights and post-Independence era, hegemonic agents have increasingly relied on the discursive efficacy of silence as a way of recouping and/or maintaining the privilege officially disavowed through legislative postures. The hegemonic gaze that was once very vocally and unabashedly enunciated—in the social, economic, political, educational, religious, scientific/medical, and cinematic practices of U.S. American racism and European imperialism—has since cloaked itself in silence as a way of concealing what James Scott calls its "hidden transcripts" (xii). In *Domination and the Arts of Resistance*, Scott notes that "The powerful, for their part, also develop a hidden transcript representing the practices and aims of their rule that cannot be openly avowed" (xii). Scott concludes that "a comparison of the hidden transcript of the weak with that of the powerful and of both hidden transcripts to the public transcript of power relations offers a substantially new way of understanding resistance to domination" (xii).

Although Scott's analysis agrees with Morrison's that subordinated groups do speak despite and beyond the restrictions of dominant groups, there are significant and instructive differences between the two analyses. While Scott imagines subordinated groups speaking behind the back of the dominant, Morrison notes that it is the dominant group—"civilization"—that hides, that is, dares not risk engaging the transcript of subordinated groups, because of its potential to expose and challenge hegemony. Second, while Scott describes a reactive stance against oppression as the locus from which this suppressed transcript emerges, Morrison identifies both proactive and reactive stances—"silence [that is] enforced or chosen"—that shape the transcripts of subordinated groups. And finally, while Scott's analysis presupposes a binary divide separating the powerful from the powerless, Morrison's endorses definitions of power and privilege that are consonant with the paradigm of growth, and that recognize power as coterminous with humanity. Nevertheless, Scott's analysis uncovers an important aspect of contemporary sociopolitical discourses: that far from abandoning the pursuit of dominance, hegemonic agents have simply taken their agendas underground. For those constituencies particularly vulnerable to endangering actions and attitudes arising from these "hidden transcripts," the need to craft a historicized and comprehensive definition of racism, one that can unveil these "transcripts," is urgent. Renewing self-possession on the part of the film's Black subjects and its viewers, Blackwood demonstrates, requires an enunciation of the silence of Miriam's London neighbors and of the "hidden transcripts" encoded therein.

While the neighborhood gaze instigates Fumi's alienation, her decision to enter the hut that symbolizes the psychic space of the culture is prompted by a verbal enunciation that ruptures the silence and exposes its hidden transcript. In observing the word "savages" painted on the sidewalk in front of their house, Fumi becomes aware of the gaze that discredits her mother and herself, which she had endorsed in her antagonistic disposition toward family members. Critical self-consciousness, the film suggests, requires an enunciation of the "hidden transcripts" encoded in "civilization's" silence. This enunciation serves as a catalyst for renewing Fumi's self-possession by prompting a simultaneous recognition and expulsion of the hegemonic gaze by which she was (dis)possessed. In the final sequence, we see signs of Fumi's renewed self-possession as the children plant seeds in the backyard, following her lead.

The establishing shot of the landscape of Miriam's London neighborhood as she walks toward her house at the beginning of the film exposes the circumscribing and encircling gaze of the White neighbors—"civilization"—as an institutional subtext that precipitates the family's psychological and spiritual destabilization. Through spatial narration, Blackwood presents the neighborhood's architectural homogeneity as a cipher for the neighbors' cultural monologism, an ideology that informs their suspicion, surveillance, and censorship of cultural difference.

In her discussion of camera-work in independent Black cinema, Toni Cade Bambara uses the term "spatial narration" to underscore its contrasting goals in relation to conventional cinema. Bambara notes, in "Reading the Signs, Empowering the Eye": "In conventional cinema, camera-work stresses hierarchy. Space is dominated by the hero, and shifts in the picture plane are most often occasioned by a blur, directing the viewer eye, controlling what we may and may not see, a practice that reinscribes the relationships of dominant ideology" (135). In contradistinction to this practice, Bambara notes that in independent Black films, "the camera-work stresses the communal. Space is shared" (135). As such, spatial narration facilitates the cinematic expression of an ethos of interconnectedness.

Spatial narration is also a strategy for articulating a Black postmodernist epistemology. As Bambara explains in "Language and the Writer": "In Hollywood space is hidden. Once you get an establishing shot—Chicago skyline, night, winter—most of the other shots are tight shots. We move up on the speaker, we then shift for a reaction shot, tight space, and the spectator is supposed to do the work and figure out what is happening outside of the frame" (144). By contrast, space has very specific significance for Black people and other circumscribed communities. Bambara notes that "for a people concerned with land, with turf, with real estate, with home, with the whole colonial experience, with the appropriation of space by the elite or by the outsider, the language of space becomes very crucial within the cinematic practice" (144). Spatial narration is, therefore, an important cinematic technique for unveiling the "language of space" as a reflection of hegemonic practices and conditions.

Bambara notes that the exploration of space coincides with and supports a rejection of a related film ideology, one that emphasizes individual/psychological causation rather than systemic or institutional/ideological causes. By contrast, the exploration of space in independent Black film-making supports a representation of space as context—institutional con-text—in addition to deconstructing domination ideologies. For example, the establishing aerial shot of Igbo Landing in *Daughters of the Dust* visually references the Middle Passage crossing and recalls the institutional subtext of Slavery that informs the family's contemporary circumstances. As Bam-bara notes, "spatial narration" enables the filmmaker to expose and analyze the institutional factors shaping the characters' situations. It is, therefore, crucial to the project of reframing Black subjects and thereby renewing self-possession among (Black) viewers.

Blackwood's use of spatial narration supports the functions identified in Bambara's analysis. The many reaction shots in *Home Away from Home* foreground the gaze of the neighbors that dominates the family's psychoso-cial space and that inculcates a discrediting view that influences Fumi's at-titude toward, and relationship with, her mother. Blackwood uses spatial narration to examine the ways in which the gaze of the neighborhood con-stitutes a destabilizing institutional context for this Black family. In fact, the mise-en-scène is repeatedly constructed to emphasize the psychological dominance of the neighborhood gaze through the use of reaction shots that frame the neighbors' distrust, discomfort, and disdain. This gaze, the cam-era reveals, has discursive power. It "speaks" to both Fumi and her mother about the prescribed definition and position of Blackness. In this environ-ment, the mother's birthday gift is discredited by the neighborhood gaze that Fumi has internalized.

Given the film's spatial narration and architectural coding of cultural monologism, Miriam's decision to respond to her own and her children's need through an architectural vehicle is doubly significant. The signifi-cance of the hut is subliminally and symbolically coded by its ubiquitous presence. Before the physical construction in the backyard, it appears in the magazine Miriam peruses in the opening scene and in the child's draw-ing on the bedroom wall. The structure creates the context and privacy for other types of encounters, with other gazes.

Miriam's hut provides the privacy for what Collins refers to as a "realm of relatively safe discourse." The very diverse examples of Mignon's conversa-tion with Esther in *Illusions,* the photographs of women that adorn Alana's apartment in *A Different Image,* Sassafrass's weaving in *Sassafrass, Cypress,*

Fumi (Ashabi Asikawo) nestles under her mother (Ellen Thomas) in *Home Away from Home*. Courtesy of Women Make Movies.

and Indigo, and Miriam's hut in *Home Away from Home* attest to the multiple ways in which this discursive realm can be constructed. There are, it should be noted, no objects in the hut. It is composed of bare earthen walls, its floor the bare earth. This space is both safe *from* discrediting discourses and safe *for* affirming discourses about, and encounters with, the Black woman self. In this space, Fumi encounters herself *as herself.* The stages of her renewed self-possession are marked by her actions, each of which traces a rerooting: covering her mother with the rejected cloth, nestling under her, whirling counterclockwise with arms extended and head uplifted, kneeling, touching and caressing the earth. These actions mimic the circular movements of ring shout performances. Historian Michael Gomez's analysis of the philosophical significance of the ring shout's kinetic patterns accentuates the significance of Fumi's movement. In *Exchanging Our Country Marks,* he notes that "ring ceremonies were very much used to invoke the presence of both ancestors and deities and served as media by which human beings entered into a shared experience with them" (118). In this space, as suggested by her circular movements, Fumi encounters ancestors and, through them, an empowering view of herself.

Although Miriam's hut is destroyed, the film depicts the family's continued recovery and growth. The film's focus on the reinvigorated familial relationships redirects the viewer's gaze away from the quest for home toward the matrilineage and reclaimed kinship network of the house of Miriam. In constructing this narrative in which Miriam does not make a physical return to Africa, and in which even the hut is destroyed, Blackwood suggests that home is not simply a physical entity or space but a set of relationships—with one's self, one's family (including ancestors), one's culture, and one's past —that are sustaining. In depicting a resolution that stems from Miriam's choice of a proactive stance, Blackwood reveals her collaboration with the protagonist in affirming the paradigm of growth. The narrative reveals that the challenges confronting Fumi and the neighbors are the same: that of figuring out if, where, how their actions and attitudes may be lacking. Like her protagonist, Miriam, Blackwood, the filmmaker, creates a discursive space in which viewers can achieve a parallel self-discovery and growth.

Like *Sugar Cane Alley* and *Daughters of the Dust*, *Home Away from Home* illustrates that Black women artists employ a variety of cinematic and narrative strategies that express an ethos of interconnectedness, and that reposition viewers and readers to embrace the philosophical, ethical, and intellectual responsibilities of the paradigm of growth. These responsibilities are consistent with a commitment to democracy and begin with self-examination, self-knowledge, and self-correction.

6

Charting Futures

Grace Nichols, Maya Angelou, and Estella Conwill Májozo

> . . . the most difficult challenge facing the activist is to respond fully to the needs of the moment and to do so in such a way that the light one attempts to shine on the present will simultaneously illuminate the future.
>
> —ANGELA DAVIS, *Women, Culture, and Politics*

In previous chapters, I have attempted to show that spirituality functions as a life-affirming ideology in Black women's art, and that, in the choices informing narrative construction and characterization, Black women filmmakers and writers embrace the role and responsibility of the priestess, bearing and distributing life-force to sustain the community of viewers and readers. This chapter pulls together the various strands of my argument by accentuating the deliberation with which Black women writers and filmmakers define and approach their responsibilities as artists. As an example, Estella Conwill Májozo's memoir—one of a very small handful of autobiographical works by Black women literary artists[1]—provides a rare insight into Black women's understanding of the relationship between their creative vision and communal roles. Similarly, in its historical and geographic trajectories, Grace Nichols's *i is a long memoried woman* underscores the artist's commitment to unveiling the possibilities of memory as a manifestation of the living past. So, too, does Maya Angelou's feature film *Down in the Delta*. The affinities among these very different works—two, fiction, one, nonfiction; one, a film, two, literary works; two from the United States, one from the Caribbean—attest to the ways in which her commitment to (the goals of) the paradigm of growth engenders particular representational and narrative choices for the Black woman artist.

The Black Woman Artist, Activist, Priestess

As the previous analyses have demonstrated, Black women's literature and cinema are explicitly crafted to present individual stories as well as a collective history by way of exploring the moral philosophy of the culture and disclosing its potential to restore a righteous equilibrium of (human) relationships. In designing the work of art to promote group preservation, the Black woman artist functions as priestess bearing life-force, thereby empowering and (re)positioning readers, viewers, other artists, and scholars to chart new futures by making more enabling choices on their own behalf.

The vision of human community informing Black women's cinema and literature arises from a complex understanding of the role of artist as an activist charged with the responsibility of producing what Toni Cade Bambara describes as "a desirable vision of the future." This is perhaps the most important of several well-defined functions the work of art must perform to support the artist's communal roles and responsibilities. These communal roles and responsibilities are connected to the tradition of the artist as activist, a tradition that has deep roots in African diaspora cultures. In the United States, for example, from its earliest beginning with the "slave narrative" genre, the African American literary tradition has been shaped by the artist's conscious intent to speak as both mediator and advocate on behalf of the cultural community. While the model of artist as activist appears to have been occasioned by the political demands of Slavery, the communal role of the artist does not begin with crisis. In fact, this cultural model predates Slavery. Consequently, its importance cannot be fully gauged when the interpretive context is restricted to the Slavery setting. Rather, a comprehensive understanding can only come from an examination within the context of a preexisting cultural paradigm.

The cultural attitudes, approaches, strategies, and ways of being displayed and deployed by enslaved Africans were not all invented during or because of Slavery. As Paris notes, and as scholarly evidence overwhelmingly confirms, preexisting cultural resources made it possible to survive Slavery.[2] While they improvised new possibilities from available materials, Africans went into Slavery equipped with the cultural resources—that is, the internal resources—that ensured their survival. These included spiritual, philosophical, ethical, and artistic traditions. In combining the roles of artist and activist in the early literary tradition, for example, enslaved Africans were acting out a cultural philosophy that emphasized the duality of functionality and aesthetics underlying artistic creation. At the same time, the destruction of relevant cultural nomenclature during Slavery gave rise to what philosophers Howard McGary and Bill Lawson describe as a "functional lexical gap," that effectively obscured the complexity and significance of a variety of communal roles. In the contemporary period, therefore, the word "activist" has frequently served as a proxy for "priestess." Black women's approach to the role of artist/activist—with their dual attention to group preservation and to envisioning a livable future—reenacts the role of artist/priestess.

In "The Priest/Artist Tradition in Achebe's *Arrow of God*," Anthonia Kalu grounds her analysis in Chinua Achebe's statements on the African view of the functional character of art.[3] In "Africa and Her Writers," a critical essay written in the early 1970s, Achebe asserts: "I will still insist that art is, and was always, in the service of man. Our ancestors created their myths and legends and told their stories for a human purpose . . . to serve the needs of their times. Their artists lived and moved and had their beings in society and created their works for the good of that society" (29). Elaborating upon and contextualizing this commentary, Kalu locates Achebe's fiction and nonfiction analyses in Igbo cosmology. She notes that "Achebe's interpretation of Igbo thought through art reveals a relationship between political and religious institutions. It is in these relationships that the Igbo artist and art traditions are most important" (51). "In recreating and revealing these connections," Kalu argues, "Achebe assumes the venerable role of Igbo priest and artist" (51). Assuming the dual roles of artist and priest involves the creation of art designed to sustain the community by highlighting the guidelines encoded within various cultural/artistic traditions. This art engages, illuminates, and interrogates the cultural philosophies that constitute a blueprint for living.

Although Kalu's analysis looks specifically at Igbo cosmology, it offers an important framework and model for evaluating the role of Black women artists as activists and priestesses throughout the diaspora. In fact, many of the principles outlined in Kalu's analysis and represented in Achebe's work have been echoed by other African diaspora artists. Like Achebe, Morrison views the role of the Black artist in communal terms. In "Rootedness," she writes: "If anything I do, in the way of writing novels (or whatever I write) isn't about the village or the community or about you, then it is not about anything. I am not interested in indulging myself in some private, closed exercise of my imagination that fulfills only the obligation of my personal dreams—which is to say yes, the work must be political" (344). Viewed through the lenses provided by Kalu's analysis, Morrison's insistence on the "political" function of her art exemplifies this awareness of, and responsibility for, group preservation. So, too, does Toni Cade Bambara's assertion that "The persistent concern of engaged artists, of cultural workers, in this country and certainly within my community, is, What role can, should, or must the film practitioner, for example, play in producing a desirable vision of the future?" Like Bambara and Morrison, other Black women artists frequently articulate their commitment to the role and responsibility of activist/priestess. In the essay "To Search for the Good and Make It Matter," poet, playwright, and collaborative public artist Estella Conwill Májozo notes, for example: "For me, the two roles exist as a single entity: the artist is the activist. . . . As the mask is for festivals, and the ground-drawing for marking sacred space, and the dance for healing and drawing energies to oneself, so, too, the rituals we perform and the monuments that we make have a function: the transformation of self and community, which is the extended self" (89). In discussing the sociopolitical function of Caribbean literature in "Challenges of the Struggle for Sovereignty," writer Merle Hodge, of Trinidad and Tobago, expresses a parallel view. "I am very confident," says Hodge, "that it is people who change the world and that people must continually engage in actions aimed at changing the world for the better. For me, there is no fundamental contradiction between art and activism. In particular, the power of the creative word to change the world is not to be underestimated" (202). Larkin offers a similar view of the artist's activist role. In "Black Women Film-makers Defining Ourselves," she writes: "We hope that with our films we can help create a new world. . . . We hope to do this, one film at a time, one screening at a time, to change minds, widen perspectives and destroy the fear of difference" (172). These statements all attest to the Black woman artist's definition of her priestess role, of her commitment to using her art to clarify and affirm the moral philosophy of the culture, and, by doing so, to advance the political goal of group preservation.

Positioning Readers and Viewers
as Agents of Transformation

In *i is a long memoried woman* (1983), Guyanese poet Grace Nichols illustrates how the Black woman artist's representation and construction of the past as a resource assist the goals of group preservation and of charting enabling futures. In this long narrative poem, the history of Slavery is revisited and represented as a well from which new and transformative options can be drawn.

One of Slavery's most crippling legacies is its characterization of African peoples as "will-less objects" devoid of human agency who consequently made no effort to free themselves. This characterization forms part of an extensive (and continuing) epistemological assault. As filmmaker Haile Gerima has observed: "For four hundred years Black people's equation of Slavery is shame. Because White people have been able to dethrone the role Black people played in freeing themselves. In the paradigm of that narrative White people actually superimpose themselves as the heroes of that story. In fact, they were the guests of the story, of that historical chapter."[4] As constructed within the master narrative of Slavery, enslaved Africans were, from the outset, the rescued—a people "saved" from benighted and primitive conditions on the "dark continent." The master narrative of Emancipation reiterated this indebtedness, again casting freed Africans as the rescued—a people "delivered" from perpetual, though benign, servitude through the unstinting efforts of White abolitionists. Both narratives negate Black people's human agency and distort the extensive history of their efforts at, and strategies for, self-emancipation. In doing so, these narratives discursively erased Black people's humanity. A recent reinscription of this subject positioning can be found in Stephen Spielberg's *Amistad* (1997), in which the focus on the efforts of the White rescuer usurps the film's ostensible focus on a group of self-emancipated Africans.[5]

Yet, as John Hope Franklin and Loren Schweninger's study *Runaway Slaves: Rebels on the Plantation* (1999) amply demonstrates, documents created by Whites in the Slavery era provide extensive evidence of widespread dissidence and resistance to enslavement. Relying on "notice[s] of runaways in newspapers and petitions to Southern legislatures and county courts" (295), Franklin and Schweninger confirm that acts of resistance were commonplace. Of the many acts they document, the most significant were those acts—such as Jacobs's resistance to the definitions of her enslaver—aimed at promoting growth, by resisting the destruction of their humanity not simply as an ideological or imagistic rendering but also as a spiritual, psychological, and ethical—that is, *internal*—reality.

This view of the internal/psychological consequences of distorted representations informs Gerima's view of the spiritual aspects of his own artistic commitment. In describing the goal of independent Black filmmaking in relation to images and understandings of American Slavery in popular culture, Gerima, like other artists, has pointed to the continuing defamation of Black people's histories. In response to this defamation, he asserts that "the spiritual revolution . . . [is] to make the film to heal yourself."[6] Gerima's focus on the healing function of Black artistic expression coincides with the vision of Achebe, Morrison, Bambara, and others. More recently, Májozo has expanded upon this vision of the artist's responsibility to assess and respond positively to the community's psychological needs. In the essay "To Search for the Good and Make It Matter," she observes that "To be able to make truly visionary art, we artists must have in our lives the crucial element called dream time, that is, time when we leave this world and go into our own sacred space, seeking the grace needed to create our work. Dream time holds the turmoil and trauma of the world at bay and allows the vision to be granted and the healing notes to attune us" (92).

Like Nichols, Angelou, and others, Májozo views the work of art as a performance space in which artist and reader/viewer collaborate in the enactment of healing transformations that affirm self. She notes that for the artist, "this deliberate pausing is also part of our work, and, in reality, it may be the only thing that distinguishes us from those community members who simply cannot make the time to take this inner space. Yet they are depending as much on us to hear the calls and sound the first responses as we are depending on them to form a chorus for the song in order to release the healing and magnify the truth" (92).

Like *Beloved, Mother of the River,* and other Black women's narratives that revisit Slavery, Nichols's *i is a long memoried woman* privileges the representation of self-affirming acts of resistance as it repositions Black people as agents in their own histories. One of the most significant aspects of this long narrative poem is its detailing of the resources and strategies used to cope with the daily challenges of Slavery. The depiction of Black women's resourcefulness and creativity in negotiating a range of psychospiritual assaults is a primary component of Nichols's strategy for positioning readers to draw new conclusions from the well of the past.

As in other Black women's texts, silence is framed as a discursive modality in *i is a long memoried woman*. In the epigraph with which the poem opens, the speaker demonstrates its complexity and efficacy.

> From dih pout
> of mih mouth
> from dih
> treacherous
> calm of mih
> smile
> you can tell
>
> **I is a long memoried woman** (4)

Silence here is multivalent. First, it functions—in conjunction with the speaker's smile—as a form of *masking*. It conceals a world of thought, a world of memory behind the speaker's mask of a "calm" demeanor. Second, it reflects the speaker's awareness of the manner in which she has been represented in the "master narrative" of Slavery—as the "smiling darky." Third, it mocks and perhaps cautions against the epistemological limitations intrinsic to the gaze and interpretive position crafted by the "master('s) narrative." Can you really "tell," the long memoried woman asks, what's behind "dih / *treacherous* / calm of mih / smile"? And finally, it unequivocally proclaims the speaker's cultural and linguistic sovereignty. By transliterating this self-declarative statement to emphasize the speaker's Caribbean nation language,[7] Nichols announces that, in breaking her silence, this long memoried woman intends to speak in her own voice, on her own terms. The epigraph, then, summarizes Nichols's project: to explore the complex *interior* world of the Black woman during Slavery in order to reveal the ways in which her reliance on cultural/spiritual traditions facilitated her survival and the ways in which the text of that history can expand the reader's options for exercising creative agency.

i is a long memoried woman details the daily assaults that Black women faced during Slavery, and the resources and strategies that assisted their survival and growth. This narrative offers an expansive view of spirituality, presenting it as the primary resource enslaved Africans relied upon for their survival. The vignette depicting the painful and ritualized execution of the "rebel woman" is instructive. In an act of visual terrorism, their enslavers compel the women to watch the painful death of Uzo, the "rebel woman," whose body has been coated in molasses. This spectacle is meant to stun them into fearful passivity. They, however, redefine and enact their own proper role and responsibility in this situation. The narrator states that "while the ants feed / and the sun blind her with / his fury / we the women sing and weep / as we work," offering an intercessory prayer to the Igbo earth goddess:

> O Ala
> Uzo is due to join you
> to return to the pocket
> of your womb
> . . . .
> O Ala
> Mother who gives and receives
> again in death
> Gracious one
> have sympathy
> let her enter
> let her rest (24)

In another instance, the long memoried woman describes the woman, raped by her enslaver, who the very first "time she knew / she was carrying / she wanted to / cry out. . . / to retch / herself / empty" (52). Her painful ambivalence toward this pregnancy is poignantly described in her plea, "Cover me with the leaves of your / blackness Mother / shed tears / for I'm tainted with guilt and / exile / I'm burden with child and maim" (53). The refrain— "Mother I need I crave your blessing / Mother I need I crave your blessing" —points to a quest for and reliance on ancestral guidance. With this assistance, the expectant mother is able to fashion a way out of her emotional crisis and to construct a redefinition of the child necessary to her psychological well-being. In this poem, Nichols reveals the type of agency enslaved Black women exerted in choosing and redefining an enabling kinship with children who are the product of rape, children fathered by their enslavers. Here and elsewhere, women are shown depending on their own spiritual consciousness and spiritual agency in combating psychospiritual assaults.

In its portrait of the inner resources that enabled them to transcend oppressive circumstances, *i is a long memoried woman* emphasizes its gendered vision of the challenges and triumphs of life in Slavery. The narrator calls attention to Black women's contributions to collective survival, praising "the women making / something from this / ache-and-pain-a-me / back-o-hardness" (13). At the same time, however, she notes that these contributions are erased and overlooked—"we the women / who praises go unsung / who voices go unheard / who deaths they sweep / aside / as easy as dead leaves." The progression from "clear fetch dig" to "sing" in the final stanza indicates that this "rememory" is both a lament and a celebration.

By way of remembering/recollecting African women's experiences, the narrative consciousness spans several perspectives, expressing a multidimensional narrative self-consciousness. Here, Nichols seeks to re-collect the dispersed aspects of African cultural history through simultaneous consideration of experiences that are multidimensional geographically, linguistically, temporally, and in gender terms. The alternating use of first-person and third-person narration indicates that while the text focuses on a single protagonist, this woman is a collective persona. After the initial emergence from the "middle passage womb," the narrator recalls that:

> . . . being born a woman
> she moved again
> knew it was the Black Beginning
> though everything said it was
> the end
>
> And she went forth with others of her kind
> to scythe the earth knowing that bondage
> would not fall like poultice from the
> children's forehead

But O she grieved for them
walking beadless
in another land (7)

The speaker's multiple locations—in the "New World" going "forth with others of her kind / to scythe the earth"; walking the Gold Coast, the Louisiana coast, the coast of Grenada "griev[ing] for them / walking beadless / in another land"—attests to the multiplicity of this "I" narrative consciousness and the variety of experiences that form part of this long memory.

Consistent with its multidimensional structure, the poem remembers several different women and men. The narrator remembers Uzo, "the rebel woman," who with a pin "stick the soft mould of her own child's head / sending the little-newborn soul winging its way back to Africa—free" (23). She also remembers the woman who, with "the cutlass in her hand / could not cut through / the days that fell / like bramble" "and the destruction that / threatened to choke / within" (11). She remembers the Black man who, like sugarcane, ". . . isn't what / he seem—/ indifferent hard / and sheathed in blades / his waving arms / is a sign for help / his skin thick / only to protect / the juice inside / himself" (32). And she remembers the revolutionary leader Toussaint L'Overture of Haiti, imprisoned in France but "dying with hope" (77).

A similar use of a multidimensional collective Black woman consciousness informs visual artist and sculptor Elizabeth Catlett's woodcut portraits *The Negro Woman Series* (1946–47). Each of the portraits of Black women ancestors—Phillis Wheatley, Sojourner Truth, Harriet Tubman, and others—features a narrative caption that underscores their collective consciousness and reliance on collective agency. In one version of the captions for the individual portraits, Catlett uses a two-sentence structure. For example, the Phillis Wheatley portrait reads: "*I'm* Phillis Wheatley. *I* proved intellectual equality in the midst of slavery" (emphasis added). The contrast between this syntax and another variant underscores Catlett's intentions in crafting these short narratives. The variant for the Wheatley portrait, for example, reads: "In Phillis Wheatley I proved intellectual equality in the midst of slavery." Similarly, the variant for the Truth portrait reads: "In Sojourner Truth I fought for the rights of women as well as Blacks." The one-sentence caption expresses a very distinct view of the speaking subject, the unidentified "I," as a collective Black woman consciousness/persona. It might also refer to a divine speaking subject—God—testifying to the expression of righteous agency through Black women's lives. Whether describing direct or indirect agency, the ancestral consciousness and voice in these portraits emanates from, and is articulated through, the artist's consciousness. Here Catlett, the artist, displays the mediational agency of the priestess. A similar structure and narrative strategy are at work in Nichols's text.

In *i is a long memoried woman,* Nichols uses a gendered symbol—waist beads—to explore and represent collective consciousness and collective history. The text introduces this image in one of the early poems when the long memoried woman laments the fact that her life, like broken waist beads, "has slipped out / of my possession" (21). The waist beads referred to here are traditionally worn by African women; they clothe, protect, and are a symbol of female authority. And unlike an amulet that forms a single linear band, waist beads consist of concentric layers of strung beads. Significantly, the individual beads are relational—that is, they form and embody a "web of kin," Nichols's term for African diaspora peoples—only when woven together. Thus, when this long memoried woman, a "Child of the middle passage womb," declares, "But I / armed only with / my mother's smile / must be forever gathering / my life together like scattered beads" (20), the text equates the loss of kinship ties and collective self-consciousness with a doubly inflected dispersion.

The protagonist's awareness of her own "beadlessness" and her queries about her own cultural/religious symbols precipitate a quest for her missing history. Logically, therefore, the journey in *i is a long memoried woman* is from the dispersion signified in the conscious "beadlessness" to the finished re-collection/restringing described in the closing piece, "Holding My Beads." This title signals the fulfillment of one of the primary objectives of the narrative: to re-collect four centuries of African diaspora history and to reclaim the heterogeneous elements of an African cultural consciousness. Its completion is announced by the narrator's calm declaration of the successful concatenation of her multiple consciousnesses and histories:

> Unforgiving as the course of justice
> Inerasable as my scars and fate
> I am here

> a woman . . . . . with all my lives
> strung out like beads
> before me (79)

Without undermining the identities of its individual constituents, the text reassembles these so that the African woman narrator leaves "*holding* her beads," having restrung them into new configurations.

> It isn't privilege or pity
> that I seek
> . . . .
> but
> the power to be what I am / a woman
> charting my own futures / a woman
> holding my beads in my hand (79)

In the epilogue that concludes her narrative, Nichols indicates, as does the title, that a pivotal aspect of the power to be one's self as an African of the diaspora lies in the power to (re)name self and experience, which in turn depends on the creation and affirmation of one's own language:

> I have crossed an ocean
> I have lost my tongue
> from the root of the old
> one
> a new one has sprung (80)

Notwithstanding the differences between the material conditions of the Slavery era and life in the twenty-first century, the psychospiritual demands of life in the contemporary era are not, Nichols suggests, categorically different from what they were two centuries ago. Then, as now, growth required a clear understanding of one's human possibilities, responsibilities, and needs. Then, as now, women had to know what their specific gendered humanity meant on its own terms. The question of an enslaved Black woman to her absent mother in the poem "Sacred Flame" is as urgent today as it was then: "What was your secret mother— / the one that made you a woman / and not just Akosua's wife" (20). The long memoried woman's answer is as significant today as it was then:

Our women
the ones I left behind
always know the taste
of their own strength —
bitter at times it might
be (20)

Nichols's narrator/priestess confirms that in addition to ancestral guidance, kinship ties, prayer, and other resources, the cultural concept and definition of an empowered womanhood is one of the primary features supporting the goals of the paradigm of growth.

Maya Angelou's *Down in the Delta* (1999) offers an expanded view of the ways in which a commitment to the goals of the paradigm of growth can inform artistic praxis. Of the films discussed in this study, *Down in the Delta* is the only one produced in Hollywood. In fact, it is one of a few Black women's films—following the path of *Daughters of the Dust* (1992), and along with Kasi Lemmon's *Eve's Bayou* (1999) and Gina Prince-Blythewood's *Love and Basketball* (2000)—to receive theatrical distribution. *Down in the Delta* attests to the commitment of the Black woman artist to empowering viewers to become agents of transformation. This analysis examines its depiction of family snapshots framed by the paradigm of growth and its implications for the future direction and development of Black women's cinema.

Down in the Delta explores intersecting crises involving a young Black woman, her two children, her mother, and members of the extended family. The Loretta (Alfre Woodard) we encounter early in the film is incapable of defining or developing right relationships, or of embracing responsibilities. She is neither a daughter to Rosa Lynn (Mary Alice) nor a mother to Thomas (Mpho Koaho) and Tracy (Kulani Hassen). In its exploration and resolution of the crisis precipitated by Loretta's self-endangering behavior and the spiritual and emotional disconnection that prompt it, the film illustrates how the past—specifically, the subtext of Slavery—can function as a resource for renewing creative agency. In so doing, it underscores the importance of interconnectedness, the importance of ancestors, the role of male nurturers, and the significance of intergenerational transfers. These aspects all converge in the centralized icon of the candelabra, "Nathan."

While Nichols's long memoried woman conceptualizes the past as waist beads, suggesting the multiplicity and interconnectedness of the individual memories that go into its construction, the past here is represented in the figure of the candelabra. The representation of the great-great grandfather in the figure of the candelabra underscores the role of ancestors and the past in anchoring the present. The candelabra, "Nathan," functions totemically in the film. Its many branches symbolize the importance of kinship ties. As an object that provides illumination, it is a visual representation of the ways in which ancestral/historical consciousness can expand vision and unveil future possibilities. Moreover, its status as a family heirloom underscores the importance of intergenerational transfers of memory and knowledge. And finally, its decorative function recalls Achebe's assessment of the duality of aesthetics and functionality, a duality informing the creation of art-as-history, art-as-archaeology, African art.

The film represents the subtext of Slavery as an enabling and empowering inheritance. Down in the Delta, on the site of oppression, definitions of Loretta's identity and possibilities are encoded and preserved. This knowledge, whose transmission is both facilitated by and associated with the ancestor Nathan, enables her to decipher and construct empowering and life-affirming relationships. The film's iconic representation of the ancestor in the figure of the candelabra illuminates the transfers facilitated through ancestor relationships. Nathan's history provides a type of illumination, understanding, and insight that are prerequisites for growth and survival. Hearing the story of how Jesse lost his father, Nathan; of his futile search to find him; and of the efforts he made to keep his family together gives Loretta a new appreciation for her mother and a new definition of her own responsibility as a mother.

Like other works discussed in this study, the film's commitment to the goals of the paradigm of growth appears in each of its many elements. Prominent among these is its concern with the figure of the male nurturer Uncle Earl (Al Freeman Jr.). Her relationship with Uncle Earl helps Loretta to regain a sense of kinship, identity, and belonging. He is also the catalyst for the recovery of her dignity and the authority that comes with exercising creative agency. Significantly, Uncle Earl plays a major role in relation to the recovery, growth, and survival of both female and male offspring. In his relationships with Loretta, Thomas, Tracy, and his wife, Annie (Esther Rolle), Angelou provides a rare and moving portrait of a nurturing man. The film expresses an ethos of interconnectedness in its insistence that women and men are equally empowered by the male nurturer.

The significance of Angelou's successful portrait of a nurturing man can be measured by the contrasting example of John Singleton's character Melvin (Ving Rhames) in *Baby Boy* (2001). In this film, Singleton sets out to provide an analysis of the factors contributing to the emotional underdevelopment of *some* young Black men and to suggest possible avenues for transformation. Singleton uses a documentary format in the opening sequence to announce the film's analytical disposition. However, what we get in *Baby Boy* is faux analysis and faux transformation.

Despite the film's implicit claim to the contrary, the surrogate father-figure, the ex-con Melvin, is an inadequate and failed model of the nurturing male needed to assist Jody's (Tyrese Gibson) transformation from emotional underdevelopment into a full adulthood. In fact, the film's premise that only a father-figure can assist emotional maturation is a dubious assumption that recurs in several of Singleton's films. In that sense, *Baby Boy* is an obvious remake of Singleton's first feature film, *Boyz in the Hood* (1991). In both works, dysfunctional behavior among young Black men is traced to a Black woman–headed household, an obvious rearticulation of the narrative of the Black matriarch. Consistent with the masculinlist narrative it upholds, the mere (and frequently uncommunicative) presence of a Black man is deemed enough to stabilize. Although Jody's mother tells us—at the end of the film— that Jody and Melvin "talked the other night," Singleton is unable to imagine and represent a conversation between a young Black man and an older father-figure.

In its deep focus on Melvin's sexual potency and prowess, the film anchors its vision of empowerment in interactions centered on a hypersexualized consciousness. To a large extent, therefore, *Baby Boy* reiterates the phallocentric definition of transformation articulated in Melvin Van Peebles's 1970s *Sweet Sweetback's Baadasssss Song*. Singleton perhaps pays tribute to Van Peebles in the model/male nurturer Melvin. Like *Baby Boy*, *Sweetback* provides audiences with a portrait of transformation in which graphic and gratuitous sex acts are meant to suggest a revolutionary disposition. Sweetback's revolutionary demeanor is represented by his sexual prowess.

In Van Peebles's Sweetback (played by himself), one can discern an attempt to replicate aspects of the psychologically complex protagonist, plot structure, and analysis articulated in Ralph Ellison's *Invisible Man*. *Sweetback*, however, failed to offer an enabling vision of possibilities for transformation—intellectual or otherwise—that the Black community could utilize. At the same time, the visual potency of its masculinist discourse was seized upon and duplicated in several imitations, most notably the *Shaft* series. As in *Sweetback*, the intellectual sources that generate a transformed/revolutionary consciousness in *Baby Boy* are equally mysterious. Like *Sweetback*, *Baby Boy*'s prominent display of sex acts caters to and reinforces a voyeuristic spectatorship. More important, it reinscribes a definition of empowered Black manhood within a masculinist framework.

Unlike Singleton's Melvin, Uncle Earl is neither muscle-bound nor testosterone-loaded. Rather, he is gifted with an understanding that "taking care of" other people is an integral part of a healthy manhood. His description of his relationship with his wife, Annie, makes it clear that this does not begin with crisis or illness but with love and with a definition of the responsibilities involved in kinship. As testimony to this vision, he recognizes the danger in Thomas's perception of guns as accessories and embraces the responsibility of instilling in him an awareness of the value of life, of what it means to lose something, someone beloved.

Uncle Earl's relationship with both Loretta and Thomas points to the many intergenerational transfers developing in this film. In its depiction of other relationships, especially the relationship between the ailing Aunt Annie and Tracy, and between Loretta and Aunt Annie, the film reveals that these transfers must expand in multiple directions to bring the process of growth full circle.

In addition to its thematic focus on an ethos of interconnectedness, *Down in the Delta* deploys spatial narration as a cinematic technique for representing diaspora communities by means of saturation. In *Understanding the New Black Poetry*, written in the early 1970s, Stephen Henderson identified "saturation" as an essential feature of Black poetry, an insight that is still instructive today. Henderson defined "saturation" as "(a) the communication of Blackness in a given situation, and (b) a sense of fidelity to the observed and intuited truth of the Black Experience" (62). The reaction of Black audiences to independent Black cinema often correlates with the filmmaker's success in spatially narrating this saturation. In the absence of saturation, Black audiences are frequently unable to recognize the space being represented as a Black text or context. The beach space in *Daughters of the Dust* is a useful example. There are no objects or markings that signal to the viewer that a Black presence occupies this landscape. The landscape isn't simply undomesticated; it is unsaturated and therefore unrecognizable for Black audiences. By contrast, *Down in the Delta* exemplifies some of the ways in which Black filmmakers can meet the challenge of spatially narrating cultural context and cultural presence.

Although *Down in the Delta* is not an independent film, it resists many of the narrative conventions that attend mainstream cinema and that undermine the viewer's autonomy. The deliberateness with which it resists an overaestheticized representation of this family is significant. So, too, is its refusal of the narrative of Black pathology typically evoked by drug addiction. By way of avoiding the prefabricated analysis the pathology narrative offers, the film points to the socioeconomic and psychological factors that fuel Loretta's alcohol/drug habit. Her failed attempt to find employment as a cashier—and the despair it unleashes—reveals a hidden angst over her own lack of training for employment. Drug addiction in the Black community, the film suggests, is neither inexplicable nor the result of some unexpurgated primeval preference for (self-)destruction. Rather, it is frequently a logical product of the despair of having no way out because of a lack of education, professional training, and employment opportunities. In its brief exposure of Loretta's despair, the film acknowledges her private hunger for creative agency, the main ingredient for her subsequent transformation. In so doing, it resists the Hollywood prescription of a utopian resolution, suggesting instead that Loretta's growth is a logical, not a "magical," outcome.

As in Angelou's film, growth and transformation are represented as logical—*not* magical—outcomes of frequently painful choices in Estella Conwill Májozo's memoir, *Come Out the Wilderness* (1999). In this autobiographical narrative, Májozo explores the new futures being envisioned and charted by Black women artists. Like *i is a long memoried woman*, Májozo's memoir is structured by a sophisticated antiphony of personal experience and cultural history. Like Angelou's film and Nichols's narrative poem, it spans two temporal realms. Here, however, the expanse is shorter—from the 1950s to the 1990s.

Come Out the Wilderness offers snapshots in the life of a Black woman-child journeying into an artist/activist/priestess adulthood. The titles of the chapters emphasize the doubling of personal experience and cultural history in this memoir. The spirituals from which the titles are borrowed exemplify this duality as well. Originating in the crucible of Slavery, they were expressions of individual grief and longing that reverberated with and gave voice to a collective sorrow. The choice of the spirituals as a titular and thematic motif underscores the centrality of voicing to Estella's development and to the work's autobiographical design. In every instance, voicing/telling becomes a vehicle and mechanism for enlarging her own and the reader's field of vision. In fact, the work depicts a symbiotic relationship between voicing and coming to vision, a pattern that emerges in a variety of experiences ranging from childhood interactions with her brothers to interactions with her two husbands, fellow artists, and fellow academics.

A primary aspect of Estella's story involves figuring out what is going on and what she therefore must do. Early in the narrative, Májozo offers an interpretation of the title and of the pedagogical goals that propel her narrative. "There are jungles and gardens everywhere," she realizes. "Each has its own potential and requires a particular bearing, and each remains a wilderness until we figure out the demeanor that will enable us to perform our creative capacity within that landscape. And at the moment of that recognition we are out of the wilderness" (25). The book then is a survey of these landscapes—of the jungles and gardens in which claiming interpretive agency is a prerequisite for exercising righteous agency. In each landscape, the narrative focuses on the artist/priestess modeling the habit of decoding/interpreting. Perhaps the most complicated and challenging of these terrains are the landscape of marriage, the contemporary professional (academic) landscape, and the landscape comprised of the artist's own public/professional arena.

Among its many insights, the book offers a definition of the work of art whose construction is carefully designed to bear and increase life-force. While taking her first course on Black women's literature, Estella realizes that "for those women who didn't have the family genealogy or model for passing on strength, the example could still be found in literature. I realized why Nikki Giovanni had taken such pains to describe the role of her grandmother, Louvenia, in her life; why Margaret Walker Alexander, in 'For My People,' labored to bring forth a vision of hope" (140). Art, she discovers, is a vehicle for distributing ancestral resources.

While it affirms and elucidates the social function of art, the memoir provides a surprisingly uncensored exploration of the difficult/problematic responsibility of having to provide "food" for all. Following an argument with her brother, sculptor Houston Conwill, Estella confesses, "I could not, as a Black woman and artist, accept what I deemed to be the stereotypical, culturally assigned role of wet-nurse for the world, feeding from my substance whatever viper voiced a loud or greedy enough demand for food" (228). While the text offers no easy resolution of this dilemma, it provides an important analysis of the risks (and responsibilities) the artist faces in her prayer: "I just want you to teach us, Lord of the wilderness, how to make of our art an offering like manna, invulnerable to the greed of those who would hoard it for themselves and control the supply and try to resell it to the needy. . . . show us how to make art that truly serves the hungry" (228).

In the name "Mâjozo," which she adopts in the latter part of the autobiography, Estella embraces a composite of roles and responsibilities derived from the examples of educator Mary Macleod Bethune; artist (musician) and activist Josephine Baker; and writer and folklorist Zora Neale Hurston. These roles encapsulate the multidimensional agenda of this memoir—a text designed to provide maps, charts, and instructions in its imperative call to readers to come out the wilderness.

Afterword

We listen to those of us who speak, write, read, to those who have written, to those who may write. We write to those who write, read, speak, may write, and we try to hear the voiceless. We are participants in a many-voiced palaver of thought/feeling, image/language that moves us to *move*—toward a world where, like Alice Walker's revolutionary petunias, all of us can bloom.

—BARBARA CHRISTIAN

The writers and filmmakers whose works have been examined here are just a few of the many Black women artists who share a commitment to the goals of the paradigm of growth. It is important to note, however, that literature and cinema are just two of the channels through which the Black woman bearing life-force and the living past fulfills her responsibility for inspiring, exemplifying, and promoting growth and thereby group preservation. Other channels frequently intersect with and help distribute the priestess's resources.

In the essay "The Highs and the Lows of Black Feminist Criticism" from which the epigraph above is excerpted, Barbara Christian reminds us that in order to stay grounded, to stay relevant, to stay true to the communities from which we gather our most critical insights and inspiration, it is incumbent upon us to make the effort to transcend the divide between the "high" and the "low" that the academy esteems and maintains. We must look beyond the academic arena (the "high world") to the many other arenas (the "low world") in which the view of spirituality as a life-affirming ideology is publicized and celebrated.

Barbara Christian's timely counsel exemplifies the ways in which what I have called in this study an *ethos of interconnectedness* can prompt us to chart new paths in our various contemporary locations. It also directs our attention to the continuities/linkages that can be forged among our various locations. Of the many contemporary Black women whose lives and careers evidence this capacity to chart new paths and forge new linkages, none is perhaps as striking as the 2004 Nobel Peace Prize laureate: the scientist, educator, activist, and—since 2003—elected member of the Kenyan government, Dr. Wangari Maathai.

Internationally renowned for mobilizing poor, rural women in Kenya to plant 30 million trees over a period of about three decades through the Green Belt Movement, Dr. Maathai was lauded by the Nobel Committee for her "holistic approach to sustainable development that embraces democracy, human rights and women's rights in particular."[1] Given her intersecting involvement in promoting sustainable economic development, environmental preservation, democracy initiatives, conflict resolution initiatives, and projects to empower poor, rural women, Dr. Maathai's career provides a most compelling example of the Black woman priestess in civil society whose political vision is informed by an ethos of interconnectedness. In addition to significant socioeconomic and political ramifications, the activity that has been at the heart of Dr. Maathai's activism—tree planting—has cultural and spiritual resonance as well. As she explained in her "Nobel Peace Prize Acceptance Speech," during the lengthy struggle to promote democratic reforms "the tree also became a symbol for peace and conflict resolution . . . in keeping with widespread African tradition. For example, the elders of the Kikuyu carried a staff from the thigi tree that, when placed between disputing sides, caused them to stop fighting and seek reconciliation." In choosing to work with a constituency that, for many, represents the quintessentially "powerless"—poor, rural, African women—Dr. Maathai has amply demonstrated how the Black woman priestess in civil society rejects the binary divide between the "powerful" and "powerless," recognizing and giving direction to her people's creative agency. Clearly, the priestess's vocation continues to evolve to fit changing needs amid changing circumstances.

NOTES

Introduction

1. Like the term "war," which is capitalized in designating specific instances of war—the Vietnam War, World War II, and so on—the term "slavery" is capitalized in referring to the event involving the abduction and commercial deportation of Africans to the Americas—North America, South America, and the Caribbean—from the sixteenth through the nineteenth century, that is, American Slavery.

2. See Truffaut, "A Certain Tendency of the French Cinema," and Wollen, "The *Auteur* Theory."

3. For a comprehensive discussion of this term and its connection to Du Bois' "second sight," see Ryan, "Contested Visions/Double-Vision in *Tar Baby*."

4. Conversation with Davis, March 2001, Delaware, Ohio.

1. Interpreting Spirituality

1. Although the paradigm of resistance, like Victor Anderson's "ontological blackness," arises from the ideology of race—what he calls "white racial ideology"—there are some notable differences between the two concepts. While Anderson presents ontological blackness, in his book *Beyond Ontological Blackness*, as a "philosophy of racial consciousness" restricting Black people's self-apprehension, the paradigm of resistance is an interpretive and pedagogical model employed by Whites, Blacks, and others. It confounds social relationships by restricting interpretive options first in the textbook/classroom, even when Blacks are neither subjects of study nor present in the textbook/classroom.

2. One of the most intense debates in twentieth-century African American literary criticism was the debate over the comparative merits of so-called "protest fiction," or resistance literature—of which Richard Wright's *Native Son* was widely considered the quintessential example—and the so-called "literature of affirmation," of which Zora Neale Hurston's *Their Eyes Were Watching God* was representative. In "Notes toward a Black Balancing of Love and Hatred" (1974), essayist and poet June Jordan provided one of the most astute commentaries on this debate when she observed that "the functions of protest and affirmation are not, ultimately, distinct: that, for instance, affirmation of Black values and lifestyle within the American context is, indeed, an act of protest" (87). Noting that these categories were part of a system of "dividing the world into unnecessary conflict," Jordan further cautioned that "we

should take care so that we will lose none of the jewels of our soul" (85). Following Jordan's analysis, resistance is here located *within* the paradigm of growth as a necessary aspect of a commitment to growth.

3. For a complete discussion, see "Slavery and the Circle of Culture" in Sterling Stuckey's *Slave Culture: Nationalist Theory and the Foundations of Black America.*

4. For discussion of early indications of this consciousness among enslaved Africans, see John Blasssingame's *The Slave Community,* and Howard McGary's "Forgiveness and Slavery" in *Between Slavery and Freedom: Philosophy and American Slavery.* In interpreting "the apparent forgiving attitude of black slaves" as an action prompted by "rational self-interest" (92), McGary points to the type of negotiations that their commitment to the paradigm of growth necessitated.

5. Morrison, "Interview with Christina Davis," 230.

6. In subsequent writings, most notably "Unspeakable Things Unspoken" and *Playing in the Dark,* Morrison fully explores the influence of this taxonomy of "race" on White writers. Indeed, the latter work explores the crisis (among some nineteenth-century White American writers) precipitated by the desire to resist/refuse the "privilege" of misnaming Black culture as the sign, symbol, and substance of "defect."

7. Throughout this discussion, the word "African" is used interchangeably with "Black" to denote cultural identity and praxis, in contradistinction from its usage to denote a collective geopolitical nationality. The term "continental African" is used to indicate the latter.

8. Among the first scholarly works to examine this subject was an article by Mildred Hill-Lubin published in 1982. In "African Religion: That Invisible Institution in African and African-American Literature," she examined novels by Chinua Achebe, James Baldwin, and Ngũgĩ wa Thiong'o, arguing that "a primary focus of these works is the impact of religion on the lives of the characters." In that sense, she concluded, "The works are essentially religious novels."

9. While the prevailing view holds that philosophies "illuminate" while ideologies "distort," at least one observer has noted the contingent nature of this distinction. In *Political Ideologies and Political Philosophies,* H. B. McCullough notes: "It is not at all uncommon to consider the political views of our adversary as ideological and the political views of our own as philosophical. We mark our adversary's views as suspicious and our own as acceptable" (2). As used throughout this analysis, therefore, "ideology" refers to a way of thinking and/or system of ideas developed by and in the interest of a specific group or constituency. Ideologies, therefore, are never neutral, but they are not always/necessarily hegemonic. Functionally, ideologies are systematic strategies for structuring social formations, group identities. As James Kavanagh defines it, "Ideology designates a rich 'system of representations,' worked up in specific material practices, which help form individuals into social subjects" (310).

10. Although I use the term "traditional" here, I agree with theologian Mercy Amba Oduyoye's critique of its implications. In "African Primal Religions," in *Hearing and Knowing*, Oduyoye writes: "I refer to traditional religion . . . as the primal religion of Africa because it is the religion of Africa unadulterated by Islam, Christianity, or any other system of belief. I do not call it 'traditional' because that word implies something 'customary,' something practiced without modification, or unthinkingly carried on just because that is how it has always been" (57).

11. In the modern world, territorial/national boundaries no longer coincide with or contain single cultural identities and linguistic traditions. Consequently, the term "cultural domain" acknowledges the continuing connectedness among globally distributed communities who claim a particular cultural identity and heritage. This means that, in addition to the African cultural domain, one can equally identify the Asian cultural domain, the European cultural domain, and so on.

12. Throughout this analysis, this term is used to mean literally and metaphysically centered on Africa, a specific cultural domain. This usage is not to be confused with the term "Afrocentric," which has accrued many pejorative meanings, apart from its own initial/intrinsic debilitation. Barbara Christian aptly summarizes these shortcomings: "In effect the use of the term *centrism* betrays the fact that Afrocentrism is generated from narrow nationalist Western thinking, that it is akin to Eurocentrism, to which it is apparently opposed but which it mimics. Thus many contemporary forms of Afrocentrism undercut the very concept they were intended to propose, that there are different interpretations of history, different narratives, depending on where one is positioned, in terms of power relations as well as distinctive cultures and that there are, given the various cultures of our world, multiple philosophical approaches to understanding life" (7). See also Cheryl Townsend Gilkes, "We Have a Beautiful Mother: Womanist Musings on the Afrocentric Idea." According to Townsend Gilkes, Afrocentrism "signifies a commitment to standing in the middle of the black experience, either in the United States or in Africa or worldwide, and starting one's thinking there" (26).

13. In *White over Black*, Winthrop Jordan discusses the eighteenth-century amalgamation of the theory of the "Great Chain of Being" and the ideology of "race."

14. Viola's disposition contrasts with that of late nineteenth-century Afro-Christian leaders and activists for whom David Walker's vision of Black people exercising creative agency—alongside of, and under, God—to liberate themselves was biblically sanctioned and exemplary.

15. A central thesis of this analysis is the integrity and, indeed, the inevitability of culturally informed and nuanced engagements with Christianity. It is, therefore, important to note the existence and integrity of Euro-Christianity, a theological range comparable to Afro-Christianity but distinguishable from what is here defined as "Christendom."

16. 2 Cor. 5:17; *NRSV.*

17. "As many of you as were baptized into Christ have clothed yourselves with Christ. There is no longer Jew or Greek, there is no longer slave or free, there is no longer male and female; for all of you are one in Christ Jesus." Gal. 3:27–28; *NRSV.*

18. It bears mentioning that Black women visual artists—like Elizabeth Catlett, Faith Ringgold, Betye Saar, and Carrie Mae Weems—have also pioneered in engaging these questions.

19. Although indigo does not permanently stain the hands, Dash has said that she wanted to use this image of stained hands "as a symbol of slavery, to create a new kind of icon around slavery rather than the traditional showing of the whip marks or the chains." As she explains, "we've seen all those things before and we've become very calloused about them. I wanted to show it in a new way" (31).

2. Embracing Responsibility

All quotations in this chapter from the works of Maria Stewart, except those identified as part of her *Meditations,* are taken from the works collected in *Maria W. Stewart, America's First Black Woman Political Writer: Essays and Speeches,* edited by Marilyn Richardson (Bloomington: Indiana University Press, 1987).

1. See Deborah Gray White's *Ar'n't I a Woman,* 131.

2. In light of the oratorical and rhetorical features of Stewart's essays and speeches, Richardson identifies her as "predecessor to Sojourner Truth, Frederick Douglass, Henry Highland Garnet, Frances Harper, and other black nineteenth-century masters of language deployed to change society" (14).

3. I am indebted to Emilie Townes for pointing out that, in keeping with the vision of the Second Great Awakening, these evangelical preachers were more concerned with the salvation of souls and saw this as the means of promoting a just social order.

4. While Meditation I is addressed to "My Friends," each of the subsequent thirteen refers to God as the explicit audience designate. The tension that one notices in these texts can be traced to their dual role as a private realm/diary that is also *intended* for public/ecclesiastical use. For the most part, complaints against others are carefully veiled in, or refracted through, biblical language.

5. In *The Life and Religious Experience of Jarena Lee, A Coloured Lady* (1836), Lee asked: "If a man may preach, because the Saviour died for him, why not the woman? seeing he died for her also. . . . Didn't Mary *first* preach the risen Saviour, and is not the doctrine of the resurrection the very climax of Christianity—hangs not all our hope on this, as argued by St. Paul?" See William L. Andrews, ed., *Sisters of the Spirit: Three Black Women's Autobiographies of the Nineteenth Century,* 36.

6. For a comparative view of theodicy in the Black church, see Anthony B. Pinn's *Why, Lord?* Unlike Paris's analysis, however, Pinn's makes no reference to, nor does it consider, the preexisting ethical and philosophical understandings that enslaved

Africans brought with them and that must have and did shape their understanding of evil.

7. This analysis echoes insights offered in W. E. B. Du Bois' *Black Reconstruction* (1935).

3. Bearing Life-Force

1. The militancy that motivated this appropriation is clearly discernible in the words of the spiritual "Go Down, Moses," first popularized for mainstream audiences by the Fisk Jubilee Singers but perhaps most memorably rendered by Paul Robeson.

2. Delores Williams's treatment of the life of the biblical Hagar, in *Sisters in the Wilderness: The Challenge of Womanist God-Talk,* reflects a parallel attempt to imagine the life of someone who is both central to, and marginalized within, the patriarchal narrative.

3. For a comprehensive analysis of "African women's participation in the public spaces from which the male-dominated colonial paradigm excluded her," see Kalu's *Women, Literature, and Development in Africa.*

4. For full discussion of these two modes of biblical appropriation and their distinct foci on liberation and survival, respectively, see *Sisters in the Wilderness.*

5. While the Bond is generally regarded as the product of a bilateral agreement, the fact that "Each of the chiefs who were alleged to have signed this document could neither read, write nor speak English, the language in which the document was drawn" (80) points to Britain's imperialist aggression.

6. This aspect of the plot recalls and highlights Aidoo's diaspora focus in her earlier play *The Dilemma of a Ghost* (1965), which explores the conflicts and possibilities of transnational/transcultural diaspora relationships.

7. See Walter Rodney's *How Europe Underdeveloped Africa.* See also John Berger's parallel analysis in *Ways of Seeing.*

8. It's important to note that while Miriam is not described as having support in her development, Moses benefits from the wisdom and protection of two ancestors, Mentu and Jethro.

4. Reversing Dispossession

1. See Clyde Taylor's insightful analysis of aesthetics as a hegemonic mechanism in *The Mask of Art.*

2. In "Friday on the Potomac," the introductory essay in the volume *Race-ing Justice, En-gendering Power: Essays on Anita Hill, Clarence Thomas, and the Construction of Social Reality,* editor Toni Morrison analyzes the psychological consequences of this positioning for the rescued.

3. In *Race, Rape, and Lynching,* Sandra Gunning identifies Thomas Dixon, the author of the novel that Griffith adapted into film, as the true pioneer. "Dixon in fact

predates Griffith on the very subject of transferring the black rapist from the page to the stage," writes Gunning. "After the success in 1905 of his third novel, *The Clansman: An Historical Romance of the Ku Klux Klan*, he formed two production companies to tour the country simultaneously performing a play version of the novel, complete with fiery crosses and hooded Ku Klux Klansmen bounding across the stage on horseback, to the delight of national audiences" (28–29). Gunning notes that it was the success of the theatrical version that inspired Griffith to create the film.

4. In "Making History: Julie Dash," Patricia Mellencamp describes Mignon as "powerful" and as having "status and influence at the studio." However, Mellencamp later concedes that "like so many women in Hollywood, what she really wants she is unable to get—film projects of her own" (101).

5. The term "ideological whiteness" comes from Toni Morrison's analysis, in "Unspeakable Things Unspoken," of the nineteenth-century formation and "successful assertion of whiteness as ideology," that is, the concept of "racial superiority, of whiteness as privileged place in the evolutionary ladder of humankind" (16–18).

6. As a participant in the "L.A. Rebellion" involving members of the Los Angeles School of Black cinema, Dash's critical interrogation of the disabling conventions of classic Hollywood cinema laid the foundation for this discursive construction. See Ntongela Masilela's "Women Directors of the Los Angeles School."

7. Larkin's feature film *A Different Image* (1982) can also be considered a self-declarative text. Its focus, however, is on images of women in the lived public arena—especially the space of public consciousness—not in the film industry.

8. While critics have complained about low-budget effects in *Illusions*, Dash's genius in crafting a plot that makes use of low-budget elements—black-and-white filming, low-key lighting, and so on—demonstrates her artistic versatility.

9. This avenue of plot development is exemplified in *Pinky*. As Elspeth kydd notes in "'The Ineffaceable Curse of Cain'": Racial Marking and Embodiment in *Pinky*," "when Pinky is revealed to be black she loses rights over her own body" (104). White men who claim the honor of "protecting" (policing) White womanhood also claim the duty of preying on (policing) Black womanhood.

5. Renewing Self-Possession

1. In an interview at the Studio Museum in Harlem in November 1992, Dash explained: "My original vision was to do a silent feature film. I wanted to push the form." Responding to questions about the implications of calling the film "science fiction," Dash stated that "The film is a historical drama, speculative fiction i.e. science fiction." Dash's coinage of the term "speculative fiction" attempts to elide connotations of the unreal or untrue that the term "science fiction" carries and to assert the possibility of engaging the past—not just the future—as a speculative project. In choosing to depict the intracommunal functions of music, Palcy, too, attempts to re-

vise Hollywood constructions of the musical and to develop an "organic musical." As I discuss below, Blackwood's new "silent film" arises from a similar impulse.

2. By way of transforming this tendency, Ménil points to the fact that "The absence of the sea is quite pronounced" (162–63).

3. See "Interview with Euzhan Palcy," by June Givanni, in which the filmmaker notes: "I am dealing with children playing, jumping, fighting in *Rue Cases-Nègres*, so I had to have a camera on their level, and it was a hand-held camera, not a steady camera moving smoothly on a dolly" (301).

4. In a gesture of associative montage, the children's recitation of the definition of Hell is deliberately timed to coincide with the arrival of Léopold's father, the plantation owner, Mr. de Thorail.

5. See discussion in *Playing in the Dark: Whiteness and the Literary Imagination*, 6–7.

6. In "The Legacy of Slavery: Standards for a New Womanhood," in *Women, Race, and Class*, Angela Davis notes that "Neither Moynihan nor Rainwater . . . invented the theory of the Black family's internal deterioration under slavery" (14). In identifying Frazier's work as the source of this distortion, Davis states that while "Frazier dramatically described the horrendous impact of slavery on Black people, . . . he underestimated their ability to resist its insinuations into the social life they forged for themselves . . . [and] also misinterpreted the spirit of independence and self-reliance Black women necessarily developed" (14).

7. As Davis notes, "it is sometimes assumed that the typical female slave was a houseservant—either a cook, maid, or mammy for the children in the 'big house.' . . . As is so often the case, the reality is actually the diametrical opposite of the myth. Like the majority of slave men, slave women, for the most part, were field workers" (5).

8. See this chapter in Taylor's *The Mask of Art: Breaking the Aesthetic Contract—Film and Literature*.

9. Quoted in Gwendolyn Audrey Foster's *Women Filmmakers of the African and Asian Diaspora*, 140.

10. In fact, technology is rarely presented as intrinsically endangering or destabilizing in Black (women's) art; rather, its impact rests on the ideological intentions behind its deployment. Morrison makes a similar observation about industrialization and urban migration in "City Limits, Village Values."

6. Charting Futures

1. Gwendolyn Brooks, Maya Angelou, Nikki Giovanni, and Audre Lorde are some of the other Black women literary artists who have written autobiographies.

2. See, for example, Paris, *The Spirituality of African Peoples*; Herskovits, *The Myth of the Negro Past*; Raboteau, *Slave Religion*; Blassingame, *The Slave Commu-*

nity; Stuckey, *Slave Culture;* Levine, *Black Culture and Consciousness;* and Gomez, *Exchanging Our Country Marks.*

3. See Anthonia C. Kalu, "The Priest/Artist Tradition in Achebe's *Arrow of God,*" 51. See also Achebe's "Africa and Her Writers," in *Morning Yet on Creation Day.*

4. Remarks made at the conference "Images of Slavery in Popular Culture," Museum of American History, Washington, D.C., March 17, 2000.

5. For a comprehensive analysis of Slavery's "master narratives" and of the ways in which Spielberg's *Amistad* resuscitates these narratives, see Judylyn S. Ryan's "Dismantling Slavery's Master-Narratives through African Diaspora Cinema."

6. Remarks made at the "Images of Slavery in Popular Culture" conference.

7. "Nation language" is the term coined by African Caribbean poet and scholar Kamau Brathwaite to designate various Caribbean vernaculars, previously—and pejoratively—referred to as "broken English." Brathwaite's coinage reflects the linguistic, grammatical, and philosophical continuities between these "New World" vernaculars and various continental African languages, as well as their role in the construction and articulation of diaspora identities. For discussion see Edward Kamau Brathwaite, *History of the Voice: The Development of Nation Language in Anglophone Caribbean Poetry.*

Afterword

1. See the "2004 Nobel Peace Prize Announcement" in Maathai, *The Green Belt Movement,* ix.

SELECTED BIBLIOGRAPHY

Achebe, Chinua. *Morning Yet on Creation Day.* New York: Anchor/Doubleday, 1975.

Aidoo, Ama Ata. *"The Dilemma of a Ghost" and "Anowa."* 1970. London: Longman, 1987.

Amadiume, Ifi. *Reinventing Africa: Matriarchy, Religion, and Culture.* London and New York: Zed Books, 1997.

Anderson, Victor. *Beyond Ontological Blackness: An Essay on African American Religious and Cultural Criticism.* New York: Continuum, 1995.

Andrews, William L., ed. *Sisters of the Spirit: Three Black Women's Autobiographies of the Nineteenth Century.* Bloomington: Indiana University Press, 1986.

Andrews, William, and Nellie McKay, eds. *Toni Morrison's Beloved: A Casebook.* New York: Oxford University Press, 1999.

Anyidoho, Kofi, Abioseh M. Porter, Daniel Racine, and Janice Spleth, eds. *Interdisciplinary Dimensions of African Literature.* ALA and Three Continents Press, 1985.

Awoonor, Kofi N. *Ghana: A Political History.* Ghana: Sedco and Woeli, 1990.

Bádéjò, Diedre L. "The Goddess Osun as a Paradigm for African Feminist Criticism." *Sage: A Scholarly Journal on Black Women* 6, no. 1:27–32.

Balibar, Etienne. "The Nation Form: History and Ideology." In *Race, Nation, Class: Ambiguous Identities,* by Balibar and Immanuel Wallerstein. New York: Verso, 1991.

Balibar, Etienne, and Immanuel Wallerstein. *Race, Nation, Class: Ambiguous Identities.* New York: Verso, 1991.

Bambara, Toni Cade. *Deep Sightings and Rescue Missions: Fiction, Essays, and Conversations.* New York: Random House, 1996.

———. "Reading the Signs, Empowering the Eye." In *Deep Sightings and Rescue Missions: Fiction, Essays, and Conversations,* by Bambara, 89–138. New York: Random House.

———. *The Salt Eaters.* New York: Random House, 1980.

Batstone, David, and Eduardo Mendieta, eds. *The Good Citizen.* New York: Routledge, 1999.

Belton, John, ed. *Movies and Mass Culture.* New Brunswick, N.J.: Rutgers University Press, 1996.

Berger, John. *Ways of Seeing.* London: BBC and Penguin, 1972.

Blassingame, John W. *The Slave Community: Plantation Life in the Antebellum South.* 1972. New York: Oxford University Press, 1979.

Bobo, Jacqueline. *Black Women as Cultural Readers.* New York: Columbia University Press, 1995.

———, ed. *Black Women Film and Video Artists.* New York: Routledge, 1998.

———. "Black Women's Films: Genesis of a Tradition." In *Black Women Film and Video Artists,* edited by Bobo. New York: Routledge, 1998.

Boyce Davies, Carole. *Black Women, Writing and Identity: Migrations of the Subject.* New York and London: Routledge, 1994.

Brathwaite, Edward Kamau. *History of the Voice: The Development of Nation Language in Anglophone Caribbean Poetry.* London and Port-of-Spain: New Beacon Books, 1984.

Brereton, Bridget. "Society and Culture in the Caribbean." In *The Modern Caribbean,* edited by Franklin W. Knight and Colin A. Palmer. Chapel Hill: University of North Carolina Press, 1989.

Brodber, Erna. *Myal.* London: New Beacon Books, 1988.

Brown, Karen McCarthy. *Mama Lola: A Voodou Priestess in Brooklyn.* Berkeley and Los Angeles: University of California Press, 1991.

Campbell, Joseph. *The Hero with a Thousand Faces.* Princeton, N.J.: Princeton University Press, 1949.

Cannon, Katie. *Black Womanist Ethics.* Atlanta: Scholars Press, 1988.

Casetti, Francesco. *Inside the Gaze: The Fiction Film and Its Spectator.* Translated by Nell Andrews and Charles O'Brien. Bloomington: Indiana University Press, 1998.

Cham, Mbye, ed. *Ex-iles: Essays on Caribbean Cinema.* Trenton, N.J.: Africa World Press, 1992.

Christian, Barbara. "Fixing Methodologies: *Beloved.*" *Cultural Critique* 12 (1993): 5–15.

———. "The Highs and the Lows of Black Feminist Criticism." In *Reading Black, Reading Feminist,* edited by Henry Louis Gates Jr. New York: Meridian, 1990.

———. "The Race for Theory." *Cultural Critique* 6 (1987): 51–63.

Collins, Patricia Hill. *Black Feminist Thought: Knowledge, Consciousness, and the Politics of Empowerment.* New York and London: Routledge, 1991.

Condé, Maryse. "Epilogue: Cinema, Literature, and Freedom." In *Ex-iles: Essays on Caribbean Cinema,* edited by Mbye Cham. Trenton, N.J.: Africa World Press, 1992.

Cone, James. "Black Theology as Liberation Theology." In *African American Religious Studies,* edited by Gayraud Wilmore. Durham and London: Duke University Press, 1989.

———. *God of the Oppressed.* New York: Seabury Press, 1975.

———. *The Spirituals and the Blues.* New York: Orbis Books, 1972.

Connor, Kimberly Rae. *Conversions and Visions in the Writings of African American Women.* Knoxville: University of Tennessee Press, 1994.

Creel, Margaret Washington. "Gullah Attitudes toward Life and Death." In *African-isms in American Culture,* edited by Joseph E. Holloway. Bloomington: Indiana University Press, 1990.

Cripps, Thomas. *Making Movies Black.* New York: Oxford University Press, 1993.

Cudjoe, Selwyn, ed. *Caribbean Women Writers.* Wellesley, Mass.: Calaloux Publications, 1990.

Dash, Julie. *Daughters of the Dust: The Making of an African American Woman's Film.* New York: New Press, 1992.

Davis, Angela. *Blues Legacies and Black Feminism.* New York: Random House, 1998.

———. *Women, Culture, and Politics.* New York: Random House, 1989.

———. *Women, Race, and Class.* New York: Random House, 1981.

Davis, Charles T., and Henry Louis Gates Jr., eds. *The Slave's Narrative.* New York: Oxford University Press, 1985.

Davis, Zeinabu irene. "Woman with a Mission: Zeinabu irene Davis on Filmmaking." *Voices of the African Diaspora* 7, no. 3 (fall 1991): 37–40.

Defoe, Daniel. *Robinson Crusoe.* 1719. New York: NAL/Penguin, 1961.

Dent, Gina, ed. *Black Popular Culture: A Project by Michele Wallace.* Seattle: Bay Press, 1992.

Diawara, Manthia, ed. *Black American Cinema.* New York and London: Routledge, 1993.

Douglass, Frederick. *Narrative of the Life of Frederick Douglass, an American Slave, Written by Himself.* 1845. New Haven: Yale University Press, 2001.

Du Bois, W. E. B. *Black Reconstruction: An Essay toward a History of the Part Which Black Folk Played in the Attempt to Reconstruct Democracy in America.* 1935. Cleveland: World Publishing Co., 1964.

———. *The Souls of Black Folk.* 1903. New York: Penguin, 1989.

Edgell, Zee. *Beka Lamb.* London: Heinemann, 1982.

Ellison, Ralph. *Invisible Man.* 1952. New York: Random House, 1990.

———. *Shadow and Act.* 1953. New York: Random House, 1994.

Erens, Patricia, ed. *Issues in Feminist Film Criticism.* Bloomington: Indiana University Press, 1990.

Evans, Mari, ed. *Black Women Writers (1950–1980): A Critical Evaluation.* New York: Anchor/Doubleday, 1984.

Foster, Frances Smith. *Written by Herself: Literary Production of African American Women, 1746–1892.* Bloomington: Indiana University Press, 1993.

Foster, Gwendolyn Audrey. *Women Filmmakers of the African and Asian Diaspora.* Carbondale: Southern Illinois University Press, 1997.

Franklin, John Hope, and Loren Schweninger. *Runaway Slaves: Rebels on the Plantation.* New York: Oxford University Press, 1999.

Gates, Henry Louis, Jr., ed. *Reading Black, Reading Feminist: A Critical Anthology.* New York: Meridian, 1990.

Giddings, Paula. "The Last Taboo." In *Race-ing Justice, En-gendering Power: Essays on Anita Hill, Clarence Thomas, and the Construction of Social Reality,* edited by Toni Morrison. New York: Pantheon, 1992.

Gilkes, Cheryl Townsend. "We Have a Beautiful Mother: Womanist Musings on the Afrocentric Idea." In *Living the Intersection: Womanism and Afrocentrism in Theology,* edited by Cheryl J. Sanders. Minneapolis: Fortress Press, 1995.

Gomez, Michael A. *Exchanging Our Country Marks: The Transformation of African Identities in the Colonial and Antebellum South.* Chapel Hill: University of North Carolina Press, 1998.

Goodison, Lorna. *Guinea Woman: New and Selected Poems.* Manchester, England: Carcanet Press, 2000.

Grant, Jacquelyn. *White Women's Christ and Black Women's Jesus: Feminist Christology and Womanist Response.* Atlanta: Scholars Press, 1989.

Guerrero, Ed. *Framing Blackness: The African American Image in Film.* Philadelphia: Temple University Press, 1993.

Guinier, Lani. *Lift Every Voice: Turning a Civil Rights Setback into a New Vision of Social Justice.* New York: Simon and Schuster, 1998.

Gunning, Sandra. *Race, Rape, and Lynching: The Red Record of American Literature, 1890–1912.* New York: Oxford University Press, 1996.

Hall, Stuart. "Cultural Identity and Cinematic Representation." In *Ex-iles: Essays on Caribbean Cinema,* edited by Mbye Cham. Trenton, N.J.: Africa World Press, 1992.

———. "Culture, the Media, and 'the Ideological Effect.'" In *Mass Communication and Society,* edited by James Curran, Michael Gurevitch, and Janet Woolacott. London: Edward Arnold, 1977.

———. "On Postmodernism and Articulation: An Interview with Stuart Hall." Edited by Lawrence Grossberg. In *Stuart Hall: Critical Dialogues in Cultural Studies,* edited by David Morley and Kuan-Hsing Chen. New York: Routledge, 1996.

Hartman, S. V., and Farah Jasmine Griffin. "Are You as Colored as That Negro?: The Politics of Being Seen in Julie Dash's *Illusions." Black American Literature Forum* 25, no. 2, Black film issue (summer 1991): 361–73.

Henderson, Mae G. "Toni Morrison's *Beloved:* Re-Membering the Body as Historical Text." In *Comparative American Identities,* edited by Hortense Spillers. New York and London: Routledge, 1991.

Henderson, Stephen. *Understanding the New Black Poetry: Black Speech and Black Music as Poetic References.* New York: William Morrow, 1973.

Herskovits, Melville J. *The Myth of the Negro Past.* Boston: Beacon Press, 1941.

Higginbotham, Evelyn Brooks. *Righteous Discontent: The Women's Movement in the Black Baptist Church, 1880–1920.* Cambridge: Harvard University Press, 1993.

Hill-Lubin, Mildred A. "African Religion: That Invisible Institution in African and African-American Literature." In *Interdisciplinary Dimensions of African Litera-*

ture, edited by Kofi Anyidoho, Abioseh M. Porter, Daniel Racine, and Janice Spleth. ALA and Three Continents Press, 1985.

Hjort, Mette, and Scott MacKenzie, eds. *Cinema and Nation*. London and New York: Routledge, 2000.

Hodge, Merle. "Challenges of the Struggle for Sovereignty." In *Caribbean Women Writers*, edited by Selwyn Cudjoe. Wellesley, Mass.: Calaloux Publications, 1990.

Holloway, Karla F. C. "*Beloved:* A Spiritual." *Callaloo* 13 (1990): 516–25.

———. *Moorings and Metaphors: Figures of Culture and Gender in Black Women's Literature*. New Brunswick, N.J.: Rutgers University Press, 1992.

hooks, bell. *Black Looks: Race and Representation*. Boston: South End Press, 1992.

Hosking, Geoffrey, and George Schöpflin, eds. *Myths and Nationhood*. New York: Routledge, 1997.

Houchins, Susan, ed. *Spiritual Narratives*. The Schomburg Library of Nineteenth-Century Black Women Writers. New York: Oxford University Press, 1988.

Hughes, Langston. "The Negro Speaks of Rivers." 1926. In *The Langston Hughes Reader*. New York: George Braziller, 1958.

Hurston, Zora Neale. "The Characteristics of Negro Expression." In *The Sanctified Church: The Folklore Writings of Zora Neale Hurston*. Berkeley: Turtle Island Foundation, 1981.

———. *Moses: Man of the Mountain*. 1939. Introduction by Blyden Jackson. Chicago: University of Illinois Press, 1984.

———. *Moses: Man of the Mountain*. 1939. Foreword by Deborah McDowell. New York: HarperCollins, 1991.

———. "The Sanctified Church." In *The Sanctified Church: The Folklore Writings of Zora Neale Hurston*. Berkeley: Turtle Island Foundation, 1981.

———. *The Sanctified Church: The Folklore Writings of Zora Neale Hurston*. Berkeley: Turtle Island Foundation, 1981.

———. *Their Eyes Were Watching God*. 1937. New York: Harper, 1990.

Idowu, E. B. *African Traditional Religion: A Definition*. London: SCM Press, 1973.

Jacobs, Harriet. *Incidents in the Life of a Slave Girl*. 1861. New York: Harcourt Brace Jovanovich, 1973.

Jaffa, Arthur. "69." In *Black Popular Culture: A Project by Michele Wallace*, edited by Gina Dent. Seattle: Bay Press, 1992.

James, Stanlie M., and Busia Abena P. A., eds. *Theorizing Black Feminisms: The Visionary Pragmatism of Black Women*. New York and London: Routledge, 1993.

Jordan, June. "Notes toward a Black Balancing of Love and Hatred." 1974. In *Civil War*, by Jordan. Boston: Beacon Press, 1981.

Jordan, Winthrop. *White over Black: American Attitudes toward the Negro, 1550–1812*. Chapel Hill: University of North Carolina Press, 1968.

Kalu, Anthonia C. "The Priest/Artist Tradition in Achebe's *Arrow of God*." *Africa Today* 41, no. 2 (1994): 51–62.

————. "Those Left Out in the Rain: African Literary Theory and the Re-invention of the African Woman." *African Studies Review* 37, no. 2 (September 1994): 77–95.

————. *Women, Literature, and Development in Africa.* Trenton, N.J.: Africa World Press, 2001.

Kavanagh, James. "Ideology." In *Critical Terms for Literary Study,* edited by Frank Lentricchia and Thomas McLaughlin. Chicago: University of Chicago Press, 1990.

King, Deborah K. "Multiple Jeopardy, Multiple Consciousness: The Context of a Black Feminist Ideology." *Signs* 14 (autumn 1988): 42–72.

Klotman, Phyllis R., ed. *Screenplays of the African American Experience.* Bloomington: Indiana University Press, 1991.

Klotman, Phyllis R., and Janet K. Cutler, eds. *Struggles for Representation: African American Documentary Film and Video.* Bloomington: Indiana University Press, 1999.

Knight, Franklin W., and Colin A. Palmer, eds. *The Modern Caribbean.* Chapel Hill: University of North Carolina Press, 1989.

kydd, Elspeth. "'The Ineffaceable Curse of Cain': Racial Marking and Embodiment in *Pinky.*" *Camera Obscura* 15, issue 43 (2000): 95–121.

Lacy, Suzanne, ed. *Mapping the Terrain: New Genre Public Art.* Seattle: Bay Press, 1995.

Larkin, Alile Sharon. "Black Women Film-makers Defining Ourselves: Feminism in Our Own Voice." In *Female Spectators: Looking at Film and Television,* edited by E. Deidre Pribram. London and New York: Verso, 1988

Lawson, Bill E. "Moral Discourse and Slavery." In *Between Slavery and Freedom: Philosophy and American Slavery,* edited by Howard McGary and Bill E. Lawson. Bloomington and Indianapolis: Indiana University Press, 1992.

Lee, Jarena. *The Life and Religious Experience of Jarena Lee, A Coloured Lady.* 1836. In *Sisters of the Spirit: Three Black Women's Autobiogaphies of the Nineteenth Century,* edited by William L. Andrews. Bloomington: Indiana University Press, 1986.

Levine, Lawrence. *Black Culture and Black Consciousness: Afro-American Folk Thought from Slavery to Freedom.* New York: Oxford University Press, 1977.

Lewis, Samella. *The Art of Elizabeth Catlett.* Claremont, Calif.: Hancraft Studios, 1984.

Lorde, Audre. *Sister Outsider: Essays and Speeches by Audre Lorde.* New York: Crossing Press, 1984.

Lubiano, Wahneema. "Black Ladies, Welfare Queens, and State Minstrels: Ideological Warfare by Narrative Means." In *Race-ing Justice, En-gendering Power: Essays on Anita Hill, Clarence Thomas, and the Construction of Social Reality,* edited by Toni Morrison. New York: Pantheon, 1992.

————, ed. *The House That Race Built.* New York: Random House, 1997.

————. "The Postmodern Rag: Political Identity and the Vernacular in *Song of Solomon.*" In *New Essays on "Song of Solomon,"* edited by Valerie Smith. Cambridge: Cambridge University Press, 1995.

Lyon, Janet. *Manifestoes: Provocations of the Modern.* Ithaca, N.Y.: Cornell University Press, 1999.

Lyotard, Jean-François. *The Postmodern Condition: A Report on Knowledge.* Translated by Geoff Bennington and Brian Massumi. University of Minnesota Press, 1984.

Maathai, Wangari. *The Green Belt Movement: Sharing the Approach and the Experience.* New expanded edition. New York: Lantern Books, 2004.

———. "Nobel Peace Prize Acceptance Speech." Oslo, Norway, December 10, 2004.

Májozo, Estella Conwill. *Come Out the Wilderness: Memoir of a Black Woman Artist.* New York: Feminist Press–City University of New York, 1999.

———. "To Search for the Good and Make it Matter." In *Mapping the Terrain: New Genre Public Art,* edited by Suzanne Lacy. Seattle: Bay Press, 1995.

Marshall, Paule. *Praisesong for the Widow.* New York: Dutton, 1984.

Masilela, Ntongela. "Women Directors of the Los Angeles School." In *Black Women Film and Video Artists,* edited by Jacqueline Bobo, 21–42. New York: Routledge, 1998.

McCullough, H. B., ed. *Political Ideologies and Political Philosophies.* Toronto: Thompson Educational Publishing, 1989.

McDowell, Deborah E. "Foreword: Lines of Descent/Dissenting Lines." *Moses: Man of the Mountain.* New York: HarperCollins, 1991.

———. "Slavery as a Sacred Text: Witnessing in *Dessa Rose.*" In *Living the Intersection: Womanism and Afrocentrism in Theology,* edited by Cheryl J. Sanders. Minneapolis: Fortress Press, 1995.

McGary, Howard, and Bill E. Lawson. *Between Slavery and Freedom: Philosophy and American Slavery.* Bloomington: Indiana University Press, 1992.

McKay, Nellie. "Nineteenth-Century Black Women's Spiritual Autobiographies: Religious Faith and Self-Empowerment." In *Interpreting Women's Lives: Feminist Theory and Personal Narratives,* edited by Personal Narratives Group. Bloomington: Indiana University Press, 1989.

Mellencamp, Patricia. "Making History: Julie Dash." In *Redirecting the Gaze: Gender, Theory, and Cinema in the Third World,* edited by Diana Robin and Ira Jaffe. Albany: State University of New York Press, 1999.

Ménil, Alain. "*Rue Cases-Nègres* or the Antilles from the Inside." Translated by Oumar Kâ. In *Ex-iles: Essays on Caribbean Cinema,* edited by Mbye Cham. Trenton, N.J.: Africa World Press, 1992.

Mitchell, Timothy. "The Limits of the State: Beyond Statist Approaches and Their Critics." *American Political Science Review* 83, no. 1 (1991): 77–95.

Mittelman, James H. *Out from Underdevelopment.* New York: St. Martin's Press, 1988.

Morley, David, and Kuan-Hsing Chen, eds. *Stuart Hall: Critical Dialogues in Cultural Studies.* New York: Routledge, 1996.

Morrison, Toni. *Beloved.* New York: Knopf, 1987.

———. "City Limits, Village Values: Concepts of the Neighborhood in Black Fiction." In *Literature and the Urban Experience: Essays on the City and Literature,* edited by Michael C. Jaye and Ann Chalmers Watts, 35–43. New Brunswick, N.J.: Rutgers University Press, 1981.

———. "Friday on the Potomac." In *Race-ing Justice, En-gendering Power: Essays on Anita Hill, Clarence Thomas, and the Construction of Social Reality,* edited by Morrison. New York: Pantheon, 1992.

———. "Home." In *The House That Race Built,* edited by Wahneema Lubiano, 3–12. New York: Random House, 1997.

———. "Interview with Christina Davis." In *Conversations with Toni Morrison,* edited by Danille Taylor-Guthrie, 223–33. Jackson: University of Mississippi Press, 1994.

———. "An Interview with Toni Morrison." By Nellie Y. McKay. *Contemporary Literature* 24 (1983): 413–29.

———. "The Official Story: Dead Man Golfing." In *Birth of a Nation'hood: Gaze, Script, and Spectacle in the O. J. Simpson Case,* edited by Morrison and Claudia Brodsky Lacour. New York: Pantheon, 1997.

———. "A Knowing So Deep." *Essence,* May 1985, 230.

———. *Playing in the Dark: Whiteness and the Literary Imagination.* Cambridge: Harvard University Press, 1992.

———, ed. *Race-ing Justice, En-gendering Power: Essays on Anita Hill, Clarence Thomas, and the Construction of Social Reality.* New York: Pantheon, 1992.

———. "Rootedness: The Ancestor as Foundation." In *Black Women Writers (1950–1980): A Critical Evaluation,* edited by Mari Evans, 339–45. New York: Anchor/Doubleday, 1984.

———. "The Site of Memory." In *Inventing the Truth: The Art and Craft of Memoir,* edited by William Zinnser, 103–24. Boston: Houghton Mifflin, 1987.

———. *Sula.* New York: Knopf, 1973.

———. "Unspeakable Things Unspoken: The Afro-American Presence in American Literature." *Michigan Quarterly Review* 28, no. 1 (1989): 1–34.

Morrison, Toni, and Claudia Brodsky Lacour, eds. *Birth of a Nation'hood: Gaze, Script, and Spectacle in the O. J. Simpson Case.* New York: Pantheon, 1997.

Naylor, Gloria. *Mama Day.* 1988. New York: Vintage, 1989.

Nichols, Bill, ed. *Movies and Methods.* Vol. 1. Berkeley and Los Angeles: University of California Press, 1976.

Nichols, Grace. *i is a long memoried woman.* London: Karnak House, 1983.

Oduyoye, Mercy Amba. *Daughters of Anowa: African Women and Patriarchy.* New York: Orbis, 1995.

———. *Hearing and Knowing: Theological Reflections on Christianity in Africa.* New York: Orbis, 1986.

Omolade, Barbara. *The Rising Song of African American Women.* New York and London: Routledge, 1994.

Overing, Joanna. "The Role of Myth: An Anthropological Perspective, or 'The Reality of the Really Made-Up.'" In *Myths and Nationhood*, edited by Geoffrey Hosking and George Schöpflin. New York: Routledge, 1997.

Palcy, Euzhan. "Interview with Euzhan Palcy." By June Givanni. In *Ex-iles: Essays on Caribbean Cinema*, edited by Mbye Cham. Trenton, N.J.: Africa World Press, 1982.

Paris, Peter J. *The Spirituality of African Peoples*. Minneapolis: Fortress Press, 1995.

Patterson, Orlando. *Slavery and Social Death*. Cambridge: Harvard University Press, 1982.

Personal Narratives Group, ed. *Interpreting Women's Lives: Feminist Theory and Personal Narratives*. Bloomington: Indiana University Press, 1989.

Peterson, Carla L. *"Doers of the Word": African American Women Speakers and Writers in the North (1830–1880)*. New Brunswick, N.J.: Rutgers University Press, 1998.

Peterson, Nancy J., ed. *Toni Morrison: Critical and Theoretical Approaches*. Baltimore: Johns Hopkins University Press, 1997.

Phillips, Kimberley L., Hermine D. Pinson, Lorenzo Thomas, and Hanna Wallinger, eds. *Critical Voicings of Black Liberation: Resistance and Representation in the Americas*. Münster, Germany: Lit Verlag, 2003.

Pinn, Anthony B. *Why, Lord? Suffering and Evil in Black Theology*. New York: Continuum, 1995.

Pribram, Deidre E., ed. *Female Spectators: Looking at Film and Television*. London and New York: Verso, 1988.

Propp, Vladimir. *Morphology of the Folktale*. 1968. Austin: University of Texas Press, 1984.

Raboteau, Albert J. *Slave Religion: The "Invisible Institution" in the Antebellum South*. New York: Oxford University Press, 1978.

Ramphele, Mamphela. "Are Women Not Part of the Problem Perpetuating Sexism?— A Bird's Eye View from South Africa." *Africa Today* 37 (spring).

Ray, Benjamin C. *African Religions: Symbol, Ritual, and Community*. Upper Saddle River, N.J.: Prentice-Hall, 1976.

Richardson, Marilyn, ed. *Maria W. Stewart, America's First Black Woman Political Writer: Essays and Speeches*. Bloomington: Indiana University Press, 1987.

Robin, Diana, and Ira Jaffe, eds. *Redirecting the Gaze: Gender, Theory, and Cinema in the Third World*. Albany: State University of New York Press, 1999.

Rodney, Walter. *How Europe Underdeveloped Africa*. Washington, D.C.: Howard University Press, 1974.

Rushdy, Ashraf H. A. "Daughters Signifyin(g) History: The Example of Toni Morrison's *Beloved*." *American Literature* 64, no. 3 (September 1993): 567–97.

Ryan, Judylyn S. "Contested Visions/Double-Vision in *Tar Baby*." In *Toni Morrison: Critical and Theoretical Approaches*, edited by Nancy Peterson. Baltimore: Johns Hopkins University Press, 1997.

———. "Dismantling Slavery's Master-Narratives through African Diaspora Cinema." In *Critical Voicings of Black Liberation: Resistance and Representation in the Americas,* edited by Kimberley L. Phillips, Hermine D. Pinson, Lorenzo Thomas, and Hanna Wallinger. Münster, Germany: LitVerlag, 2003.

Ryan, Judylyn S., and Estella Conwill Májozo. "*Jazz* . . . On 'The Site of Memory.'" *Studies in the Literary Imagination* 31, no. 2 (fall 1998): 125–52.

Ryan, Michael, and Douglas Kellner. *Camera Politica: The Politics and Ideology of Contemporary Hollywood Film.* Bloomington: Indiana University Press, 1988.

Sanders, Cheryl J., ed. *Living the Intersection: Womanism and Afrocentrism in Theology.* Minneapolis: Fortress Press, 1995.

Schwarz-Bart, Simone. *The Bridge of Beyond.* 1972. London: Heinemann, 1982.

Scott, James C. *Domination and the Arts of Resistance: Hidden Transcripts.* New Haven: Yale University Press, 1990.

Sedgwick, Eve Kosofsky. *Epistemology of the Closet.* Berkeley and Los Angeles: University of California Press, 1990.

Shange, Ntozake. *For Colored Girls Who Have Considered Suicide When the Rainbow is Enuf.* New York: St. Martin's Press, 1975.

———. *Sassafrass, Cypress, and Indigo.* New York: St. Martin's Press, 1983.

Shohat, Ella, and Robert Stam. *Unthinking Eurocentrism: Multiculturalism and the Media.* New York: Routledge, 1994.

Smith, Sidonie. 1998. "Autobiographical Manifestos." In *Women, Autobiography, Theory,* edited by Sidonie Smith and Julia Watson, 433–40. Madison: University of Wisconsin Press, 1998.

Smith, Sidonie, and Julia Watson, eds. 1998. *Women, Autobiography, Theory.* Madison: University of Wisconsin Press, 1998.

Smith, Theophus H. *Conjuring Culture: Biblical Formations of Black America.* New York: Oxford University Press, 1994.

Smith, Valerie, ed. *New Essays on Song of Solomon.* Cambridge: Cambridge University Press, 1995.

———. *Not Just Race, Not Just Gender: Black Feminist Readings.* New York: Routledge, 1998.

Snead, James. *White Screens/Black Images.* New York: Routledge, 1994.

Spillers, Hortense, ed. *Comparative American Identities.* New York and London: Routledge, 1991.

Stewart, Maria W. *Maria W. Stewart, America's First Black Woman Political Writer: Essays and Speeches.* Edited and with an introduction by Marilyn Richardson. Bloomington: Indiana University Press, 1987.

———. *Meditations.* In *Spiritual Narratives,* edited by Susan Houchins. The Schomburg Library of Nineteenth-Century Black Women Writers. New York: Oxford University Press, 1988.

Stuckey, Sterling. *Slave Culture: Nationalist Theory and the Foundations of Black America.* New York: Oxford University Press, 1987.

Taylor, Clyde. *The Mask of Art: Breaking the Aesthetic Contract—Film and Literature.* Bloomington: Indiana University Press, 1998.

———. "New U.S. Black Cinema." In *Movies and Mass Culture,* edited by John Belton. New Brunswick, N.J.: Rutgers University Press, 1996.

———. "Paths of Enlightenment: Heroes, Rebels, and Thinkers." In *Struggles for Representation: African American Documentary Film and Video,* edited by Phyllis R. Klotman and Janet K. Cutler. Bloomington: Indiana University Press, 1999.

Taylor-Guthrie, Danille, ed. *Conversations with Toni Morrison.* Jackson: University of Mississippi Press, 1994.

Truffaut, François. "A Certain Tendency of the French Cinema." In *Movies and Methods,* vol. 1, edited by Bill Nichols. Berkeley and Los Angeles: University of California Press, 1976.

Turner, Graeme. *Film as Social Practice.* New York: Routledge, 1988.

Walker, Alice. *In Search of Our Mothers' Gardens: Womanist Prose.* San Diego: Harcourt Brace Jovanovich, 1983.

Walker, David. *David Walker's Appeal to the Coloured Citizens of the World, but in particular, and very expressly, to those of the United States of America.* 1830. Baltimore: Black Classic Press, 1993.

Welbon, Yvonne. "The State of Black Independent Film." *Sundance Film Festival Magazine 2001:* 69–78.

West, Cornel. *Democracy Matters: Winning the War against Imperialism.* New York: Penguin Press, 2004.

———. "The Moral Obligations of Living in a Democratic Society." In *The Good Citizen,* edited by David Batstone and Eduardo Mendieta. New York: Routledge, 1999.

White, Deborah Gray. *Ar'n't I a Woman: Female Slaves in the Plantation South.* New York: Norton, 1985.

Williams, Delores. *Sisters in the Wilderness: The Challenge of Womanist God-Talk.* New York: Orbis Books, 1993.

Williams, Patricia J. *Seeing a Color-Blind Future: The Paradox of Race.* New York: Farrar, Straus, and Giroux, 1997.

Wilmore, Gayraud S., ed. *African American Religious Studies: An Interdisciplinary Anthology.* Durham and London: Duke University Press, 1989.

Wiltse, Charles M., ed. *David Walker's Appeal to the Coloured Citizens of the World . . .* 1829. New York: Hill and Wang, 1965.

Winfrey, Oprah. *Journey to Beloved.* New York: Hyperion, 1998.

Wollen, Peter. "The *Auteur* Theory." In *Movies and Methods,* vol. 1, edited by Bill Nichols. Berkeley and Los Angeles: University of California Press, 1976.

Young, Lola. *Fear of the Dark: "Race," Gender, and Sexuality in the Cinema.* London: Routledge, 1996.

Zeusse, Evan M. *Ritual Cosmos: The Sanctification of Life in African Religions.* Athens: Ohio University Press, 1979.

Zinnser, William, ed. *Inventing the Truth: The Art and Craft of Memoir.* Boston: Houghton Mifflin, 1987.

Zobel, Joseph. *Black Shack Alley.* Translated by Keith Q. Warner. Boulder, Colo.: Lynn Reiner Publishers, 1997. Originally published as *Rue Cases-Nègres* (1950).

FILMOGRAPHY

Baby Boy. Directed by John Singleton. Culver City, Calif.: Columbia/Tri-Star Pictures, 2001.

Birth of a Nation. Directed by D. W. Griffith. Chicago: International Historic Films, 1915.

Boyz in the Hood. Directed by John Singleton. Burbank, Calif.: Columbia Pictures, 1991.

Compensation. Directed by Zeinabu irene Davis. New York: Women Make Movies, 1999.

Cycles. Directed by Zeinabu irene Davis. New York: Women Make Movies, 1989.

Daughters of the Dust. Directed by Julie Dash. New York: Kino International, 1992.

A Different Image. Directed by Alile Sharon Larkin. New York: Women Make Movies, 1982. Burbank, Calif.: Miramax, 1999.

Down in the Delta. Directed by Maya Angelou. Burbank, Calif.: Miramax, 1999.

Eve's Bayou. Directed by Kasi Lemmons. Santa Monica, Calif.: Trimark Pictures, 1997.

Finding Christa. Directed by Camille Billops and James V. Hatch. New York: Third World Newsreel, 1991.

Home Away from Home. Directed by Maureen Blackwood. New York: Women Make Movies, 1993.

Illusions. Directed by Julie Dash. New York: Women Make Movies. 1983.

Imitation of Life. Directed by John Stahl. Universal City, Calif.: Universal Studios, 1934.

Kiss Grandmama Goodbye. Directed by Debra J. Robinson. New York: Women Make Movies, 1992.

Losing Ground. Directed by Kathleen Collins. Washington, D.C.: Mypheduh Films, 1982.

Love and Basketball. Directed by Gina Prince-Blythewood. New York: New Line Cinema, 2000.

Mother of the River. Directed by Zeinabu irene Davis. New York: Women Make Movies, 1995.

Pinky. Directed by Elia Kazan. Los Angeles: Twentieth Century Fox, 1949.

A Powerful Thang. Directed by Zeinabu irene Davis. New York: Women Make Movies, 1991.

Remembering Wei Yi-Fang, Remembering Myself. Directed by Yvonne Welbon. New York: Women Make Movies, 1995.

Sankofa. Directed by Haile Gerima. Washington, D.C.: Mypheduh Films, 1993.

Sidet: Forced Exile. Directed by Salem Mekuria. New York: Women Make Movies, 1991.

Sugar Cane Alley. Directed by Euzhan Palcy. New York: New Yorker Filmworks, 1985.

Sweet Sweetback's Baadasss Song. Directed by Melvin Van Peebles. Los Angeles: New World Pictures, 1970.

Watermelon Woman. Directed by Cheryl Dunye. New York: First Run Features, 1996.

Within Our Gates. Directed by Oscar Micheaux. Washington, D.C.: Smithsonian Video, 1919.

Zajota and the Boogie Spirit. Directed by Ayoka Chenzira. New York: Red Carnelian Home Video, 1989.

INDEX